Welfare Discipline

Welfare Discipline

DISCOURSE,
GOVERNANCE, AND
GLOBALIZATION

Sanford F. Schram

 Temple University Press
PHILADELPHIA

Temple University Press
1601 North Broad Street
Philadelphia PA 19122
www.temple.edu/tempress

∞ The paper used in this publication meets the requirements of the American National Standard for Information Sciences—Permanence of Paper for Printed Library Materials, ANSI Z39.48-1992

Library of Congress Cataloging-in-Publication Data

Schram, Sanford.
    Welfare discipline : discourse, governance, and globalization / Sanford F. Schram.
        p. cm.
    Includes bibliographical references and index.
    ISBN 1-59213-301-0 (cloth : alk. paper) — ISBN 1-59213-302-9 (pbk. : alk. paper)
    1. Public welfare. 2. Social policy. 3. Public welfare—United States. 4. United States—Social policy—1993– 5. Public welfare—Europe. 6. Europe—Social policy. 7. Globalization—Social aspects. 8. Discourse analysis. I. Title.

HV31.S34   2006
361.6'1–dc22   2005050659

2 4 6 8 9 7 5 3

To Tracey Krulcik

Contents

Acknowledgments

Many people helped me finish this book. I wish to thank them all and hope to the next time I see them. For now I want to express my thanks to several people for reading and commenting on parts of the manuscript: Rosemary Barbera, Jane Bennett, Nina Berven, Fred Block, Stephen Bronner, Wesley Bryant, Nancy Campbell, William Corlett, Barbara Cruikshank, Anne Dalke, Kennan Ferguson, Richard Fording, Erica Honneycut, Patrick Kaylor, Michal McCall, Marlena Melhunek, Paul Meshejian, Anne Norton, David Osten, Melania Popa, Dorit Roer-Strier, Joan Schram, Ryan Schram, Jack Schram, Corey Shdaimah, Joe Soss, Roni Strier, Jennifer Stotter, Carl Swidorski, John Tambornino, Brianne Wolfe, and Charlie Wolfe. Frances Fox Piven once again challenged me to make my manuscript better. I am forever in her debt for her willingness to share not only her knowledge and insights but also her honesty. Roland Stahl read the entire manuscript in drafts and provided extensive commentary. His close readings and insightful criticisms are most appreciated. Tia Burroughs provided critical research assistance that made a real difference in the manuscript, particularly Chapter 4. I thank all of the students in my political science and social work classes who have challenged me to rethink ideas I have developed in this book. I continue to treasure the opportunity not just to teach my students but to learn from them as well. I want to make a special note of appreciation for my editors at Temple University Press, Peter Wissoker and Alex Holzman. Peter provided not only careful editing but also critical suggestions for framing the manuscript. Peter is a great editor and he has a great sense of humor, too. Alex understood what I was trying to do and helped make it happen. I am forever in his debt. Last, I want to thank Tracey Krulcik for getting back in touch with me after so many years and providing the motivation to write this book. Tracey's commitment to writing and to writing to make a difference is inspiring. I can only hope that this book reflects some of that inspiration.

Chapter 4 is a revision of "Contextualizing Racial Disparities in American Welfare Reform: Toward a New Poverty Research," *Perspectives on Politics* 3, 2 (June 2005): 253–68.

Introduction

The essays in this book are about new approaches to welfare in an era of globalization. By *approaches*, I mean both forms of governance and ways of studying them.

Charles Lemert has eloquently reminded us that we need new methods of study for these times of globalization.[1] For Lemert, "global methods" means getting close while achieving critical distance at the same time so as to better understand diverse people and practices in the fluid contexts of globalization. It could be argued that we should have been practicing this sort of double work whether there was globalization or not. Placing social action in context to make it interpretable is an idea that finds strong resonance in certain traditions in the social sciences.

My particular approach emphasizes the importance of examining the power of discourse to invoke contexts that make some actions seem appropriate and others not. Discourse situates isolated actions in context so as to give them a meaning they would not otherwise have. Discourse invokes context in the way it frames, narrates, and positions policymakers, their policies, and the effects those policies have on people. The terms of contemporary welfare policy discourse, such as "dependency," "self-sufficiency," "personal responsibility," "labor activation," and even "contract," or "asset-building," invoke historical and social contexts associated with western, liberal capitalism that impart particular meanings to isolated actions. While discourse is open to multiple readings, some resonate more than others to invoke more widely shared, established contexts. The power of discourse is represented in iterated discursive practices that reinforce themselves to the point that we can say they "make themselves real," privileging their way of saying and doing things, while marginalizing others. Iterated discursive practices can make for a vicious cycle of self-fulfilling prophecies. The

---

1. Charles Lemert, *Social Things: An Introduction to the Sociological Life* (Lanham MD: Rowman and Littlefield, 2002), pp. 176–206. Also see Michael J. Shapiro, *Methods and Nations: Cultural Governance and the Indigenous Subject* (New York: Routledge, 2003).

power of discourse extends to the social identities associated with class, gender, and race. Discourse makes class, gender, and racial identities. While people may be encouraged to internalize how they are positioned in discourse to have a certain identity, perhaps more important is how class, gender, and race get performed as people enact the relevant discursive practices, whether they are concerning work, care, welfare, and so on.

Research that fails to attend to the self-fulfilling power of discourse is incomplete and cannot address the major questions of social welfare policy. In this book, I focus on getting beyond the limitations of conventional welfare policy research by highlighting how discourse is a critical form of power for shaping policy. By attending to the power of discourse, we can obtain critical distance on the context of social welfare policy while creating opportunities to leverage change in specific instances. The specific instances that concern me in this book are related to how welfare policy is changing in a globalizing world.

As for governance, Mark Bevir and others have alerted us to the issue of governance in an era of globalization.[2] For Bevir, governance emerges in the context of globalization where international institutions and sources of power constrain the latitude of the nation-state to act independently, while simultaneously the nation-state increasingly relies on civil society and the private sector both to provide social welfare and to impose social control. The nation-state is increasingly limited by international linkages and dependence on organizations in civil society. With the term "governance," Bevir means to capture the new forms of power that emerge in this context. His thinking follows closely that of Michel Foucault when he speaks of "governmentality" as the dissemination of state power through the institutions of civil society for disciplining the civilian population in ways required by the late modern social order.[3] I focus on the new forms of welfare policy that are critical for disciplining populations in an era of globalization.[4] My entry point for understanding the new forms of welfare governance is to focus on the growing influence of an American welfare

---

2. See Mark Bevir, ed., *Encyclopedia of Governance* (http://igov.berkeley.edu/projects/encyclopedia.html).

3. Michel Foucault, "Question of Method" and "Governmentality," in *The Foucault Effect: Studies in Governmentality with Two Lectures by and an Interview with Michel Foucault*, Graham Burchell, Colin Gordon, and Peter Miller, eds. (Chicago: University of Chicago Press, 1991), pp. 73–104.

4. For an analysis of welfare-to-work as an example of local privatized service delivery that is "rescaling" state power to create new forms of governance in an era of globalization, see Jamie Peck, "Political Economies of Scale: Fast Policy, Interscalar Relations, and Neoliberal Workfare," *Economic Geography* 78, 3 (July 2002): 331–60.

policy discourse that is framed around impugning "welfare dependency" so as to justify as necessary the retrenchment of welfare in the face of growing global economic competition. Welfare reform discourse simultaneously helps legitimate the idea that globalization is inevitable while repositioning those who are disadvantaged by globalization as deficient persons who need to be subject to new disciplinary practices that fit them into the emerging economic order.

The first essay makes the case for discourse analysis as a useful way for understanding the globalization of U.S. social welfare policy discourse in recent years. I examine how the idea of economic globalization has significantly influenced U.S. social welfare policy discourse especially as it relates to the dramatic welfare reforms of the last decade.[5] I do not dispute that economic globalization is happening; but I suggest that a discourse of globalization has made it seem inevitable so as to require scaling back the welfare state in the name of local economies becoming more internationally competitive. This globalization discourse has been characterized as reflecting the ideology of "neoliberalism" that has rationalized globalization as the road to economic prosperity for all, when in fact it has increased inequality at home and abroad.[6] I make the case that the United States has led the way in championing the necessity of attacking welfare dependency and scaling back the welfare state in the face of globalization, and nowhere has the idea of globalization had as devastating consequences for social policies for the most vulnerable in society as in the United States. Globalization looks more and more like a process that starts with a story about the rest of the world that the United States has told itself in no small part to produce a welfare state retrenchment right here at home, resulting in the United States becoming a model for other welfare states. First through iteration and then through emulation, globalization discourse makes itself real, becoming in the United States the self-fulfilling prophecy it did not need to be. Failure to account for its role in conditioning the choices of policymakers only reinforces the power of globalization to operate as a taken-for-granted context for action. I conclude by cautioning against missing the "forest" of globalization discourse when trying to understand the "trees" of welfare policy change.

---

5. See Frances Fox Piven, "Globalization, American Politics, and Welfare Policy," in *Lost Ground: Welfare Reform, Poverty and Beyond*, Randy Albelda and Ann Withorn, eds. (Cambridge: South End Press, 2002), pp. 27–42.

6. See Sandra Morgen and Jeff Maskovsky, "The Anthropology of Welfare Reform: New Perspectives on U.S. Urban Poverty in the Post-Welfare Reform Era," *Annual Review of Anthropology* 32 (October 2003): 315–38.

In the second essay, I pursue this question further and examine in detail the debate about whether western European welfare states are being Americanized by U.S.-style globalization discourse and the growing penchant in European countries to articulate social welfare policy change in an American idiom of reducing welfare dependency. I note that European countries have developed a discourse focused on "labor activation" to promote work among the unemployed.[7] In Europe, welfare dependency is increasingly seen as reinforcing "social exclusion," and the solution there is to increase the labor participation of welfare recipients. Yet, depending upon how it is done, labor activation risks creating what Joel Handler calls the "paradox of inclusion," where the unemployed are put to work but in ways that reinscribe their subordination. Nonetheless, for the most part, European labor activation policies are less draconian and as not focused on single mothers with children as is welfare reform in the United States. I conclude that there is indeed an Americanization of welfare discourse afoot in Europe and that it is leading to a greater likelihood that assistance to the unemployed will be conditioned in more countries with work requirements. Yet, I also suggest that the changes in policy taking place vary widely across welfare states and that nowhere are they as draconian as in the United States. Discourse is never univocal and is always open to multiple readings. I argue that other welfare states have developed their own variations that are almost always far less punitive than the U.S. version. Given their stronger welfare states, Europeans overall have been better able to resist the idea that we must now give up on the welfare state.

The third essay examines the growing concern about issues of care as a sign that the gender inequities of social welfare provision unavoidably come to the fore as women increasingly are expected to work as paid laborers outside the home. As labor activation becomes the increasing focal point of welfare policy discourse, mothers, like other women in recent years, are increasingly seen primarily as potential workers. As a result, concern about issues of care point to what is at risk of being neglected when work is increasingly emphasized. I rely on a number of prominent feminist theorists to highlight how there are gender biases operating in the globalizing dependency discourse.[8] I examine policy innovations in Sweden and Norway

---

7. See Joel Handler, *Social Citizenship and Workfare in the U.S. and Western Europe: The Paradox of Inclusion* (Cambridge, UK: Cambridge University Press, 2004).

8. Martha A. Fineman, *The Autonomy Myth: A Theory of Dependency* (New York: New Press, 2004); Joan Williams, *Unbending Gender: Why Family and Work Conflict and What to Do about It* (New York: Oxford University Press, 2000); and Nancy Fraser, "After the Family Wage: Gender Equity and the Welfare State," *Political Theory* 22, 4 (November 1994): 591–618.

that demonstrate that, regardless of whether recent policy changes in even the most progressive welfare states are gender-neutral or gender-sensitive, they are but a beginning to the struggle to realize gender justice. I emphasize that policy needs to be contextualized and account for its relationship to deeply embedded gender biases that operate in the broader society. I conclude this essay with consideration of what it would take for the welfare state to better promote gender justice.

The fourth essay investigates in detail how racial disadvantage is reproduced even, or especially, via the ostensibly neutral discourse of welfare reform.[9] This chapter focuses on how conventional public policy research fails to interrogate the silences of U.S. welfare policy discourse so as to leave unchallenged the way such discourse operates as a self-legitimating, self-fulfilling prophecy. As racial and ethnic diversity become growing issues in Europe, the problem of ostensibly neutral but latently race-biased policy grows larger for other countries as well. In the U.S., a welfare policy discourse that articulates the problem of welfare dependency as if it were simply a question of enforcing work irrespective of the distinctive societal barriers confronting low-income single mothers of color is a discourse that helps reinforce the idea that these "welfare queens" are deviants not like "normal," white middle-class mothers and are undeserving of our support. I argue that the ostensibly neutral discourse of welfare reform operates as its own form of what Loïc Wacquant calls "racemaking," which works to reinforce the idea that race is a marker highlighting real, durable differences between blacks and whites regarding things like intelligence, ability, and effort.[10] New forms of governance require new forms of analysis and only a policy research that places findings about racial disparities under welfare reform in a historical and social context will enable us to highlight the processes of "racemaking" of ostensibly neutral welfare reform discourse.

The fifth essay interrogates one of the most innovative developments in recent years in welfare policy discourse: the asset-building approach to fighting poverty.[11] Assets-building discourse is yet another instance of how U.S.-style welfare reform is increasingly a global phenomenon, as it now

---

9. On the issue of racial representation in ostensibly neutral contexts, see Naomi R. Cahn, "Representing Race Outside of Explicitly Racialized Contexts," *Michigan Law Review* 95, 4 (February 1997): 965–1004.

10. Loïc Wacquant, "From Slavery to Mass Incarceration: Rethinking the 'Race Question' in the US," *New Left Review* 13:1 (2003): 41–60.

11. See Michael W. Sherraden, *Assets and the Poor: A New American Welfare Policy* (Armonk, NY: M. E. Sharpe, 1991).

spreads from the United States to Europe, Latin America, and other parts of the world. I focus on its most dramatic application in the United States in the set of policy initiatives to make homeownership more common among low-income families. The asset-building approach assumes that low-income families cannot begin to act middle class until they start to acquire assets that enable them to grow an investment, increase savings, and create capital that they can use to promote the long-run economic fortunes of their families and to pass on wealth to their children. Then low-income families will begin to model middle-class families in their economic practices and will begin to leave poverty behind in the next generation, if not sooner. The main asset most middle-class families in the United States have is their home, and so the main focus of the asset-building approach has increasingly become making homeownership more accessible to low-income families. I examine the various policy initiatives that have arisen of late to increase the homeownership among low-income families in the United States, and I survey the research that indicates the limitations of this asset-building strategy. I question why this approach has become so popular with researchers, funders, and policymakers. I find fault in the implicit assumptions of asset-building welfare policy discourse more generally because they resonate with earlier culture of poverty arguments that saw the poor as lacking middle-class values, living too much for today, not being able to plan for the future, and lacking the discipline needed to acquire savings, capital, wealth, and assets that could be used to get a family out of poverty. The asset-building approach to fighting poverty has floundered on the economic realities confronting low-income families, but its failure most significantly begins with its unreflective victim-blaming discourse that assumes the problem is in the capital management of the poor rather than in the inequitable economic practices that limit the ability of low-income families to be able to buy homes or acquire other assets that might actually over time prove to be good investments for generating future wealth for their families.

The sixth essay deconstructs dependency discourse to begin the process of posing alternatives to the new forms of governance. I step back for a moment from welfare policy to reflect on Roman Jakobson's analysis of aphasia as a model for understanding the underlying principles of language and suggest it as a methodology for examining the role of discourse in welfare policymaking today.[12] Jacokson's studies of aphasia led him to

---

12. Roman Jakobson, "Two Aspects of Language and Two Types of Aphasic Disturbances," in *The Norton Anthology of Theory and Criticism*, Vincent B. Leitch, ed. (New York: Norton, 2001), pp. 1265–71.

suggest that metaphor and metonymy were central to the uses of language. Metaphors referenced how a signifier was like a signified object and metonymy referenced how one signified object was contiguous to another. Often the after-effect of brain trauma, aphasia came in two forms in either being not able to reference the metaphoric or the metonymic principle. My thesis in this chapter is that dependency is a form of metonymy where it displaces poverty as the topic that is discussed. I examine the persistence of the dependency metonymy over the past 200 years since it was first popularized by Thomas Malthus in late 18th-century England through the writings of Charles Murray in the 1980s in the United States. I point to how today the dependency metonymy is expressed in a highly medicalized idiom that sees it as the social welfare policy equivalent of a chemical dependency or addiction. I argue that the medicalization of dependency facilitates its treatment in therapeutic, rather than economic, terms. I further suggest that the medicalization of welfare dependency also helps assimilate it to the new forms of governance operating in civil society's social agencies that are designed to help people become self-disciplined selves who can fit into the social order as needed in an era of globalization. Discourse analysis can help resist the medicalization of welfare dependency as an established fact and thereby destabilize the new forms of governance in regimenting people into the emerging low-wage workforce of the globalizing economy.

The seventh essay asks whether "compassionate conservatism" is the best way to make social welfare policy more caring.[13] I do agree that more compassion in social welfare policy is needed but fear that compassionate conservatism does little more than rationalize the disciplinary practices of the new forms of governance operating via private service, often charitable, agencies, where compassion often takes the form of a "tough love" to help people acquire the personal fortitude to practice greater personal responsibility and become more self-disciplined. As an alternative, I offer the idea of "harm reduction," taken from various alternative treatment communities as a practice designed to resist judging others so as to help them live their lives better on their own terms. I suggest that a compassionate emphasis on reducing harm rather than the tough love of insisting on the enforcement of certain moral standards regarding work and family would enable us to allow for diversity to flourish even as we build community. This may take us beyond the conventional modern liberal

---

13. Marvin Olasky, *Compassionate Conservatism: What It Is, What It Does, and How It Can Transform America* (New York: Free Press, 2000).

discourse of justice and rights to get there. In the process, we may come to see even the entitlement right to a basic income as grounded in a need to compensate those excluded from first-class citizenship in the political economy for making the privileges of the included possible.

Taken together, these essays suggest that new forms of governance require new methods of analysis. Each essay in its own way highlights how social welfare policy discourse is an insidious form of power that can become its own self-fulfilling prophecy. By examining what is said and unsaid in welfare policy discourse today, these essays seek to contribute to collective efforts to resist the embedded biases of such discourse and to help articulate alternative public policies. By using new approaches to the study of welfare policy, we can better promote alternatives to the new forms of governance.

Welfare Discipline

1

The Truth of Globalization Discourse

A Self-Fulfilling Prophecy

"[T]he moment one seriously questions the existing liberal consensus, one is accused of abandoning scientific objectivity for the outdated ideological positions. This is the point that one cannot and should not concede: today, actual freedom of thought must mean the freedom to question the predominant liberal-democratic postideological consensus—or it means nothing.... Lenin's wager—one that is today, in our era of postmodern relativism, more relevant than ever—is that universal truth and partisanship, the gesture of taking sides, are not only not mutually exclusive but condition each other. In a concrete situation, its universal truth can only be articulated from a thoroughly partisan position; truth is by definition one-sided."

—Slavoj Žižek, "A Plea for Leninist Intolerance," *Critical Inquiry* 28, 2 (Winter 2001): 542–66.

A very capable student once reminded me that when she asked in class how I define "truth," I lamely replied that the truth was at best... "mushy." More than fifteen years later, the former student attended a lecture I gave at a university in the metropolitan region where she had moved. Her children now grown, she was seeking to reconnect to her academic past. Her attendance in part prompted my revisiting the truth question. I began by quoting Slavoj Žižek. Now the truth was no longer mushy but, perhaps no more reassuring, it had become... "one-sided."

If anyone is looking for consistency in my thinking, I guess we can say that I remained against "truth," at least as it is often characterized, as objective and independent of human intervention. (I recognize that this might not entirely be the case for Žižek, whose own version of Marx's dialectical materialism is centered on an understanding of universal truth that finds, at its most profound level, the abyss to be, paradoxically, a real absence present in our lives.) Instead, the truth remains for me best understood as an artifact of discourse. In other words, truth, whatever it may be ultimately, is, for humans, apprehensible first and foremost as a discursive practice. Bracketing the ultimate nature of truth, I prefer to situate my truth-studies in the ways in which discourse presents things to us as if they were true. With Michel Foucault, I am more interested in how discourse makes some things out to be true, regardless of whether they are.[1] And still with Žižek I am interested most critically in how the prevailing neoliberal consensus today discourages the interrogation of these discursive practices such that what is taken to be true by that consensus reigns supreme and unchallenged even as it forecloses, simultaneously effacing and erasing, alternative world views, perspectives, and discursive practices that could allow us to understand our social, political, and economic relations differently.[2]

Did Somebody Say Dependency? The Globalization of Welfare Policy Discourse

Today, the one-sided nature of truth is not most dramatically represented in a worldwide proletariat whose actions, as a class "in-itself" acting "for-itself," were to serve as the basis for universal emancipation, according to Lenin, as Žižek reminds us, and, we should add, according to Marx before him.[3] Instead, today, a more questionable one-sided truth is ascendant: the monolithic discourse of globalization that has come to dominate political debate all over the world but especially where I argue it was originally most aggressively championed—in the United States.[4] For several decades, U.S. politics has drowned in a torrent of globalization talk, incessantly and consistently drenching us in a fear of the coming global economic competition and our resultant need to attack the alleged problem of "welfare dependency" and to retrench the welfare state.[5] I call

1. Michel Foucault, *Power/Knowledge: Selected Interviews and Other Writings, 1972–1977*, New York: Pantheon, 1980), p. 133: " 'Truth' is to be understood as a system of ordered procedures for the production, regulation, distribution, circulation and operation of statements."

2. See Kathy Ferguson and Phyllis Turnbull, "Portable Sovereignty, National Internationalism, and the Peaceful Arms Trade: The Bush Doctrine in Foreign Policy" (paper presented at the annual meeting of the Western Political Science Association, Portland, OR, March 11, 2004) for the point that discourse simultaneously effaces and erases.

3. Also see Shlomo Avineri, *The Social and Political Thought of Karl Marx* (London: Cambridge University Press, 1968).

4. Frances Fox Piven and Richard A. Cloward, "Eras of Power," *Monthly Review* 49 (January 1998): 11–24.

5. John Agnew, *Hegemony: The New Shape of Global Power* (Philadelphia: Temple University Press, 2005); and Manfred B. Steger, *Globalism: A New Market Ideology* (Lanham, MD: Rowman and Littlefield, 2002).

this way of framing social welfare policy deliberations "globalization discourse."

My argument is that starting as early as the mid-1970s, globalization discourse began helping to create the pretext for the U.S. welfare state retrenchment.[6] The emerging ideology then was what came to be referred to as "neoliberalism," which championed the idea of freeing local markets from nation-state regulation to pursue greater opportunities for economic growth globally.[7] The need to attack welfare dependency by way of welfare retrenchment became a popular corollary in this argument.[8] That retrenchment was most significantly represented in the eventual passage of the Personal Responsibility and Work Opportunity Reconciliation Act of 1996. The 1996 law ended welfare as an entitlement; imposed time limits, work requirements, and other punitive policies; and eventually resulted in massive declines in the numbers of welfare recipients as growing numbers of them ended up in low-wage jobs that kept them in poverty. It has given birth to a "Work First" welfare reform regime that puts in place a series of "get-tough" policies designed to reduce the problem of welfare dependency.[9] As a result, the number of recipients receiving what is now called TANF (Temporary Assistance for Needy Families) fell from 13,242,000 in 1995 to 5,334,000 in 2002—a decline of 59.7 percent.[10] And while welfare reform has been widely declared a success, it has largely replaced the welfare poor with the working poor, even though many of the welfare poor were working before welfare reform and many of the working poor need more social welfare assistance than they have been getting.[11]

6. Frances Fox Piven, "Globalization, American Politics, and Welfare Policy," in *Lost Ground: Welfare Reform, Poverty and Beyond*, Randy Albelda and Ann Withorn, eds. (Cambridge: South End Press, 2002), pp. 27–42.

7. Jamie Peck, "Political Economies of Scale: Fast Policy, Interscalar Relations, and Neoliberal Workfare," *Economic Geography* 78, 3 (July 2002): 331–60.

8. Sandra Morgen and Jeff Maskovsky, "The Anthropology of Welfare Reform: New Perspectives on U.S. Urban Poverty in the Post-Welfare Reform Era," *Annual Review of Anthropology* 32 (October 2003): 315–38.

9. Thomas Gais and R. Kent Weaver, *State Policy Choices Under Welfare Reform*, Welfare Reform & Beyond: Brief No. 21 (Washington, DC: Brookings Institution, April 2002).

10. *Statistical Abstract of the United States* (Washington, DC: U.S. Bureau of the Census, 2002), p. 354.

11. See Sanford F. Schram and Joe Soss, "Success Stories: Welfare Reform, Policy Discourse, and the Politics of Research," in *Lost Ground: Welfare, Reform, Poverty, and Beyond*, Randy Albelda and Ann Withorn, eds. (Boston: South End Press, 2002), pp. 57–78.

Explicit calls for the retrenchment of welfare on the grounds that growing global economic competition necessitated it were many from the mid-1970s on right up until the passage of the welfare reform law in 1996.[12] Yet welfare reform was tied to the alleged need to respond to globalization in ways that went well beyond claims that we had to reduce welfare dependency to restore the work ethic among welfare recipients. It also went beyond claims that welfare imposed excessive tax burdens on the economy. Instead, welfare reform was part of a larger restructuring of the political economy that made workers in general more vulnerable. Welfare reform was matched by retrenchment in other social protections, including increased restrictions in unemployment insurance and a variety of other programs.[13] Protections for unions declined as well. Further, welfare reform meant more than increasing the pool of low-wage labor. It also could help further increase the vulnerability of all workers and drive down wages. By reducing the social safety net for the poor, all workers were affected. A strong signal was sent that workers had less on which they could fall back if they resisted accepting the declines in pay and job security.

Welfare reform was arguably part of a larger restructuring in other ways as well. There is also the argument that welfare reform facilitated new forms of governance that represented a "rescaling" of nation-state power and its policies to create greater flexibility for growing local pools of low-wage workers as allegedly was required for competing in the emerging global economy.[14] Welfare reform not only ended the national entitlement to public assistance for poor families but also devolved major

12. E. J. Dionne notes that President Bill Clinton, as a "New Democrat," successfully championed welfare reform in part as a response to the public's anxiety about globalization. See E. J. Dionne, *They Only Look Dead: Why Progressives Will Dominate the Next Political Era* (New York: Simon and Schuster, 1997), pp. 94–102. For a blatant example of linking the need for welfare reform with globalization, see Murray Wiedenbaum, " 'No Way Out' of Global Markets," *Christian Science Monitor* (October 19, 1995): 20. For analysis of claims like this, see Morgen and Maskovsky, "The Anthropology of Welfare Reform," pp. 315–38; Stephen Turner, "Globalization on Trial: The Third Way," *Society* (January/February 2005): 10–4; and Betty Reid Mandell, "The Future of Caretaking," *New Politics* 9, 2 (Winter 2003) 61–77. For the extent to which increased global economic competition was invoked as justification for the necessity of welfare cutbacks in Canada, see Lea Caragata, "Neoconservative Realities: The Social and Economic Marginalization of Canadian Women," *International Sociology* 18, 3 (2003): 559–80.
13. See Michael B. Katz, *The Price of Citizenship: Redefining America's Welfare State* (New York: Metropolitan Books, 2001).
14. See Peck, "Political Economies of Scale," pp. 331–60. For the argument that welfare reform's emphasis on decentralized administration via private providers is in response to demands that national welfare assistance be retrenched as an impediment

responsibility for welfare to the states, where it has been administrated locally largely by private providers. Devolution and privatization have worked hand-in-glove with the supposedly inevitable globalization to create more flexible local labor markets at the low end of the wage structure.

My argument is that welfare reform was legitimated in part by politically questionable concerns about economic globalization. I do not deny that economic globalization was occurring; instead I am arguing that what I am calling globalization discourse helped make it seem in the United States that economic globalization of necessity required scaling back the welfare state in the name of being able to compete internationally. Welfare state retrenchment was made possible in no small part because the issue was framed in the United States in terms of a "crisis narrative" on the necessity of welfare policy retrenchment in the face of growing international economic competition, making it seem unavoidable that the United States retrench welfare provision.[15] U.S. globalization discourse had created its own specter of a debilitating global economic competition that required welfare state retrenchment as part of the necessary response.

From Iteration to Emulation

My argument goes further to suggest that the ultimate irony of what I am calling globalization discourse operated as a form of circular causality in that it operates as a self-fulfilling prophecy.[16] The United States has led the way in championing the necessity of scaling back the welfare state in the face of globalization, and nowhere has the idea of globalization had as devastating consequences for social policies for the most vulnerable in society as in the United States. Nonetheless, while globalization discourse looks like a process that starts with a story about the rest of the world that

---

to growing local pools of low-wage workers for an emerging globally integrated economy, see Theodore J. Lowi, "Think Globally, Lose Locally," *Boston Review* (April/May 1998): http://www.bostonreview.net.

15. On crisis narratives, see Murray Edelman, *Politics as Symbolic Action* (New York: Academic Press, 1967); and Deborah Stone, *Policy Paradox: The Art of Political Decision Making* (New York: W. W. Norton & Company, 2002). On crisis narratives and the roots of globalization discourse in the United Kingdom, see Colin Hay, "Narrating Crisis: The Discursive Construction of the Winter of Discontent," *Sociology* 30, 2 (May 1996): 253–77.

16. On circular causality as an important, if understudied, topic in the social sciences more generally, see, Anne Norton, *95 Theses: Politics, Culture, & Method* (New Haven: Yale University Press, 2004).

the United States has told to itself in no small part to produce a welfare state retrenchment right here at home,[17] the result is that the United States became a model for other welfare states.[18] The globalization of welfare policy discourse has come to involve both the high degree to which welfare policy was framed in terms of the necessity to retrench in order to compete internationally *and* the dissemination of that perspective to other countries. Both forms of the globalization of welfare policy discourse are occurring. Now that the United States as a world economic leader has so dramatically begun to scale back its social protections in the name of making itself more able to compete in a global economic competition, other countries have developed similar discourses, often in the name of "labor activation," to promote work and reduce reliance by the unemployed on state benefits. The irony here, I argue, is that the dissemination of U.S.-style globalization discourse ends up coming back home to reinforce concerns in the United States about the need to retrench its social welfare policies.

In this way, globalization discourse could very well become its own self-fulfilling prophecy. Like a ghost of a not-yet-fully-born world system, globalization discourse haunted the political imagination of the west until preoccupation with its very idea furthered the possibility of it materializing in practice. For someone like Jacques Derrida, globalization discourse is therefore a form of melancholy more than mourning: by anticipation, we were regretting what had not yet happened, rather than waiting to grieve after a loss occurred.[19] The crisis narrative of welfare retrenchment as a necessary consequence of economic globalization implied to its audience a subject position as a concerned party who must

---

17. For analysis that suggests that the United States press prematurely presented welfare state retrenchment in Europe in ways that delegitimated liberalizations in social welfare policy in the United States, see Janet C. Gornick and Marcia K. Meyers, "Lesson-Drawing in Family Policy: Media Reports and Empirical Evidence about European Developments," *Journal of Comparative Policy Analysis* 3, 1 (June 2001): 31–57. For Gornick and Meyers, this misreporting significantly distorted U.S. policy deliberations, especially regarding family leave policies.

18. On the United States becoming a model for other welfare states, see Joel Handler, *Social Citizenship and Workfare in the U.S. and Western Europe: The Paradox of Inclusion* (Cambridge, UK: Cambridge University Press, 2004).

19. For a meditation on the counter idea of Marxism as a ghostly specter that haunts the western capitalist imagination, oftentimes to make credible the prospect of a threat that needs to be beaten back, see Jacques Derrida, *Specters of Marx: The State of The Debt, The Work of Mourning, and the New International*, translated by Peggy Kamuf, with an introduction by Bernd Magnus and Stephen Cullenberg (New York: Routledge, 1994). The distinction between melancholy and mourning was a concern

share the narrative's sense of urgency and must accept that drastic actions need to be taken to avoid the impending catastrophe before it arrives. Therefore, irrespective of how much increased global economic activity was occurring, the crisis narrative of welfare state retrenchment in the face of economic globalization became in the United States its own pretext. Irrespective of whether all western welfare states had actually already entered into what has been called a "race to the bottom" stemming from global economic competition, the idea has created anticipation to the point that the retrenchment in social welfare protections that did take place has increased the currency of the very same idea to the point that scaling back has become what has to be done in order to compete successfully in a new global economy.[20] In a vicious cycle, globalization discourse makes itself real.

This U.S. discourse of welfare state retrenchment as unavoidable in the face of economic globalization has to varying degrees with varying effects become a model to be emulated by policymakers in other advanced industrial societies.[21] In Europe, welfare reform is focused on "labor activation," which

---

for Sigmund Freud, whose focus on mourning was inverted by Derrida to emphasize the importance of melancholy as a heightened awareness that something was at risk of being left out by the exclusionary practices of discourse. For a critique, see Slavoj Žižek, "Melancholy and the Act," *Critical Inquiry* 26, 4 (Summer 2000): 657–81.

20. On the idea of an international "race to the bottom" by western welfare states, see Fritz W. Scharpf, "The Viability of Advanced Welfare States in the International Economy: Vulnerabilities and Options," Working Paper 99/9 (Cologne, Germany: Max Planck Institute for the Study of Societies, September 1999). On the parallel domestic U.S. "race to the bottom," see Sanford F. Schram and Joe Soss, "Making Something Out of Nothing: Welfare Reform and the New Race to the Bottom," *Publius: The Journal of Federalism* 28, 3 (Summer 1998): 67–88, and "The Real Value of Welfare: Why Poor Families Do Not Migrate," *Politics and Society* 27, 1 (March 1999): 39–66. Also see Sanford F. Schram and Samuel H. Beer, *Welfare Reform: A Race to the Bottom?* (Baltimore: Woodrow Wilson Center Press, 1999). Actual levels of welfare migration by recipients moving from one state to another for better benefits are low and do not affect welfare cutback decisions by state government policymakers in the different states in the United States but the idea of welfare migration is still nonetheless exploited by state policymakers to justify cutbacks.

21. For a detailed and positive discussion on the extent to which Wisconsin Governor Tommy Thompson's mid-1990s welfare reforms became an influential model that European policymakers widely discussed as a logical response to the supposed pressures of global economic competition, see Jay Hein, "Ideas as Exports," *American Outlook* (Summer 2002) (http://www.americanoutlook.org/index.cfm?fuseaction= article_detail&id=1877). Hein calls this an example of an emerging "global domestic policy" discourse where ideas circulate across the developed world, in this case from Wisconsin to Europe as the basis for understanding welfare reform as a necessary and effective response to the alleged growing pressures of global economic competition.

implies, like the U.S. "welfare dependency," that the unemployed are passive and need to be made active participants in the workforce.[22]

There is therefore both economic globalization and the Americanization of welfare discourse spreading around the developed world.[23] Both are occurring, and the second is helping make the first a *fait accompli*. As the latter spreads around the world, its globalization, as it were, helps make a self-fulfilling prophecy of the idea of attacking welfare dependency to retrench the welfare state in the face of global competition. And as the latter spreads around the world, it also increases consideration of policies of welfare state retrenchment, albeit in some countries more than in others, including most especially, and perhaps not ironically, the United States, where the discourse of globalization and its preoccupation with welfare state retrenchment as an unavoidable corollary were first most aggressively championed. The causal chain is not linear.

Paul Pierson, a prominent welfare state analyst, and others have suggested that in Europe, where there has been retrenchment, it is more attributable to internal economic, social, and demographic changes, such as declining birth rates and increasing life expectancy, whereas immigration participation in the welfare state remains limited and still a hotly debated topic.[24] As a result, concern about the solvency of pensions in particular has led to revisions. Pierson and others have argued from a historical-institutional perspective that the "path dependency" of each

---

22. See Frank Vandenbroucke, "Promoting Active Welfare States in the European Union," (presentation at the "New Approaches to Governance in EU Social and Employment Policy: Open Coordination and the Future of Social Europe" Workshop, The European Union Center, University of Wisconsin-Madison, October 31, 2003) (http://eucenter.wisc.edu/Conferences/OMCnetOct03/VandenbrouckeLecture.htm).

23. In Europe, there is also Europeanization given the growing role of the European Union in influencing its member states' social welfare policies. Clare Annesely, however, argues that while Americanization involves a "one-way" transaction disciplining welfare recipients to take work, Europeanization involves a "two-way" contractual obligation where the state supports workers to become more active so as to contribute more to the economic growth of the nation. I emphasize that both focus on what the Europeans call "labor activation," although in Europe labor activation is generally less punitive and less insistent when it comes to single mothers than in the United States. See Clare Annesley, "Americanised and Europeanised: UK Social Policy Since 1997," *British Journal of Politics and International Relations* 5, 2 (May 2003): 143–65.

24. See Paul Pierson, "Introduction: Investigating the Welfare State at Century's End," in *The New Politics of the Welfare State*, Paul Pierson, ed. (Oxford, UK: Oxford University Press, 2001), pp. 1–16. Also see David Pozen, "Race to the Bottom? Globalization and European Welfare Regimes," in *Parallax: The Journal of Ethics and Globalization* (December/January 2004) http://www.parallaxonline.org. Pozen concedes that if any European welfare states are vulnerable to retrenchment due to

welfare state's policies forces policymakers to respond to these internal pressures by taking advantage of the efficiencies or "increased returns" of working with existing policies and established practices to make cutbacks in ways that are specific to the politics associated with particular policies in each country.[25] External factors such as the competitive pressures stemming from economic globalization are therefore secondary in influencing welfare retrenchment decisions.

My thesis includes the idea that economic globalization is neither objective nor external in the sense that its effect is captured in quantitative indicators of international economic activity. I am more interested in what I am calling globalization discourse, which operates within and across national policy arenas to structure choices about what responses policymakers will choose to internal factors like a surplus of retirees and a lack of low-wage workers. Analysts who insist that welfare cutbacks have occurred because policymakers in each country are responding in some causal way to internal economic and demographic changes, each in their own path-dependent way, overlook that globalization discourse structures and limits the choices that policymakers make to scale back the welfare state in each country, each in their own way. Policymakers may be responding to internal demographic and economic pressures more so than to objective, external economic pressures stemming from globalization, and they may indeed be relying on past practices to respond to these internal changes. Yet, I argue that this is at best an incomplete explanation that represents a classic case of "missing the forest for trees." Statistically, it might be true that the welfare states most integrated into the world economy are not the most likely to be making welfare state cutbacks. But those statistics need to be placed in context.[26] First, policymakers are

<hr>

concern about globalization, it is Scandinavian ones because their policies are so much more generous. Chapter 3 examines Sweden and Norway and notes that Norway has cut back on Transitional Allowances for lone mothers while initiating aid for all mothers with children aged 1 to 3 so as help buffer the effects of work on care. Pierson does acknowledge the influence of the European Union in influencing welfare state restructuring in Europe, noting that it makes its member states "semi-sovereign" in this policy area. See Stephan Leibfried and Paul Pierson, *European Social Policy: Between Fragmentation and Integration* (Washington, DC: The Brookings Institution, 1995). It is arguably the case that the European Union itself has achieved such influence on member state social welfare policies in no small part due to concerns about the competitiveness of Europe in a globalizing world economy.

25. Paul Pierson, "Increasing Returns, Path Dependence, and the Study of Politics," *American Political Science Review* 94, 2 (June 2000): 251–67.

26. For a good critique of decontextualized statistics, see Lawrence M. Mead, "Comment on Rank and Hirschl, 'Rags or Riches,'" *Social Science Quarterly* 82, 4 (December 2001): 670–5. Also see Chapter 4.

making choices at least as much as they are being forced inexorably to respond to internal demographic and economic pressures. Second, their choices are being structured by a politically convenient and self-serving globalization discourse that implies welfare state retrenchment is the inevitable necessary consequence of increased international economic competition.[27] The rationality of policy choice needs to be appropriately contextualized.

Social scientists more often than not focus their studies on how choices get made, sometimes using "rational choice" models to predict what factors lead decision-makers to make what choices. Such issues are often also studied using quantitative information to test various causal models that end up demonstrating that the choices in question have been determined by particular inexorable, objective factors. The study of welfare state cutbacks is no different and results in suggesting that policymakers are somehow fated to follow a particular path down a road of retrenchment, varying only to the degree that economic, social, and demographic factors allow. What gets lost in such analyses is the extent to which policymakers have discretion to play with the idea of globalization as a politically convenient excuse that makes cutbacks seem more necessary than perhaps they are. In particular, what is especially glaringly neglected is how globalization is used by policymakers to suggest that cutbacks in domestic programs that they had already wanted to execute are now unavoidable.[28]

The problem is simply more complicated than conventional analyses would allow. Failing to account for the pervasive role of globalization discourse in structuring how policymakers choose to respond to internal demographic and economic changes is a serious oversight in ways that involve both an impersonal determining structure and the volition that comes with having personal agency. In one sense, failing to account for globalization discourse overlooks how it facilitates making the policy choices that lead to making welfare state cutbacks seem inevitable when instead the choice of how to respond to internal pressures is much more open-ended than the neoliberal discourse of capitalist welfare states would allow. Therefore, the emphasis on internal pressures over the external forces of globalization overlooks that globalization as a politically convenient discourse is pervasively and readily available to structure debate about what to do about internal demographic and economic changes. As a

---

27. See Anne Gray, *Unsocial Europe: Social Protection or Flexploitation?* (London: Pluto Press, 2004).

28. For the argument that the war in Iraq has had the same domestic effect leading to prior plans for cutbacks to be accelerated, see Frances Fox Piven, *The War at Home: The Domestic Roots of Bush's Militarism* (New York: New Press, 2004).

result, globalization as a discourse, more so than as an inexorable, objective economic force, can help create the conditions under which welfare cutbacks seem to be the only logical response, especially for political and economic elites who see opportunities to be exploited by restructuring their welfare states so that their economies can be more competitive in the global economy, not because they have to but because they want to. Globalization discourse structures policy choices, making them seem to be the logical and even inevitable ones.

Globalization discourse was, therefore, arguably a story the United States told about the rest of the world to itself and which ended up fueling welfare state retrenchment back at home in America. It is distinctly possible that U.S. corporate leaders could champion globalization so successfully because they did not confront much resistance from a debilitated labor movement, further distinguishing them from their European counterparts, who have often had to elaborate social welfare policy changes in ways that supported workers rather than simply pushing them into low-wage jobs. In any case, globalization discourse helped also frame European responses to what were taken to be deterministic economic, social, and demographic forces. Colin Hay and Matthew Watson capture this role of globalization discourse in framing welfare retrenchment deliberations in the United Kingdom when they write:

> [G]lobalisation acts as so pronounced a constraint upon the autonomy of government precisely because the government believes that it does; the merely contingent is rendered necessary only through the discourse and politics of globalisation.
>
> An image of inexorable economic forces is often summoned in order to explain the emergence of globalisation's logic of inevitability. Once a more dialectical understanding of the relationship between the material and the ideational is emphasised, however, a rather different picture emerges. Political outcomes are not structurally-determined by a globalisation process for which there is, in any case, only superficial evidence. The political is far more than merely residual to a determining economic essence. Indeed, in the absence of decisive, facilitating political interventions, the material processes of globalisation would be unsustainable. Consequently, we argue that it is necessary to focus not only on empirical measures of the extent to which economic relations have, or have not, been globalised.[29]

---

29. Colin Hay and Matthew Watson, "Globalisation and British Political Economy" (paper presented at the British Political Studies Association Annual Meeting, 1998). The longer version of the presented paper was entitled "The Discourse of Globalisation and the Logic of No Alternative: Rendering the Contingent Necessary in the Downsizing of New Labour's Aspirations for Government."

As this quotation suggests, globalization is more than an empirical question. Further, globalization discourse is, like any discourse, self-fulfilling, making itself real by iteration. In the case of welfare state retrenchment, it is as if the United States conveniently created its own foreign threat that it then convinced itself it had to fear, producing the desired economic insecurity at home and abroad, and eventually making itself real and becoming its self-fulfilling prophecy, in the U.S. and then in Europe as well. Globalization discourse is in this sense self-legitimating. It is also a conspiracy of its own special sort.

Globalization Discourse Is More Than Talk

What we can call the conspiracy of discourse is a potent force for making the world the way it is because discourse is more than mere talk or propaganda. It is also different than ideology. Discourse is arguably more powerful than ideology. Ideology characterizes an alleged preexisting reality, but discourse constitutes that reality.[30] Although the distortions of ideology can be challenged by pointing to inconsistent facts, discourse operates more insidiously to constitute those facts, to become those facts. Of his own work on discourse, Foucault wrote:

> [T]he target of analysis wasn't 'institutions,' 'theories,' or 'ideology,' but practices—with the aim of grasping the conditions which make these acceptable at a given moment; the hypothesis being that these types of practice are not just governed by institutions, prescribed by ideologies, guided by pragmatic circumstances—whatever roles these elements may actually play—but possess up to a point their own specific regularities, logic, strategy, self-evidence and 'reason.' It is a question of analyzing a 'regime of practices'—practices being understood here as places where what is said and what is done, rules imposed and reasons given, the planned and the taken for granted meet and interconnect.[31]

Discourse is more than talk; it is what is said and what is done. It is lived language that is materialized in practice. Discourse involves discursive practices that we practice in our daily lives as we go about making sense of what we do and doing what we do in terms of how we make sense of it, as when we become convinced that economic growth in an era of global-

---

30. See Wendy Brown, *States of Injury: Power and Freedom in Late Modernity* (Princeton: Princeton University Press, 1995), p. 142, fn. 13.

31. Michel Foucault, "A Question of Method," in *The Foucault Effect: Studies in Governmentality with Two Lectures by and an Interview with Michel Foucault*, Graham Burchell, Colin Gordon, and Peter Miller, eds. (Chicago: The University of Chicago Press, 1991), p. 75.

ization is dependent upon workers taking low-wage jobs to the point that there are only low-wage jobs for certain workers to take. And once we move past the point of seeing some jobs as being paid low wages and start seeing those jobs as essentially low-wage jobs, then discourse has made itself real and those jobs become low-wage jobs that will not likely be paid better wages anytime soon.

In this sense, hegemonic discourse naturalizes and materializes its reality, via social practices, custom, and the power of economic relations, thereby making it hard to see what is taken as essentially a low-wage job as anything other than that, even though it just happens to be a job for which low wages are paid (probably in no small part because workers are not unionized to fight for higher wages). Discourse then not only naturalizes and materializes its reality by giving it an essential nature but also erases and effaces the possibility of alternative natures that reality might have, as in the case of unionized workers being paid decent wages for doing what is "essentially" seen as low-wage work. That has now, in an age of globalization, become unthinkable, at least in the United States.[32] Paying decent wages to people who work in low-wage jobs would be going against the facts of the situation as they have come to be constituted; it would result in workers earning more than their "true" wage, which of course in the current era of globalization is now in free fall, as transnational corporations and other firms increasingly "outsource" jobs to low-paying labor markets in the Third World and increase downward pressure on those jobs at home.[33]

That only the United States has naturalized the idea of the low-wage job as much as it has among western nation-states also reminds us that discourse, even as it materializes the reality of which it speaks, is never univocal and is given to infinite variation.[34] Discourse may be a self-fulfilling prophecy but it speaks in multiple tongues. Some welfare states have developed far less draconian policies in the face of the globalization of Americanized retrenchment discourse. If discourse is a conspiracy, it is one where there are many leaks, defections, and resistances. Nonetheless,

32. David Shipler, *The Working Poor: Invisible in America* (New York: Alfred A. Knopf, 2004).
33. For an analysis that contrasts structural Marxism and poststructural discourse analysis to critique the framing of welfare retrenchment as a *fait accompli* of globalization, see Colin Hay, "Globalisation, Welfare Retrenchment and 'the Logic of No Alternative': Why Second-Best Won't Do," *Journal of Social Policy* 27, 4 (October 1998): 525–32.
34. See Handler, *Social Citizenship and Workfare in the U.S. and Western Europe*, pp. 144–5, 233–6.

a dominant discourse operates as a main theme from which there can be only minor variations.

Therefore, given the pervasiveness of globalization discourse in welfare policymaking today, it may be that neither structural Marxism nor liberal empiricism is telling us the full story. Attention to discourse in all its varieties may be just what we need in order to understand globalization's role in the story of international welfare retrenchment.[35] Perhaps then discourse analysis does in fact have something to offer politics designed to resist the idea that there the alleged immutable forces of economic globalization requiring welfare state retrenchment.

Conclusion

U.S.-style globalization discourse has singled out welfare dependency as a problem that must be attacked by scaling back social assistance so that local economies can become more competitive internationally. This is a discourse that has made itself real first by iteration in the United States and then by emulation in part elsewhere, making it seem inevitable to the point that it becomes a self-fulfilling prophecy, especially in the United States.

The lesson of this I argue is that the truth, whatever it may be ultimately, comes to us as a self-fulfilling and self-legitimating artifact of discourse. Discourse's self-fulfilling and self-legitimating circular causality operates as a potent form of power helping to make what its takes to be true real and determinative, obdurate and factual. The truth is a form of power says Foucault, and globalization discourse would be a primary case in point, especially when it comes to understanding welfare state retrenchment in the United States in recent years. Therefore, not only might the truth be one-sided but its edge cuts deep and hard, for better or, as is often the case, for worse. The truth is not "mushy" after all. Neither is globalization discourse, which operates as its own hard-edged self-fulfilling prophecy.

---

35. See Colin Hay and David Marsh, eds., *Demystifying Globalization* (New York: St. Martin's Press, 2000). For an example of discourse analysis applied to the British Labour Party's uncritical reproduction of the retrenchment discourse in England that facilitated Margaret Thatcher's rise to power, see Hay, "Narrating Crisis: The Discursive Construction of the Winter of Discontent," pp. 253–77.

2 Reversed Polarities

The Incomplete Americanization of European Welfare Policy

I have a confession to make. For over two decades, I have discussed with students that the research literature was filled with references to the United States as a "welfare-state laggard."[1] Research study after research study provided copious statistical documentation on the fact that the United States spent far less on social welfare policies to combat poverty and did less to aid the poorest members of U.S. society than did most, if not all, other industrialized societies.[2] The major implicit normative subtext of such objective social science studies was more often than not the idea that the United States would, it was hoped, eventually "catch up" to European welfare states that had often started earlier, say with Bismarck's plan for social security in the 1880s, than the U.S. welfare state that was seen as being founded with the Social Security Act of 1935.

The metaphor of lagging behind in time was palpable in a social science literature that was assumed to be providing an objective, factual presentation of reality. Claims to objectivity not withstanding, distance and time metaphors have long been popular in social welfare policy discourse of liberal, individualistic, capitalistic societies for suggesting that some people,

1. Mary Ruggie has pointed out that Harold Wilensky was the first to call the United States a "welfare state laggard." See Mary Ruggie, "Rich Democracies: Political Economy, Public Policy, and Performance by Harold L. Wilensky," *Political Science Quarterly* 118, 2 (Summer 2003): 355–56. Wilensky actually originally called the United States a "reluctant welfare state." See Harold L. Wilensky, "The Problems and Prospects of the Welfare State," in *Industrial Society and Social Welfare*, Harold L. Wilensky and Charles N. Lebeaux, eds. (New York: Free Press, 1965), pp. xii–xxv. Also see Bruce S. Jansson, *The Reluctant Welfare State*, 4th edition (Belmont: Wadsworth/Brooks Cole, 2001); Diane Sainsbury, *Gender, Equality and Welfare States* (Cambridge: Cambridge University Press, 1996), pp. 28–29; Richard Titmuss, *Essays on the Welfare State* (London: Allen & Unwin, 1958); and Gosta Esping-Andersen, *The Three Worlds of Welfare Capitalism* (New York: Polity Press, Cambridge, 1990).

2. For a recent and thorough example of such research, see Lee Rainwater and Timothy M. Smeeding, *Poor Kids in a Rich Country: America's Children in Comparative Perspective* (New York: Russell Sage Foundation, 2003).

states, or policies lag behind others and are at risk of being "left behind," implying that there is some path or track that is to be followed in some timely way. The idea of a race seems to have been always there beneath the surface, implicitly reinforcing the idea of competition that is so fundamental to liberal, individualistic, capitalistic discourse.[3]

There also has been the very popular idea among welfare state analysts that as welfare states "matured," they would become more alike.[4] The effectiveness of this aging metaphor in suggesting that welfare states actually do mature depended in no small part on the implied origination or birth date of the welfare state in question. The U.S. welfare state was seen as immature because its assumed birth date was 1935, with the passage of the Social Security Act, relatively late in comparison to the welfare states of Europe and even Canada.[5] The likelihood that with time welfare states would become more alike was also articulated with the spatial metaphor of "convergence," which also became a major research subject.[6] The spatial metaphor buttressed the time metaphor. Then again, you could say that the aging metaphor reinforced the distance and time metaphors, because as lagging welfare states aged, they caught up to others. This mixing of

---

3. No better example of the salience of the lagging-behind metaphor and its implicit referencing of competition exists in the United States today than the No Child Left Behind Act of 2002. It imposes standardized testing on public school students and then holds schools accountable for the scores, without providing those schools with the necessary funding to overcome disparities with other schools that, in all likelihood, are the major cause for the low test scores. Punishing school districts by denying them the aid that they were deprived of in the first place is its own vicious cycle and perpetuates the myth of a fair race or competition that is implicit in the No Child Left Behind Act.

4. See Paul Pierson, "The New Politics of the Welfare State," *World Politics* 48, 2 (1996): 143–79.

5. Theda Skocpol has made the case for locating the origins of the U.S. welfare state further back in time, tracing it to the Civil War pensions of the later 19th century and the Mothers' Pensions that states adopted in relatively rapid fashion after 1910. See Theda Skocpol, *Protecting Soldiers and Mothers: The Political Origins of Social Policy in the United States* (Cambridge: The Belknap Press of Harvard University Press, 1992). For the argument that the origins of the U.S. welfare state lie in the development of 19th-century orphanages, see Matthew Crenson, *Building the Invisible Orphanage: A Prehistory of the American Welfare System* (Cambridge: Harvard University Press, 1998).

6. The major proponent of the idea of welfare state convergence as a discernible trend has been Harold Wilensky. See Harold Wilensky, *The Welfare State and Inequality: Structural and Ideological Roots of Public Expenditure* (Berkeley: University of California Press, 1975). For his latest restatement of this argument, see Harold Wilensky, *Rich Democracies: Political Economy, Public Policy, and Performance* (Berkeley: University of California Press, 2002).

metaphors did not undercut, but instead consolidated, the subtextual message of the objective social science literature: the United States was a welfare state laggard that should, and would, it was hoped, with time come to resemble the more progressive welfare states of Europe.

In the midst of this metaphorical confusion, I structured my discussions with students around the prospects for the United States developing a more inclusive, solidaristic, social-democratic welfare state that effectively sheltered all citizens from the economic insecurities associated with capitalism. We debated whether the United States would become like Europe. Yet, in recent years, changes in social policy in the more-developed societies suggest that perhaps it is more likely that the opposite is happening. Instead of the United States becoming more like Europe, Europe is becoming more like the United States. In particular, there is a movement in European countries toward a U.S.-style welfare reform with its emphasis on conditioning the receipt of aid on participation in welfare-to-work programs. It looks like I had it the wrong way around—metaphorically speaking, that is.[7]

Or so it seems. This chapter makes the case for discourse analysis as a useful way to understand the global social welfare policy change in recent years. I focus on key metaphors associated with the globalization of welfare policy discourse. By globalization, I really mean the Americanization of welfare policy discourse that focuses on reducing welfare dependency by enforcing work so as to increase economic competitiveness.[8] I show that while European nation-states have come to increasingly articulate their social welfare policy reforms in ways that reflect the American obsession with the "welfare dependency" metaphor, they have done so by using their own critically chosen allusive metaphor of "labor activation." And when they talk of labor activation they vary from the United States with its more punitive approach that is directed primarily at lone mothers.[9] The European focus is more about activating the long-term unemployed, is less punitive than the U.S. approach, and varies

---

7. For a similar argument about the Americanization of European penal discourse, see Loïc Wacquant, "How Penal Common Sense Comes to Europeans: Notes on the Transatlantic Diffusion of Neoliberal *Doxa*," *European Societies* 1 (1999): 319–52.

8. See Clare Annesley, "Americanised and Europeanised: UK Social Policy Since 1997," *British Journal of Politics and International Relations* 5, 2 (May 2003): 143–65.

9. See Joel Handler, *Social Citizenship and Workfare in the U.S. and Western Europe: The Paradox of Inclusion* (Cambridge, UK: Cambridge University Press, 2004), pp. 112–13; Anne Gray, *Unsocial Europe: Social Protection or Flexploitation?* (London: Pluto Press, 2004); and Jamie Peck, *Workfare States* (New York: Guilford Press, 2001).

across welfare states in ways that are not associated with objective internal demographic and economic changes or external ones like integration into the world economy.

My goal in this chapter, therefore, is not to prove that European welfare states are inexorably becoming more like the United States. European welfare states have over the past decade indeed moved toward what are called labor activation policies that emphasize placing welfare state recipients in employed positions.[10] Many policymakers in Europe are allowing themselves to get caught up in globalization discourse as a way of justifying welfare cutbacks. Yet, while many emphasize policies to increase economic flexibility and enhance global competitiveness, others seek to do so without undermining needed social supports for workers and their families. This chapter provides detail that the discourse of globalization operates as that form of the crisis narrative that encourages people to accept welfare state retrenchment as the *fait accompli* it need not be.[11] But the varied responses in Europe provide the evidence that welfare state retrenchment need not be the inevitable result.

I start this analysis by focusing on the growing penchant in most European countries to articulate social welfare policy change in an American idiom of reducing welfare dependency by requiring active labor market participation. Included here are the metaphors of the active welfare state as it is championed in Europe today. "Activation" has developed into a compelling discursive practice over the past decade in Europe, and European policymakers, like those in the United States, have developed an interest in scaling back welfare provision, especially to the unemployed, so as to grow a pool of low-wage laborers that enable their economies to be more competitive in an increasingly global economy. I suggest that the discourse of activation trades on the implicit idea that welfare recipients are by definition passive simply by virtue of their receiving assistance and

10. See Rebecca Blank, "U.S. Welfare Reform: What's Relevant for Europe?" *CESinfo Economic Studies* 49, 1 (2003): 26.

11. On the role of globalization discourse in making welfare retrenchment seem unavoidable, see Colin Hay and Matthew Watson, "Globalisation and British Political Economy" (paper presented at the British Political Studies Association Annual Meeting, 1998). The longer version of the presented paper was entitled "The Discourse of Globalisation and the Logic of No Alternative: Rendering the Contingent Necessary in the Downsizing of New Labour's Aspirations for Government." Also see Colin Hay, "Globalisation, Welfare Retrenchment and 'the Logic of No Alternative': Why Second-Best Won't Do," *Journal of Social Policy* 27, 4 (October 1998): 525–32. On crisis narrative in the formative period of globalization discourse, see Colin Hay, "Narrating Crisis: The Discursive Construction of the Winter of Discontent," *Sociology* 30, 2 (May 1996): 253–77.

not being able to provide for themselves and their families through paid employment. The discourse of activation implies that welfare recipients are in need of outside instigation to become active and achieve self-sufficiency. They need to sign "welfare contracts" requiring work so they can become full members of the "social contract." In this way, they will overcome their "social exclusion." Such a discourse of activation erases consideration of alternative understandings of why welfare recipients are not active in the labor force and excluded from mainstream society in the first place. The discourse of activation becomes a new way of blaming the victims of capitalism all over again. It enacts what Joel Handler calls the "paradox of inclusion," because activation policies include the unemployed in the work-first society but in ways that risk reinscribing their subordination.[12] Including the unemployed but only as a class of low-wage workers, can ensure their continued marginality.

I suggest that the discourse of activation has the potential to be a European version of the American discourse of welfare dependency that developed increasingly from the 1970s on to repudiate welfare recipients as passive, lazy, and, therefore, undeserving. Welfare dependency discourse was never an accurate representation of a preexisting reality, but over time made itself real. With time, U.S. policymakers increasingly came to see that they had a crisis of welfare dependency even as the duration of welfare use for the average recipient did not change substantially.[13] As suggested, it is as if saying made it so. And with time, other welfare states in the western world felt the need to see welfare dependency as a problem existing in their midst. This is why I have suggested that there is the distinct prospect that Americanization of welfare discourse is occurring to varying degrees in different European countries. This discourse provides European policymakers with a way of making sense of how to respond to their growing welfare burdens given their countries' declining birth rates and increasing longevity rates. They look to a justification for promoting greater labor activation policies. While an international race to the bottom in welfare retrenchment is distinctly possible under such circumstances, I detail in what follows that the variations reflecting past commitments to welfare state protections remain important and point to how different countries develop their responses

---

12. See Handler, *Social Citizenship and Workfare in the U.S. and Western Europe*, p. 8.
13. Robert A. Moffitt and Peter T. Gottschalk, "Ethnic and Racial Differences in Welfare Receipt in the United States," in *America Becoming: Racial Trends and Their Consequences, Volume I*, Neil J. Smelser, William Julius Wilson, and Faith Mitchell, eds. (Washington, DC: National Academy Press, 2001), pp. 152–73.

that result in less than American-style reforms.[14] The European experience shows that the "welfare contract" can affirm as well as deny the "social contract" depending on how it works to overcome "social exclusion" through employment.

While globalization discourse about the necessity of welfare policy retrenchment is a story about what must and is happening around the world, it has operated most powerfully here at home. I emphasize that while European countries have gotten caught up in the Americanization of welfare policy discourse, I conclude by highlighting how the power of discourse is real but not total, as is demonstrated by the lack of convergence among European welfare states in moving toward a more reduced form of social provision in the era of globalization.

The Americanization of European Welfare Policy Discourse

The Americanization of European welfare policy discourse is now a subject of in-depth study.[15] A good example is Ireland, where its inclusion in the European Union led to rapid economic development and a debate about what public policies will best help sustain Ireland's economic bubble. The debate is widely known as the "Boston/Berlin" debate and concerns whether Ireland should move toward being more like the United States with its neoliberal free market economic policies or more like Germany with its social democratic policies that regulate business and protect workers.[16] Ireland is awash in concerns about the need to privatize even its successful and profitable state-owned enterprises such as its national airline Aer Lingus. The Irish political leadership has initiated a campaign to promote "personal responsibility," not so much in terms of promoting work and family values among the poor as much as in terms of getting the heads of all families to save for their retirement so that the government can reduce the extent to which it has to fund state pensions. There is even the beginning of discussions in Parliament on the adoption

---

14. On national variation in the character of capitalism as it relates to policies that affect labor markets such as welfare reform, see Susan Christopherson, "Why Do National Labor Market Practices Continue to Diverge in the Global Economy? The 'Missing Link' of Investment Rules," *Economic Geography* 78, 1 (January 2002): 1–20.

15. See Handler, *Social Citizenship and Workfare in the U.S. and Western Europe*, pp. 15–16.

16. On the Boston/Berlin debate and related issues, see Karin Gilland, "Irish Euroscepticism," *European Studies: A Journal of European Culture, History and Politics* 20, 1 (January 2004): 171–91.

of an immigration policy to allow the growing numbers of needed migrant workers from other countries (including some from England) to eventually gain citizenship and the entitlement rights that come with it. Ireland is seeking to sustain its economic miracle of recent years by integrating itself into the world economy.

The "Boston/Berlin" debate is an explicit example showing that globalization discourse is about the issue of Americanization in ways that quickly imply issues for social welfare state reorganization. This debate flows quite logically from the dissemination of U.S. globalization discourse.[17] It is true that this is not the first time that U.S. ideas on social welfare have spread to Europe. The dissemination of U.S. ideas about social welfare harkens back at least to the "Atlantic Crossings" Daniel Rodgers identified in his study of the Progressive Era exchange of ideas concerning the reform of capitalism.[18] Rodgers, however, convincingly demonstrated that the ideas flowed both ways across the Atlantic. That seems less so today.

Yet, I argue that when European welfare states Americanize they also transform that American discourse in ways more appropriate for their social democratic politics, being not marked as much by the separation of political and economic rights as is the case in the United States with its political ideology of uniqueness and moral superiority (often referred to as "American exceptionalism"). Since its founding, the United States has told its origin story about how it is a special place for realizing the ideal of freedom and democracy, and this has discouraged us from learning from others outside the United States about many things, even welfare-to-work schemes.[19] American policymakers continue for the most part to be uninterested that European work requirement policies for the poor tend to be not as draconian, less focused on punishing single mothers with

---

17. See Jay Hein, "Ideas as Exports," *American Outlook* (Summer 2002) (http://www.americanoutlook.org/index.cfm?fuseaction=article_detail&id=1877). Hein notes how welfare reform was in the mid-1990s a popular idea that spread from Wisconsin to Europe for responding to the perceived (correctly in his mind) pressures of economic globalization. He calls this an example of an emerging "global domestic policy" discourse where ideas circulate across the developed world.

18. Daniel T. Rodgers, *Atlantic Crossings: Social Politics in a Progressive Age* (Cambridge: The Belknap Press of Harvard University Press, 1998).

19. See Jonathan Zeitlin, "Introduction," in *Governing Work and Welfare in a New Economy: European and American Experiments*, Jonathan Zeitlin and David Trubek, eds. (New York: Oxford University Press, 2003), p. 7. Zeitlin notes the differences between European countries that share information on welfare-to-work via the European Union's Open Method of Coordination and the United States, which evidences a lack of interest in what other countries are doing.

children, and more focused on activating unemployed youth, the long-term jobless, and, to a lesser extent, the disabled.[20]

In fact, in European hands, the American discourse can be pointed in progressive directions as is the case with the British appropriation of the American idea of switching from income support to asset building.[21] Asset-building policies are seen to encourage more personal responsibility and less welfare dependency over the long haul by, for example, giving families funds to build assets, like a college fund for the children's education rather than providing them with welfare payments. The difference in the British case is that the welfare state is involved in financing significant amounts of assets for needy families while the United States provides only symbolic gestures that remind the poor they are supposed to act more middle class and save on their own.

Nonetheless, as Jamie Peck makes clear in his *Workfare States*, there is definitely something to an Anglo-American affinity operating in the area of social welfare policies such that Australia, Canada, and Great Britain can be seen as joining the United States in retrofitting their welfare policies for the poorest members of their societies to put greater emphasis on work requirements and welfare-to-work programming.[22] The Anglo-American axis has led the way in forging a "Third Way" between a social democratic welfare state and a laissez-faire free-market approach to fashion policies that will prod the poor into taking the low-wage jobs being offered in the globalizing economy.[23] Canada, England, and even Australia seem keen to follow the lead of the United States but to make their versions of the new emphasis on "workfare" more consistent with their own welfare state traditions. As a result, their welfare reforms are far less draconian than the "get-tough" approach of the United States with its strict time limits and penalties for noncompliance. More emphasis is also given to providing training than in the United States. Still, the brave new world of workfare is being rolled out in each of these countries. For Peck, a distinctive discourse that emphasizes the importance of taking whatever

---

20. See Handler, *Social Citizenship and Workfare in the U.S. and Western Europe*, pp. 6–8.

21. See *Asset Building and the Escape from Poverty: A New Welfare Policy Debate* (Paris: Organization for Economic Co-operation and Development, November 2003). For a critique of U.S. asset building, see Chapter 5.

22. See Peck, *Workfare States*, pp. 1–27.

23. The "Third Way" is championed by British Prime Minister Tony Blair and is the brainchild of social theorist Anthony Giddens as the best available response out of the crisis of the welfare state created by the postindustrial global economy. See Anthony Giddens, *The Third Way and Its Critics* (Cambridge, UK: Polity Press, 2000).

work the market provides is being adopted in all of these countries, and it is a discourse in service of those corporate interests that have the most to gain from regimenting citizens into low-wage labor markets. From this perspective, the Third Way offers the poorest members of society almost no way to make a decent living or to gain the needed support from the state when they need it. Peck writes: "Stripped down to its labor-regulatory essence, workfare is not about creating jobs for people that don't have them; it is about creating workers for jobs that nobody wants. In a Foucaldian sense, it is seeking to make 'docile bodies' for the new economy: flexible, self-reliant, and self-disciplining."[24]

Rebecca Blank suggests that the U.S. model of welfare reform is likely to increasingly resonate beyond the Anglo-American countries with their more individualistic cultures. Blank provides a number of reasons:

First, *European nations have been facing more budgetary limits in recent decades*. In part, this is due to slower economic growth rates. In part, it is due to demographic changes that are producing an aging population and growing strains on budgets. In part, it is due to the economic effects of monetary union within Europe, which has forced nations to pay closer attention to budget deficits.... It is exactly a tighter budget environment in which concerns about welfare dependency and over-use of public assistance programs might be expected to arise.

The long-term slower macroeconomy has also affected the European conversation around welfare. As more and more analysts have become convinced that European labour markets are too inflexible and over-regulated, this has produced broad-scale interest in ways to introduce more efficiency into the economies. Not surprisingly, concern with disincentive effects of assistance programs are one response.

Second, the *emerging economic co-operation within the European Union* has produced concern about the response to national social policies if labour becomes more mobile across Europe. While little progress has been made in EU conversations about social policy convergence, there is nervousness about the extent to which more generous programs in some countries will induce migration. The "race to the bottom"—a long-discussed concern in the U.S.—argues welfare benefits will be underprovided if there is a threat of "welfare migration" across states.

Third, *racial issues are becoming more prominent in Europe*.... [There is reason to] suggest that race is a primary reason for a more limited system of public support in the U.S. Europe has become much more diverse in recent decades as well. Tensions around the presence of immigrants have been much discussed, particularly the influence of these tensions on the rise of right-wing politicians.[25]

---

24. Peck, *Workfare States*, p. 6.
25. Blank, "U.S. Welfare Reform: What's Relevant for Europe?" pp. 68–70.

Blank's analysis is insightful but perhaps a bit too uncritical in its assumption that the forces she cites are objective and real. Instead, if there is globalization in the sense of Americanization, it is not because objective forces are pushing Europe in that direction. Instead, I argue for a more constructivist perspective that suggests that changes in discourse are facilitating reframing the issues of the welfare state in these terms. Rather than a matter of necessity, it is a matter of politically convenient language choice that articulates welfare state issues in terms of limiting benefits to those "other" people who are not doing what we want them to do in order for us to grow a low-wage labor force to compete for larger profits in a globalizing economy. Blank's objectivistic social science discourse itself prevents her from taking her insightful analysis far enough to get to the gritty issues of the power of discourse to help usher in a new economy that will benefit corporate interests more than ordinary workers.

Colin Hay agrees that the United Kingdom in particular has come over time to emulate significant features of the American approach to framing the welfare state as a problem of welfare dependency. Yet he sees this not as an inevitable response to the objective forces of globalization or to any other objective forces but instead as choices policy elites have made in part because of how globalization discourse has framed the problem. Hay sees the problem as beginning as early as 1979, when the economic turmoil under the Callaghan Labour government was framed in a crisis narrative of "our winter of discontent." Hay notes how the mass media help position voters in the crisis narrative as discontented with the demands of striking labor unions to the point that Margaret Thatcher's rise to power was made that much more likely.[26] Colin Hay and Matthew Watson build on the idea of globalization as a crisis narrative to state:

> [Our objective] is to demonstrate that, "trans-continental" airlines and "international" bankers notwithstanding, there is *no* conclusive proof that we now live in a truly globalised world. Indeed, it would be possible to cite from the secondary literature on globalisation any number of statistical measures which show fairly unequivocally that claims for globalisation cannot be substantiated. Yet, to engage with the empirical arguments and nothing else may well be to miss the most important aspect of the globalisation debate.... Thus, as Frances Fox Piven suggests, "the explanation [of globalisation] itself has become a

---

26. Colin Hay uses Louis Althusser's concept of "interpellation" to emphasize that crisis narratives implicitly provide their audience with a subject position that they are expected to take in order to interpret the narrative and thereby identify with its sense of urgency that something needs to be done in order to save them from that crisis. See Hay, "Narrating Crisis: The Discursive Construction of the Winter of Discontent," pp. 253–77.

political force helping to create the institutional realities it purportedly merely describes...." [G]lobalisation acts as so pronounced a constraint upon the autonomy of government precisely because the government believes that it does; the merely contingent is rendered necessary only through the discourse and politics of globalisation.[27]

Under Tony Blair's leadership, the Labour Party became "New Labour," where as Blair stated in 1996: "The key to New Labour economics is the recognition that Britain...[has]...to compete in an increasingly international market place.... Today's Labour Party, New Labour, is the political embodiment of the changed world—the new challenges, the new policies and the new politics."[28]

But as Hay and Watson suggest: "New Labour's search for alternatives to the now ascendant paradigm of neo-liberal economics has been less than exhaustive. This not so much because such alternatives do not exist, but because the space within which such alternatives might be framed is simply not perceived to exist. Once again, the rhetorical force of globalisation's 'logic of no alternative' becomes a self-fulfilling prophecy."[29]

Ruth Lister notes that Blair's New Labour government founded its responses to globalization by invoking the imported American idiom of "welfare dependency" as an ill that had to be treated by enforcing work and family responsibility via its New Deal program that was centered on a "new contract for welfare."[30] Lister notes that key policy documents were filled with metaphors of space and time indicating that welfare dependency "held back" the country from achieving its economic goals and created an excluded class "cut off from the mainstream of society" and its values.[31] And while New Labour's American-sounding "New Deal" program of welfare reforms followed U.S. welfare reform in reducing access to benefits and trying to promote required paid employment outside the home by lone mothers, the U.K. approach in this area has been much less draconian than in the United States, with programs providing services that support work along with benefit reductions rather than focusing only on setting stiff work

27. See Hay and Watson, "Globalisation and British Political Economy," p. 3.
28. Tony Blair, speech to the BDI Annual Conference, Bonn, Germany, June 18, 1996, as quoted in Hay and Watson, "Globalisation and British Political Economy," p. 4.
29. Hay and Watson, "Globalisation and British Political Economy," p. 7.
30. Ruth Lister, "The Responsible Citizen: Creating a New British Welfare Contract," in *Western Welfare in Decline: Globalization and Women's Poverty*, Catherine Kingfisher, ed. (Philadelphia: University of Pennsylvania Press, 2002), pp. 110–27.
31. Lister, "The Responsible Citizen: Creating a New British Welfare Contract," pp. 113–14.

requirements. Although lack of public funding for affordable child care becomes just another burden for lone mothers leaving welfare in the United States, the same shortage of public funding of child care in the United Kingdom has reduced pressure to impose harsher policies. Nonetheless, the United Kingdom in many ways has led Europe in adopting the U.S. "welfare dependency" discourse as a way of vilifying welfare receipt and structuring welfare reform. The rest of Europe has been caught up more in the related but somewhat broader discourse of labor activation. You could say that the mobilizing of "activation" for the purposes of reforming welfare requires the agency of key policy actors in each country which is to also say that the discourse is never univocal.

Activating Discourse: Each in Its Own Way

A discourse of labor "activation" has helped frame welfare reform in Europe in recent years. This is potentially another discourse of welfare dependency that operates as a politically and economically convenient way to reinscribe deficiency among low-income welfare recipients and ends up blaming them for their alleged idleness. It does this while simultaneously manufacturing a pool of low-wage labor. Europe's new discourse of labor activation has spawned talk on behalf of new "active welfare state" that focuses on promoting economic efficiency and competitiveness by delegitimizing welfare taking as inherently passive and negative, while overvalorizing low-wage work as inherently active and positive. The European versions of this discourse, however, contrary to that of the United States, are for the most part rarely are as draconian and moralistic as in the United States.[32]

Nonetheless, I argue that European labor activation discourses perform important work in the public sphere by its reinscribing passivity and thereby underservingness among those who need to depend on the state for assistance. The unemployed as welfare recipients are by definition people who are not able and need to be enabled. In this discursive formation, they are "othered" by the mere act of receiving assistance. The enabling state creates

---

32. Former Belgian Minister for Employment and Pensions Frank Vandenbroucke coined the term "active welfare state" and stresses supportive work programs. See Frank Vandenbroucke, "Promoting Active Welfare States in the European Union" (presented at the "New Approaches to Governance in EU Social and Employment Policy: Open Coordination and the Future of Social Europe" Workshop, The European Union Center, University of Wisconsin-Madison, October 31, 2003) (http://eucenter.wisc.edu/Conferences/OMCnetOct03/VandenbrouckeLecture.htm).

its own passive clients who serve as the basis for making its own preferred solutions seem necessary. These solutions can range from expensive investments in human capital development, including in particular serious support for education and training, to cheap work requirements without many social supports. The cheap and easy solution is to simply require work of recipients. This is the American approach and it has been emulated in different ways to varying degrees by most European countries in recent years; if outside the United States, it is often more supportive in promoting work rather than simply insisting on it.

Therefore, European countries have not in all instances followed the United States down the road of welfare state reorganization and the imposition of a punitive workfare regime to the degree one could imagine.[33] Social democracies have proved to varying degrees much more resilient than some observers have noted, even if there are policy changes in various countries that pantomime the U.S. style of welfare retrenchment.[34] It is also important to note that some countries have followed the United States more than others but none have gone as far as the Americans. This variation is itself noteworthy because it highlights that what globalization discourse posits as necessity is really choice and that different countries will choose differently based on their history, culture, political economy, and welfare state traditions. In particular, the rhetoric of moving from a "passive" welfare state that provides benefits to an "active" welfare state that emphasizes labor "activation" and labor market "insertion" policies leads to many different understandings of an "active" welfare state that are being enacted in Europe today, with some putting increased stress on providing needed social supports.[35]

---

33. See Christopherson, "Why Do National Labor Market Practices Continue to Diverge in the Global Economy?" pp. 1–20.

34. See Peter Taylor-Gooby, "Polity, Policy-Making and Welfare Futures," in *Welfare States Under Pressure*, Peter Taylor-Gooby, ed. (London: Sage Publications, 2001), pp. 171–88; and Giuliano Bonoli, Vic George, and Peter Taylor-Gooby, *European Welfare Futures: Toward a Theory of Retrenchment* (Cambridge: Polity Press, 2000).

35. See Vandenbroucke, "Promoting Active Welfare States in the European Union," for an insistence that an "active welfare state" means for the originator of the term greater commitment to social welfare assistance than that of the proponents of the "Third Way." "Insertion" refers to the French 1988 *Revenu minimum d'insertion* (RMI) law that created work requirements and supports for a category of claimants under that universal income policy for all persons whose incomes fall below the legislated minimum. "Insertion contracts" to facilitate integration into the workforce are not mandatory. See Handler, *Social Citizenship and Workfare in the U.S. and Western Europe*, pp. 15–16.

Comparisons can be difficult, especially regarding work requirement policies. Several broad indicators, however, suggest the United States is distinctive in its use of a "get-tough" approach in pursuing labor activation policies for single mothers in particular. First, it is important to bear in mind that there is substantial variation across welfare states in terms of their level of commitment to providing social welfare benefits and the ways in which they do it, with the United States continuing to be much more limited in most policies areas in its extension of benefits to those who cannot provide for themselves through the market. Second, variation in the generosity and coverage of benefits across European welfare states is considerable but most often still exceeds that provided in the United States even after the welfare reforms of recent years have been imposed. Third, U.S. welfare reform has been distinctively focused on primarily, but not entirely, reducing access to assistance and requiring work by lone mothers who receive welfare, what is now called Temporary Assistance for Needy Families (TANF), whereas welfare reform in Europe has been concentrated more on increasing the employment of the broader population of recipients of unemployment benefits. Further, where welfare reform has involved reducing benefits to lone mothers, it has often been aggressively resisted, as in the United Kingdom, or has been met with generous supports for caregiving, as in Norway.[36]

With these points in mind, it is not surprising then that the United States generally has a more punitive approach to moving the unemployed into the workforce. Giuliano Bonoli and Jean-Michel Bonvin compared sanction rates under work schemes in the United States with those in Denmark, Germany, and the United Kingdom and with the average for the 30 more-developed countries that belong to the Organization of Economic Cooperation and Development (OECD). The United States stands out in its more frequent use of sanctions for unemployed claimants who fail to fulfill the requirements of their welfare contracts.[37]

An important source of variation across the countries is the target group. Most European countries have concentrated their welfare reforms on reducing unemployment among selected populations such as the long-term unemployed. This focus contrasts with that of the United States,

---

36. See Chapter 3.

37. For further details, see Giuliano Bonoli and Jean-Michel Bonvin, "Who Is to Be Activated? A Comparison of Active Labour Market Policies' Target Groups in Four Countries" (paper presented at the workshop "Social Exclusion, Minimum Income Support and Workfare in Europe," at the 5th Conference "Visions and Divisions" of the European Sociological Association, Helsinki, August 28–September 1, 2001).

where the most dramatic reforms have been in moving single mothers off welfare. In Germany, there is no requirement and not much support for mothers of young children who want to take paid employment. In England, the program for lone mothers is voluntary and is accompanied with a robust child care program to facilitate single mothers taking paid employment. Denmark has relatively stiff requirements for single mothers who are receiving assistance, but at the same time it provides substantial supports to help them eventually obtain decent-paying jobs. While France has retained better benefit levels and protections for the unemployed relative to countries like the United Kingdom, it also has moved toward increased emphasis on labor activation but without including single mothers among the groups who are required to work.[38] Overall, the United States tends to have a much more punitive approach to workfare that is distinctively focused single mothers.

Table 2-1 compares the United States with Denmark, Germany, and the United Kingdom regarding the extent to which their welfare policies have been revised to affect particular target groups: the young unemployed, single parents, older workers, and disabled workers. This table reports measures on the extent to which the country requires labor market participation, conditions benefits, and provides positive incentives to take employment, such as tax credits on earnings. For each target group, the United States imposes more conditions and provides fewer incentives than the European countries listed. The United States is particularly distinctive in its punitive approach to workfare for single parents. Denmark ranks the same as the United States in being the most punitive to single mothers, but two important points made this similarity disappear. First, Denmark provides substantial social supports, scoring 3 in positive incentives, whereas the United States does not provide such incentives and scores only 1. Second, the Danish policy begins only after paid family leave is exhausted. The United States does not have paid family leave and therefore has only its more punitive workfare to offer single mothers. Workfare in the United States is generally more punitive than in the other countries, and this is especially the case for single parents.

Deviation from the American model is apparent even with the alleged "Dutch miracle" of a more active welfare state that has replaced the "Dutch disease" of a passive welfare state that allegedly allowed too many

---

38. See Jochen Clasen and Daniel Clegg, "Unemployment Protection and Labour Market Reform in France and Great Britain in the 1990s: Solidarity versus Activation," *International Social Policy* 32, 3 (2003): 361–81.

TABLE 2-1. Intensity of Activation in Relation to Selected Target Groups

	Young unemployed			Single parents			Older workers			Disabled workers		
	Exposure to market	Benefit conditionality	Positive incentives	Exposure to market	Benefit conditionality	Positive incentives	Exposure to market	Benefit conditionality	Positive incentives	Exposure to market	Benefit conditionality	Positive incentives
Denmark*	1	3	3	1	3	3	1	1	2	1	1	2
Germany	2	2	2	1	1	1	1	1	1	1	1	2
UK	2	3	2	1	1	2	2	2	2	1	1	1
US	3	3	1	2	3	1	3	3	2	2	2	1

*Single parents are considered after parental leave.

Scoring procedure: Scores range between 1 and 3. 1 = pressure to work is weak; 3 = pressure to work is strong.

Exposure to market:

(1) The relevant group has access to comparatively generous benefits;

(2) The relevant group has access to benefits that are very modest, and/or limited in time and/or difficult to obtain; and

(3) The relevant group does not have access to income replacement benefits.

Benefit conditionally:

(1) Benefits are granted unconditionally;

(2) There are work/training conditions attached to benefits, but these are not strictly enforced; and

(3) Conditions are strictly enforced, and non-compliance results in sanctions.

Positive incentives:

(1) No additional advantage for individuals who move into paid work;

(2) Moderate incentives, like tax credits, access to advice, etc.; and

(3) Wide-ranging set of policies supporting employment of the relevant group (including policies available to other groups as well).

Source: This table is reprinted with permission from Giuliano Bonoli and Jean-Michel Bonvin, "Who is to be Activated? A Comparison of Active Labour Market Policies' Target Groups in Four Countries," (A paper presented at the workshop "Social Exclusion, Minimum Income Support and Workfare in Europe," at the 5th Conference "Visions and Divisions" of the European Sociological Association, Helsinki, August 28–September 1, 2001). http://www.shakti.uniurb.it/eurex/esa/PDF/ESA-Bonvin.pdf.

people to receive assistance in lieu of working. In some respects, the Dutch did follow the U.S. model of using work requirements and sanctions to compel work. The Dutch did begin to tighten work-related criteria for social welfare benefits in the 1980s; and they conditioned the receipt of unemployment insurance starting in 1996 and then social assistance in 1997 with a sanctioning process for noncompliance with work-related obligations such as job searching. Yet, as Dutch Sociologist Wim van Oorschot indicated:

> Only a few activation measures are solely aimed at the unemployed individuals themselves. Wage supplements for those accepting a job with a lower wage level, reorientation interviews aimed at designing individual reorientation plans (*heroriënteringsgesprekken*), and 'social activation' (unpaid, so-called *Melkert III* jobs) are the only measures that do not require the immediate co-operation of employers. All other schemes do, in the sense that they try to encourage employers to employ long-term unemployed mainly by means of temporary or permanent wage subsidies and reduction of taxes and social security contributions. Apparently, the perceptions and attitudes of employers and their related selection behaviour are seen as more of a concern than the motivations and qualifications of the unemployed.[39]

As van Oorschot suggests, the Dutch deviated from the narrow U.S. focus on the unemployed person as suffering from some disease of welfare dependency or passivity and instead placed greater stress on job creation as the key to solving the problem of nonwork. The Dutch saw the Dutch disease as just that—a disease of the economy rather than a disease of the individual. Stagnation of the job market more than passivity of the individual was the disease that had to be treated.

That said, it is important to note that the Dutch changes also demonstrate that the success of their labor activation policies is subject to some debate. There is more than meets the eye to the supposed Dutch miracle. After more than a decade and a half of stagnation, job growth accelerated rapidly in the Netherlands in the 1990s. Yet, the miracle cure is somewhat illusory. According to van Oorschot, it turns out that many of the newly created jobs were part-time and temporary, creating a new tier of more vulnerable workers with less pay, fewer benefits, and fewer protections from the uncertainties of a changing economy.[40] In addition,

---

39. Wim van Oorschot, "Work, Welfare and Citizenship: Activation and Flexicurity Policies in the Netherlands" (paper presented at COST Action 13 meeting, Aalborg University, Aalborg, Denmark, November 2–4, 2001), p. 15.
40. Oorschot, "Work, Welfare and Citizenship: Activation and Flexicurity Policies in the Netherlands." p. 14.

women, non-Dutch ethnic workers, and less-educated workers were overrepresented in the new part-time and temporary positions, further reinforcing the division between the full-time and part-time workers.

Last, it is likely that labor activation policies themselves played only a limited role in this mixed success story. van Oorschot has written:

> In conclusion, from a citizenship perspective, the Dutch activation policies of the 1980s and 1990s can not be regarded as a great success. Although many thousands of people found (additional) work through activation measures, the aggregate effect of such measures on the labour market participation of unemployed people does not appear to be very great. In the second half of the 1990s, the decrease in the number of beneficiaries was much lower than the explosive growth in the number of jobs; the outflow chances of unemployed people have not improved and those of disabled people have even worsened. The reintegration of the most vulnerable groups, such as the long-term unemployed, older unemployed, disabled workers, ethnic minorities, and the under-skilled, is "stagnating." The activation trend also seems to have led to increasing feelings of social isolation and uselessness among unemployed and disabled people. It seems that activation measures have, at best, further facilitated the labour market participation of those who might have got jobs anyway in the period of strong job growth.[41]

The Dutch story is noteworthy for what it tells us about variation in the new world of an active welfare state as it is evolving in Europe. One important point that comes through is that European countries are likely to fashion their own versions of labor activation policies that are often going to be less focused than those in the United States on changing the behavior of recipients through a system of sanctions and penalties. Nonetheless, the Dutch miracle is somewhat an exaggeration. New policies may be making welfare recipients more active participants in the labor force but in ways that are only increasing their economic marginalization and vulnerability. Part-time and temporary employment for already vulnerable groups sounds more like a cure for a profit-seeking economy than it is a cure for any condition an individual might have.

These issues have not gone unnoticed among the Dutch, who continue to debate whether the major policy changes that have led to the growth of part-time and temporary employment are consistent with their commitment to inclusive social welfare state. In particular, the 1995 "flexicurity agreements" that have allowed employers greater freedom in dismissing full-time employees in exchange for extending legal entitlement rights

---

41. Oorschot, "Work, Welfare and Citizenship: Activation and Flexicurity Policies in the Netherlands."

and benefits to part-time workers in particular continue to receive critical scrutiny.[42]

From Flexicurity to Euroskepticism

The Dutch are not alone in increasing labor force participation via labor activation policies that include work requirements in new welfare contracts recipients must fulfill. European welfare states have been getting an additional nudge by the EU, which began to emphasize the importance of innovation in this area via the Open Method of Coordination (OMC) that does not require but encourages policy change via the sharing of ideas among member states. Jonathan Zeitlin notes: "This approach, which also seems particularly well-adapted to the problems of pursuing broad common concerns under conditions of institutional diversity among participating units, was pioneered by the European Employment Strategy (EES) during the late 1990s. But the OMC in various forms has now become a virtual template for EU policy-making in other complex, politically-sensitive areas, including not only social inclusion, pensions, and health care, but also macroeconomic management, education and training, research and innovation, immigration and asylum."[43]

The EES was adopted in 1997 at the Amsterdam Intergovernmental Conference to address growing welfare expenditures in the face of persistently high unemployment levels and economic stagnation. The goal of the policy was to encourage member states to find ways to promote employment while maintaining social welfare protections. How effective the EES policy has been via the OMC in producing the desired changes in the various European welfare states is still much debated.

A particular concern is the quality of jobs that have been created; many are like the ones that are behind the alleged Dutch miracle—part-time and temporary. A related concern is the social protection associated with these jobs. There are also concerns of equity and of whether workers in these jobs will be accorded the same sort of entitlements of full-time workers. Issues of gender equity and fairness to immigrants are often mentioned as well. There is a growing concern that the EU-backed policy changes risk creating second-class citizenship in

---

42. See Bill Jordan, "Citizenship and the New Politics of Welfare" (paper presented at COST Action 13 "Changing Labour Markets, Welfare Policies and Citizenship" meeting, Ljubljana, Slovenia, June 8–9, 2001); and V. Spike Peterson, *A Critical Rewriting of Global Political Economy: Integrating Reproductive, Productive and Virtual Economies* (New York: Routledge, 2004), pp. 59–70.

43. See Zeitlin, "Introduction," in *Governing Work and Welfare in a New Economy*, p. 5.

the various member states.[44] The idea of requiring recipients to work off a "welfare contract" is increasingly seen as putting at risk the idea of the "social contract." As a result, there is talk of spreading "Euroskepticism" among voters in the different member states, with an increasing number voting to resist EU policies that are seen as a threat to member nations' welfare states.[45] The discourse of labor activation may yet deconstruct.

Given the growing resistance to EU activation policies, we could suggest that EU policies, and not globalization discourse, are behind the simultaneous development of different activation policies in the welfare states of Europe. But the fact that some countries preceded the EU in pursuing activation aside, the distinction between the EU policies and globalization discourse is chimerical. The EU is itself a creature of globalization discourse. The pressure that the EU puts on member states to get on the activation bandwagon is but a response to the pervasive influence of globalization discourse in producing the EU, its drive for integration, and its interest in rationalizing welfare state policies across the member states in order to grow a European economic engine on the world stage. As the EU strives to realize its global destiny as scripted in globalization discourse, member states increasingly find resistance to the pressures for conformity where it means sacrificing prior national commitments to citizenship entitlement rights. The idea of an alien outside force, once again, this time in the form of the EU, takes hold. Globalization discourse creates its own resistance. Its power is real but not total.

In fact, there is ample research demonstrating that welfare states continue to vary widely even in the era of globalization.[46] Vicente Navarro, John Schmidt, and Javier Astudillo have noted:

---

44. See Jordan, "Citizenship and the New Politics of Welfare"; and David Etherington and John Andersen, "Workfare or Inclusion?" Cost A15 Workshop, "Reforming Social Protection Systems in Europe: Comparing Dynamics of Transformation of Social Protection Systems in Context of Globalization and European Construction," Nantes, France, 2002).

45. See Ian Black, "EU Searches for an Answer to Apathy: Governments Survey the Damage," *The Guardian* June 15, 2004 (http://www.guardian.co.uk/eu/story/0,7369,1239023,00.html); and George Pagoulatos, "A Comprehensive Reform Agenda: Report and Conclusions on the Conference Proceedings," in *UK/Greece: New Look at Relations*, George Pagoulatos, ed. (Athens: ELIAMEP—Hellenic Foundation for European and Foreign Policy, London School of Economics, British Embassy, and British Council, 2001), pp. 73–100.

46. For compelling evidence and a review of related research demonstrating that welfare states continue to vary widely in the era of globalization, see Vicente Navarro, John Schmidt, and Javier Astudillo, "Is Globalization Undermining the Welfare State?" *Cambridge Journal of Economics* 28, 1 (January 2004): 133–52.

The data presented in this paper show that, for the most part, welfare states of most developed capitalist countries have not converged during the globalization period towards a reduced welfare state. On the contrary, over the globalization period, whether measured as a share of GDP or by public employment, welfare states have grown across the large majority of the world's richest economies. Also, during this period welfare states have continued to be different, retaining their individual characteristics, shaped primarily by the dominant political tradition that governed each country during the pre-globalisation period. . . . Some aspects of the globalization process, however, have affected the composition of the revenues through which states fund their welfare states, as well as affecting their economic and social policies. The deregulation of capital markets, for example, has changed considerably the ability of social democratic governing parties to follow a key component of supply-side socialism—their credit policies. Also, in the 1990s, the globalization of trade might have provided the rationale or justification for the decline in the social security and payroll taxes to fund their welfare states. . . . In both cases, however, the political colour of their governments has played the major role in the states' responses to these situations, to ensure that the welfare state is not reduced. Politics do indeed matter.[47]

For Navarro, Schmidt, and Astudillo, globalization may indeed be providing a self-serving rationale in some countries to reduce commitments to the welfare state, but globalization is not uniformly affecting the way in which different countries continue to structure their forms of social protection such that a convergence of welfare states in the era of globalization is not occurring. Instead, the globalization rationale for welfare state retrenchment plays differently in different countries with variation for the most part contingent upon major political differences such as different traditions of supporting the welfare state.

The Danish Alternative

Denmark, as shown in Table 2–1, has labor activation policies that lead to more social supports rather than less. Denmark, like other European countries, has responded to EU initiatives to develop its own labor force activation policies. The Danish alternative involves using welfare contracts that require work of the unemployed but in ways that minimize what Handler calls the "paradox of inclusion." David Etherington and John Andersen underscore the strengths of the Danish approach by

---

47. Navarro, Schmidt, and Astudillo, "Is Globalization Undermining the Welfare State?" p. 151.

contrasting its activation policies with the Neal Deal active labor program of the United Kingdom.[48] The contrast merits a detailed description.

According to Etherington and Andersen, the British reforms, such as the New Deal for the Unemployed, are much more one-sided in pushing work because they leave in place substantial cutbacks in social supports that ironically make the transition to relying on paid employment that much harder for the unemployed. The New Deal for Lone Parents is particularly vulnerable to criticism because of shortages in the availability of child care, much like in the U.S. The Third Way of the British New Deal claims to be overcoming the social exclusion of the economically marginal by including them in the workforce, but it does so in a way that reinforces class disadvantages associated with accessing decent-paying jobs. As a result, U.K. active labor participation policies end up shifting the blame for economic marginalization to the very people who are being marginalized by the growth of a low-wage economy. Rather than promoting social inclusion, such an activation policy reinforces exclusion, sequestering the economically marginal in low-wage jobs with limited social supports.

Denmark's labor activation policy takes place in a much more supportive context.[49] As a result, even after the imposition of new activation policies that restrict unlimited access to unemployment benefits, in most cases recipients can receive benefits up to seven years. Denmark's corporatist political structure retains a role for labor unions, producing a negotiated welfare state. This negotiated system includes labor union-controlled unemployment funds that, although administered locally, provide nationally legislated non-means-tested entitlement benefits to the unemployed. It is true that union influence over various components like training has declined and that policies allowing firms greater latitude to introduce layoffs have been implemented. Workfare requirements for the

---

48. Etherington and Andersen, "Workfare or Inclusion?" Also see David Etherington, "Welfare Reforms Local Government and the Politics of Social Inclusion: Lessons from Denmark's Labour Market and Area Regeneration Programmes," Research Paper 4/03 (Institut for Samfundsvidenskab og Erhvervsøkonomi, Roskilde University, Denmark); and John Andersen, "Social Exclusion and Inclusion in the Globalized City" (paper for World Social Forum, Mumbai, India, 2004, reprinted as Research Paper 3/2004) (Department of Social Sciences, Roskilde University, Roskilde, Denmark) (http://www.ssc.ruc.dk/workingpapers).

49. On the importance of accounting for context in assessing reform across welfare states, see Yuri Kazepov, "Introduction," in *Cities in Europe: Changing Contexts, Local Arrangements and the Challenge to Social Cohesion*, Yuri Kazepov, ed. (Oxford, UK: Blackwell, 2004), pp. 3–5.

unemployed were introduced in 1994 but they were in the form of conditioning continued receipt of benefits in terms of acceptance of various offers including educational leave and/or employment training. A training and job placement package was introduced that included paid leave schemes comprising educational, sabbatical, and child care. The 1999 Social Policy Act gave increased responsibility local councils for those dropping out of the unemployment system and moving onto social assistance, and it became required that Individual Action Plans (i.e., welfare contracts) be developed for each of these clients. The plans included the choice from a menu of job training and vocational training opportunities. In addition, the Danish system still includes both substantial social supports such as child care and cash assistance and higher minimum wage and benefit standards. The new labor activation contracts in the Danish case are much more supportive than are those in many other countries.

As a result, the attempt to balance greater market flexibility with social welfare protections in the form of a "flexicurity" policy has been more effectively implemented in Denmark. The Danish system has been characterized as producing politics "against *and* along with markets" as it increases labor market flexibility while preserving social welfare protections.[50] The developments in Denmark suggest that the country is finding a way to make labor activation policies actually work to promote inclusion rather than have such policies rationalize the social exclusion and marginalization being manufactured by the new economy of unprotected and insufficiently subsidized low-wage work. Denmark serves as another example of how there are a variety of European responses to the new discourse of an active welfare state—some better at making inclusion real, some better at saying "inclusion" but practicing exclusion.[51]

The Welfare Pendulum

The foregoing analysis suggests that the changes in the welfare state in recent years attributable to the globalizing discourse of welfare dependency

---

50. For an in-depth analysis of the Danish approach to labor activation, see Etherington and Andersen, "Workfare or Inclusion?"

51. For analysis of the discourse of "rights and responsibilities" in helping shift social welfare policy in Denmark, see Erik Christensen, "The Rhetoric of Rights and Obligations: Workfare and Citizens' Income Paradigms/Discourses in Denmark in a Labour History Perspective" (paper presented at the Basic Income European Network VIIIth International Congress, Berlin, Germany, October 6–7, 2000).

point to the continuing relevance of that old adage: the more things change, the more they stay the same. The retrenchment of welfare rights, the shift from welfare assistance to work requirements, and the movement from protecting caregivers to incentivizing active labor force participants are but a shifting back of the historic pendulum of welfare capitalism that Frances Fox Piven and Richard Cloward characterized decades ago.[52] We are not moving beyond the welfare state, as some might wish, as much as we are accentuating the work enforcement dimension of the existing welfare state.[53] And the differences between countries remain as they all shift toward labor activation policies, with the United States being in its own more market-centered world of welfare capitalism compared with the others. While the new work policies are touted as a way to address the "social exclusion" of various economically and socially marginal groups, depending on the structure of the new policies, they can end up including marginal groups in ways that reinforce their subordination. Inclusion is not necessarily the solution to exclusion; it all depends on how it is done.[54] The end result may be new policies that perpetuate old practices of regimenting welfare recipients into the bottom rungs of capitalist labor markets, thereby ensuring their continued economic marginalization and the deleterious social consequences associated with it.

On this point, it is important to note that given the Europeans' stronger commitment to a universalistic welfare state, the discourse of welfare reform for them tends to imply changes that will affect potentially all constituencies—not just single mothers or low-income families but also the retired, the disabled, and even working families. As a result, welfare reform plays differently in Europe than it does in the United States, where it implies a targeted focus on limiting access to public assistance by low individuals, most especially nonwhite, single mothers. In Europe, "welfare reform" implies something much broader in its effects as posing a potential threat to universalistic entitlement rights. Even policies designed to target long-term unemployed to take paid employment can be treated skeptically in Europe if they are seen as a potential wedge to

52. See Frances Fox Piven and Richard A. Cloward, *Regulating the Poor: The Functions of Public Welfare* (New York: Vintage Books, 1971).

53. For an argument that we are moving beyond the welfare state to an "enabling state" that imposes obligations to work, see Neil Gilbert, *The Transformation of the Welfare State: The Silent Surrender of Public Responsibility* (New York: Oxford University Press, 2002).

54. On the exclusionary practices implicit in policy designed to promote inclusion, see Barbara Cruikshank, *The Will to Empower: Democratic Citizens and Other Subjects* (Ithaca: Cornell University, 1999).

winnowing welfare state entitlements more generally. As a result, welfare reform at this time still means something very different in Europe than in the United States and can attract more opposition more easily. In late summer 2004, the most dramatic example of continuing "Euroskepticism" was the Hartz demonstrations throughout Germany to protest the "Hartz IV" reforms to greatly reduce the time for receipt of unemployment benefits (i.e., the fourth stage of implementing workfare policies labeled after a commission led by Peter Hartz, personnel director at Volkswagen).[55] Under these conditions, labor force activation policies for the unemployed and other target groups are often likely to be examined in terms of their possibility for creating tiers of entitlement rights among citizens that can lead to accentuating class differences and thereby weakening the commitment to a solidaristic and inclusive social welfare state. The European analysts I have reviewed exhibit a strong concern about the consequences of targeted labor activation policies for the commitment to a universalistic welfare state. And the continuing commentary about "Euroskepticism" suggests that the general public in a number of countries also worries about how far welfare reform will go in creating second-class citizenship with reduced entitlement rights. For these reasons, it is premature to conclude that welfare reform discourse in Europe will lead to end of the welfare state or, if not that, then, its Americanization.

Conclusion

If the welfare state is in crisis today, then it is a crisis that is in large part one of discourse. It is a crisis-mongering discourse of globalization that creates the insistence that capitalist societies must learn to live beyond the welfare state. The dissemination of American-style discourse has given increased emphasis to "welfare dependency" as connoting a stigmatized condition that makes an individual a deviant and the society as a whole less productive, less efficient, and less able to compete globally. Legitimate reasons for needing public assistance are increasingly hard to articulate in such a discourse, and the positive benefits to one's family and society are as well. In Europe, the discourse of welfare dependency has given birth to a preference for an active welfare state where receipt of public assistance is seen as passive and negative. Labor activation policies are being implemented in country after country to counteract the alleged deleterious

---

55. "It's Those People, All Over Again," *The Economist*, August 12, 2004 (economist .com/displayStory.cfm?Story_ID=3092887).

effects to both the individual and society. The metaphors of active and passive operate in the globalizing discourse of welfare dependency to re-inscribe hierarchies of privilege and position those in need of public assistance as less than worthy until they become "active" and are "inserted" into the labor force. In the new discourse of the active welfare state, there is the risk that work at any job will become the only legitimate solution to one's alleged passivity. A discourse of labor activation enrolls the unemployed in seeking inclusion in the society on terms that reinscribe their subordination as those who need to be disciplined if they are to ever achieve self-sufficiency. In this way, welfare reform can give rise to new forms of governance for regimenting subordinate populations to the emerging social order in an era of globalization.

There is no question that welfare reform in Europe is occurring. Part of the reason is that the welfare states of Europe do have fiscal issues. There are real challenges to the welfare state in the form of aging populations, worsening dependency ratios, labor shortages, and the like; however, these demographic changes need not necessitate welfare state retrenchment and are addressable within the confines of welfare state policy changes of a relatively modest sort. Social security and state pension programs are the primary problem policies here, and they can be adjusted with changes in contributions and benefits. The changes required, however, can be agonizing for political systems to negotiate.

Yet, the changes are already happening in a number of countries without abandonment of the idea that the social welfare state must protect citizens from the arbitrary practices of an unregulated market. Some states have moved further away from their welfare state commitments while others are actually increasing them, if often in ways that tie benefits more toward supporting those who seek work. Therefore, it is simply wrong to conclude that there is a convergence toward repealing the welfare state in the era of globalization. European welfare states have not come close to matching the United States in adopting punitive welfare reforms.

Nonetheless, things could change. Globalization discourse is affecting how welfare is being framed in Europe. Europeans continue to debate to how to enforce work like the U.S. welfare reform program while still ensuring access to social welfare protections. If European countries end up emphasizing more Boston than Berlin, it will not be because it is an unavoidable necessity of the impersonal economic forces of globalization but instead because globalization discourse made such choices seem to be so. Policymakers looking to cut costs and to manufacture new pools of workers who are required to take lower paying jobs can make those choices if they want to and if they find the political power to do so.

Globalization discourse is an important and insidious source of power simultaneously rationalizing these choices as unavoidable necessities while making the inevitability they claim already exists all the more likely. We do not have to collaborate in growing a low-wage workforce to feed the coffers of corporate leaders seeking new sources of profit in an emerging global economy. Discourse just makes it seem that we do.

The active welfare state can be empowering in disempowering ways, forcing the long-term unemployed, youth, lone mothers, immigrants, and even the disabled into dead-end jobs without social supports and with the increased stigmatization and exploitation associated with being stuck in those marginal jobs. The welfare-to-work contract can become the quintessential discursive practice operating as a ritual of denigration for the purposes of reinscribing on welfare recipients the stigmatized identity of a passive citizen who needs to be forced by the state into being a more active contributor the nation's productivity. The welfare-to-work contract can perform its own "paradox of inclusion."[56]

Yet, it does not have to be this way—an active welfare state does not have to always mean the same thing. And it does not, as is evident from an analysis of the copious literature on the subject. While the power of a discourse is great, it is not total as the incomplete Americanization of social welfare policy in Europe shows us. Labor activation means different things in England, Holland, and Denmark. Each has responded to globalization discourse in its own way independent of objective internal or external forces. Each spins its own version of globalization discourse and how to respond. Therefore, the globalizing discourse of welfare dependency and its call for welfare state retrenchment need not be a *fait accompli*. If Europe can resist this self-fulfilling prophecy, perhaps so can the United States. So far, there continues to be a significant difference between the United States and Europe on welfare state policies overall, with the United States providing far more limited coverage and benefits. There also continues to be significant differences within Europe. Some countries continue to offer far more limited social welfare protections than others. And some countries have been more responsive to the siren calls of globalization and the discourse of labor activation. Our job is to appreciate that and to exploit its incompleteness so as to highlight how it is still possible to choose the welfare state as an act of social justice. Learning from Europe is one way to do this that would be most appropriate in an era of globalization. We have a chance to learn that not only do politics

---

56. Handler, Social *Citizenship and Workfare in the U.S. and Western Europe*, pp. 6–8.

matter (in the sense of leading different countries to have different welfare states) but also it should matter (in the sense that resisting a globalizing discourse of welfare retrenchment promotes the capacity of citizens to decide for themselves the public policies that best serve their needs).

3 Truth Is a Woman

Care as the Real Absence in the Post-Industrial Welfare State

I teach in a graduate school of social work at a women's college. Students in my classes are continually using an important dichotomy to turn discussions of the growing emphasis in social policy on work into debates about care. The emphasis on work glosses over the importance of care as students are wont to remind me, again and again. You would think I would learn that by now. They have a point. To emphasize one part of the dichotomy risks neglecting the other. Sending more and more women, especially mothers of young children into the workforce, puts at risk our ability to provide needed care. The growing emphasis in welfare reform on turning women into workers in the official economy risks removing needed caregivers from unofficial economy of the home and the community. Work requirements of welfare reform have the potential to undermine women's caregiving roles and to devalue that activity even more than its already marginal status in the work-oriented capitalist societies of the western world.

Most of these students are quick to remind me that they are not suggesting that women by virtue of biology or socialization should be sequestered into caregiving roles because that is what women naturally or socially are best at doing. They support gender equity, including the right to work and earn as much money as men. Yet, they also believe that gender equity includes supporting caregiving as much as breadwinning. When we discuss the globalization of work-oriented welfare policy discourse, these students often see this as further evidence that caregiving is an important service to society that continues to be devalued even, or especially, in a post-feminist era of a growing female workforce.

It is true that welfare states in Europe have often done a better job than the social policy regime in the United States in recognizing the need to promote and support caregiving. And, as discussed in the last chapter, welfare reform in Europe is not singularly focused on getting single mothers with children into the workforce or into marriages. And cutbacks on aid to lone mothers were much more actively resisted in countries like the United Kingdom in than the United States, resulting in a less drastic retrenchment in access to benefits. In fact, most European countries do not have policies that put emphasis on moving single mothers with young children from welfare to work. Further, paid family leave, child allowances, and family services are more widely available in European welfare states. Welfare reform in Europe may be work oriented, but European welfare states tend to be much more pro-family and supportive of child-rearing and caregiving by mothers.

Yet, today, welfare reform across welfare states is focused on labor activation, and female welfare recipients are not just affected in the United States. As a result, an emerging issue at the heart of welfare reform discourse is what is at risk of being forgotten: caregiving. The core issue of welfare reform's globalizing discourse of work is, therefore, what will happen to care. Ultimately, the more emphasis that is given to work, the more we need to worry about care and the more it must become an issue to be confronted in Europe as well as the United States.

But why is this such a women's issue? While the work/care dichotomy need not be gendered, it is. At least, that is how it has been down through the ages, in the western world as well as elsewhere.[1] To neglect care is to devalue work that women often are required, expected and even want to do. Welfare reform that emphasizes work at the expense of care risks reinscribing gender inequity by denying recognition and support to the important work that women do more often than men. Real welfare reform would support caregiving as it promotes work. Otherwise, it will only add gender injustice to the injustice it does in the name of class.

My focus for this chapter grows from realization that the globalization of work-oriented welfare policy discourse risks increasing the already growing strain on women to balance work and family, a problem that is slowing coming into focus, first in Europe and now, if more slowly, in the United States. This is a problem that despite foot-dragging by policymakers has become an issue of crisis proportions in the United States, where welfare reform mandates work for single mothers but expects them in large part to shoulder their care responsibilities while taking paid employment that has been shown to not pay enough to cover child care

1. Joan Tronto, "Who Cares? Public and Private Caring and the Rethinking of Citizenship," in *Women and Welfare: Theory and Practice in the United States and Europe*, Nancy J. Hirschmann and Ulrike Liebert, eds. (New Brunswick, NJ: Rutgers University Press, 2001), pp. 65–83.

costs associated with trying to support a family.[2] The problem of supporting caregiving while working is a growing issue elsewhere as well, because women are increasingly going into the workforce not only because they can but also because they must in the face of a globalizing economy that drives down wages and increases the need for multiple wage earners in families.[3] The jobs that women often find do not pay well and do not provide the benefits needed to cover their caregiving responsibilities. There is growing evidence that a workplace that is not gender fair or gender friendly is at risk of becoming more so under globalization discourse that discourages the proliferation of social welfare benefits. Further, globalization in no small part thrives on the proliferation of low-wage jobs that are disproportionately filled by women, often immigrants and often working under inadequate conditions and without health insurance and other protections.[4] Overall, it is an important question whether globalization will affect the ability of employers to structure jobs so as to be more accommodating to women who have to balance work and family. An equally important question is whether social policy will recognize and support caregiving as much as it should in an era of emphasizing work.

This chapter first looks at what Martha Fineman calls "dependency discourse," its bias in favor of making invisible the dependencies of male breadwinners, and its prejudices in focusing attention on the dependencies of female homemakers.[5] I further this discourse analysis by using Joan Williams' critique of the "ideal worker model" implicit in the welfare state that assumes benefits are earned by a breadwinner in a traditional two-parent family.[6] I extend the analysis by relying on Nancy Fraser's critique of what she calls the "family wage logic" of the social welfare state.[7] All of these theoretical perspectives inform an argument on behalf of what Joan

2. See Gwendolyn Mink, "Violating Women: Rights Abuses in the Welfare Police State," in *Lost Ground: Welfare Reform, Poverty and Beyond*, Randy Albelda and Ann Withorn, eds. (Boston: South End Press, 2002), pp. 95–112.
3. Randy Albelda and Chris Tilly, *Glass Ceilings and Bottomless Pits: Women's Work, Women's Poverty* (Boston: South End Press, 1997), pp. 33–45.
4. Saskia Sassen, *Globalization and Its Discontents: Essays on the New Mobility of People and Money* (New York: The New Press, 1998), pp. 81–109.
5. Martha A. Fineman, *The Autonomy Myth: A Theory of Dependency* (New York: New Press, 2004).
6. Joan Williams, *Unbending Gender: Why Family and Work Conflict and What to Do About It* (New York: Oxford University Press, 2000).
7. Nancy Fraser, "After the Family Wage: Gender Equity and the Welfare State," *Political Theory* 22, 4 (November 1994): 591–618.

Tronto calls "rights through care," where a nongendered understanding of citizenship is defined as including the right to be supported in fulfilling one's caregiving responsibilities.[8] This amounts to a paradigm shift from a breadwinner model of the "workerist welfare state" where families are supported on the basis of the breadwinner's work contributions to society to a homemaking model of a "caring state" where citizens are supported to fulfill their caregiving responsibilities in ways that are not limited to supporting just the traditional two-parent family.

I then examine how the welfare state remains gender-biased in no small part due to neglect of the issues of care and how this remains especially the case in the face of globalization discourse and its emphasis on labor activation. Relying on the work of Diane Sainsbury, Ann Shola Orloff, and Ruth Lister, I highlight how the various welfare states in the western world today still, even in their most progressive and universalistic forms, do not operate in a gender-fair way to support care and establish rights through care.[9]

I build on these feminist critiques of the welfare state to examine attempts by leaders in this area, Sweden and Norway, to incorporate rights to care into the welfare state in gender-fair ways. My main thesis is that gender policy in the welfare state is inevitably tied more widely to gender relations in civil society. The attempts to value and support care via either gender-neutral or gender-sensitive public policies will inevitably risk reinscribing gender differences as to who does care work and how it will be valued, unless they are tied to broader efforts to challenge the embedded gender biases operating in the wider society.

Care policy is unavoidably contextual, embedded, and nested in the gendered dichotomies used to structure social relations more broadly. Care policy in this sense is intertextual, referencing other gendered discourses that need to be invoked in order for that policy to be articulated with gendered family and market relations. Any attempt to build care into the welfare state needs to be sensitive to these discursive relays. Otherwise, the promise of a gender-fair welfare state that supports the rights to care will be infinitely deferred.

---

8. Tronto, "Who Cares? Public and Private Caring and the Rethinking of Citizenship," pp. 65–83.

9. Diane Sainsbury, *Gender Equality and Welfare States* (Cambridge, UK: Cambridge University Press, 1996); Ann Shola Orloff, "Gender and the Social Rights of Citizenship: The Comparative Analysis of Gender Relations and Welfare States," *American Sociological Review*, 58 (1993): 303–28; and Ruth Lister, "Dilemmas in Engendering Citizenship" (paper presented at the Crossing Borders Conference, Stockholm, Sweden, May 27–29, 1994).

Gender Bias in Dependency Discourse

In the United States, welfare reform is forcing millions of single mothers into low-wage jobs that have distinctive characteristics associated with globalization. Besides low-wages, these jobs often include no benefits, unsafe working conditions, inflexible production schedules, and a myriad of other characteristics that make it increasingly difficult for these women to balance the competing pressures of work and family. Welfare reform makes low-income single mothers with children seem like the ideal workers for the new low-wage economy in an era of globalization.[10] Saskia Sassen has emphasized that the gender dimension of globalization needs to be given greater emphasis and the exploitation of women, immigrants as well as citizens, via the low-wage jobs that have proliferated with globalization is a critical factor in making globalization the exploitive form of economic development that it is.[11] Welfare reform proponents' solutions to these problems are not to provide better support for caregiving while work is being required. Instead, for those women who cannot shoulder the dual responsibilities of breadwinning and caregiving on their own with minimal support from the state, the solution being emphasized of late in policy discussions is . . . marriage. Women who cannot make it on their own ought to get married.[12]

The basic assumption behind this perspective is that people fulfill their personal responsibility regarding issues of work and family via a married relationship. Through marriage, couples can combine breadwinning and homemaking, balancing work and care responsibilities without need of anyone else. The traditional two-parent family with a male breadwinner and a female homemaker is still held out as the ideal for best fulfilling personal responsibility.

Martha Fineman effectively debunked what she calls the dependency discourse that animates this policy perspective that privileges the tradi-

---

10. See Aihwa Ong, *Flexible Citizenship: The Cultural Logics of Transnationality* (Durham: Duke University Press, 1998).

11. Sassen, *Globalization and Its Discontents*, pp. 81–109, as quoted in Kathleen R. Arnold, *Homelessness, Citizenship and Identity* (Albany: SUNY Press, 2004), p. 143. Also see V. Spike Peterson, *A Critical Rewriting of Global Political Economy: Integrating Reproductive, Productive and Virtual Economies* (New York: Routledge, 2004), pp. 21–43.

12. See Patrick F. Fagan, Robert W. Patterson, and Robert E. Rector, *Marriage and Welfare Reform: The Overwhelming Evidence that Marriage Education Works* (Washington, DC: Heritage Foundation, Policy Backgrounder No. 1606, October 25, 2002).

tional two-parent family with a male breadwinner and a female home-maker.[13] Fineman is critical of the autonomy myth that she says is ascendant in the western culture, especially American culture, and operates to privilege a specific form of family as more deserving of state support. She calls it a foundational myth for it plays a role of legitimating the existing structure of society and its institutions, such as the family, by imputing a fantastic fable-like origin to society and those institutions. The idea of autonomy performs a legitimating role in a mythical origin story and does so in a way that serves as a foundation for the current social structure and its institutions.

Fineman first critiques the assumption that people who rely on the necessary interdependencies of family relationships should be seen as independent. In particular, she invalidates the idea that the male bread-winner should be seen as independent. Instead, Fineman points out that everyone, including male breadwinners, are interdependent beings, reliant on others, including female homemakers, to be able to practice what passes for a self-sufficient autonomous being. Therefore, for Fineman, requiring single mothers to mimic the self-sufficient autonomy of male breadwinners without being able to rely on support from others is more than unfair; it is an unrealistic policy that will result in prejudicing our assessments of the deservingness of these single mothers when they fail to effectively balance the dual responsibilities of breadwinner and home-maker and as a result fail to lift their families out of poverty.

Second, Fineman questions why we assume that being in a particular type of family relationship makes one seem to be not only independent but also deserving of state support. We see the interdependent breadwinner not only as autonomous but also as deserving. The welfare state is organized around supporting the traditional two-parent family, and citizens qualify for welfare state benefits often in terms of their relationship to a breadwinner in such a family. This includes unemployment benefits, disability, social security, and other policies. Fineman has referred to this as a bias in favor of the "sexual family."[14] The sexual family defines family relationships in terms of married couples rather than in terms of caring relationships, such in a parent and children or an adult child and aging parents. What is privileged in such a discourse is the sexual relationship between the breadwinner on the one hand and the homemaker, as op-

---

13. Fineman, *The Autonomy Myth*, pp. 143–204.
14. Martha Albertson Fineman, *The Neutered Mother, the Sexual Family, and Other Twentieth Century Tragedies* (New York: Routledge, 1995).

posed to the caregiving relationships between caregivers and their dependents. The result is a nuclear family-centered discourse of autonomy that essentially privatizes the idea of interdependence and biases it in favor of particular individuals in certain types of families. The critically important caring relationships in families are too significant to be reduced to being organized and identified largely in terms of the sexual relationship between a husband and wife, and families should be able to qualify for state support to engage in nurturing relationships independent of that sexual relationship.

Fineman sees the discourse of the sexual family and its blinkered view of who is autonomous and dependent being accentuated by welfare reform that insists women on welfare should to a great degree assume their caregiving responsibilities as a private matter of the family, just as the work required by the welfare reform legislation is assumed to be a private matter fulfilled by participating in the formal economy. American-style welfare reform reinforces the traditional American bias in favor of relying on the family and the market for fulfilling care and work responsibilities. Welfare reform insists on, more than supports, caregiving through the family and work through the market as if both of these are largely private matters determined by the degree to which people fulfill their personal responsibilities. It does so, Fineman argues, because reliance on the market and on the family are fundamental background assumptions, as she calls them, of the highly individualistic and capitalistic version of the social contract that undergirds the American welfare state. And welfare reform is about reinforcing these background assumptions rather than promoting state intervention that can help people fulfill those responsibilities when market and family conditions do not allow for them to do so as well as they need to in order to ensure their well-being and that of their children and partners.

For Fineman as long as welfare policy discourse is indebted to the autonomy myth, the centrality of caregiving relationships to the well-being not just of families, but of society in general, will be short-changed. She proposes redefining families in terms of caregiving relationships and then supporting caregivers in fulfilling those relationships as the critical service they provide not just to their families but also to society as a whole. Welfare policy ought to be structured not to reinforce the privatization of caregiving as a responsibility that is imposed on families to fulfill on their own without support. Instead, welfare policy ought to do the opposite and make caregiving a degendered publicly-supported practice that society crucially depends on and needs to promote regardless of what sort of family relations are involved in helping make that caregiving happen. In fact, all of society, especially the market and the workplace, as well as the welfare state, needs to be reorganized to recognize the importance of caregiving and to support it with policies that assume all citizens and workers have caregiving responsibilities regardless of their gender and their specific family roles, ties, and relationships. Fathers as well as mothers, sons as well as daughters, corporate executives as well as their administrative assistants, all need to be assumed to be people who have caregiving responsibilities and have the support of the state, their employers, and the rest of society so that they can fulfill those responsibilities.

Further, Fineman's analysis suggests that social welfare policy ought to reflect the fact that breadwinners owe homemakers a debt of interdependence that should be compensated via a basic entitlement right to provide care as essential to the functioning of the work-first society, which ought to be recognized really as the care-first-so-people-can-work society. Any policy that does not do this is a policy that keeps caregiving behind closed doors as a private practice and, in so doing, given the gendered nature of family roles, keeps women, who do most of the caregiving, subordinated in the role of providing a service on which society depends but does not support. Instead, we need to compensate caregivers for making the work-first society possible.[15] As of now, the privatization of caregiving perpetuates the subordination of women who must shoulder this special responsibility without equitable compensation while foregoing opportunities that go to men who do not have to take on those undercompensated caregiving responsibilities.

Another feminist legal theorist, Joan Williams, critiques what she calls the "ideal worker model" implicit in social welfare policies.[16] Williams highlights how ostensibly neutral social policies, such as unemployment compensation, implicitly assume that the unemployed person is a married male breadwinner. Therefore, single mothers can in some states be terminated from receiving unemployment benefits when they turn down a full-time job because unemployment policy does not recognize the need to take part-time work in order to balance the dual responsibilities of breadwinning and homemaking. Failure to accept a full-time job is seen as avoiding work. The implicit biases of the policy become explicit when

---

15. See Chapter 7 for an analysis of how the dichotomy between universal entitlements that are allegedly earned versus targeted compensation benefits that are granted acts of compassionate charity deconstructs once we highlight that the existing welfare state is biased in favor of supporting those who have worked in paid employment. We then see the role that those not in paid employment played to make workers' alleged independence and self-sufficiency possible.

16. Williams, *Unbending Gender*, pp. 4–6.

applied to single mothers in these instances. The implicit biases not only are gendered but also reinforce the privileging of work over care as the basis for being seen as a deserving and entitled citizen.

A similar critique is offered by Nancy Fraser, who suggests that the entire political economy is organized around articulating a particular set of relationships between the family, the market, and the state.[17] State policies privilege the traditional two-parent family as the most appropriate for the smooth functioning of our market system. Fraser has called this the "family-wage system" that emphasizes families should be able to support themselves by combining the efforts of a breadwinner and a homemaker and that state support for other families will be discouraged as rewarding behavior and practices that are inefficient as well as irresponsible. Such a policy supports two-parent families because they are functional was well as moral.[18]

Fraser notes that the current welfare state in the West is passé because it is based on the family-wage logic and assumes viability of the traditional two-parent family ideal, when in fact most families in this post-industrial era no longer conform to that model of a male breadwinner and a stay-at-home female who tends to the homemaking responsibilities. Nonetheless, the welfare state remains anachronistically structured according to what she calls the "universal breadwinner" model, which assumes families most often conform to the traditional two-parent family ideal of a male breadwinner and a female homemaker and qualify for unemployment, disability, survivor, or retirement benefits based on the earnings of the breadwinner.

Fraser seeks to move us beyond the limitations of evaluating the welfare state according to this anachronistic standard that does not account for the changes of a post-industrial society and the changing nature of gender relations in the family, the market, and society in broader terms. She is animated to confront the challenges of what she calls "post-socialism," where the Left can no longer rely on the dream of socialist society as the solution to problems with capitalism. More critically, she sees that in the post-socialist age, it is no longer meaningful to organize political struggle for a just social welfare state strictly around issues of class conflict. Instead, issues of recognition of identities and the way in which differences are used to manufacture otherness must be addressed in the way that they contribute to issues of redistribution so as to achieve a just allocation of

---

17. Fraser, "After the Family Wage," pp. 591–618.
18. For the argument that morality is functional, see Charles Murray, "The Coming White Underclass," The *Wall Street Journal*, October 29, 1993, p. A-14.

resources. Fraser therefore seeks to bridge the divide between those who emphasize a multicultural politics of recognition and those who still give priority to a class politics of redistribution.

Fraser is most interested in highlighting the gender bias of the family wage logic, the workerist welfare state, and the system of redistribution that reinscribes male privilege. Fraser combines the need to recognize gender bias in the welfare state to inform efforts to achieve redistribution in the face of the insecurities visited on workers and families by the class system of capitalism. Therefore, the passing away of the relevance of the universal breadwinner model in a post-industrial era is to be greeted as an opportunity to degender the welfare state as a way to begin to obtain economic distributive justice.

Fraser introduces an alternative "caregiver parity" model that structures social welfare protections so that caregivers will earn entitlement rights just as do breadwinners, because care work will be seen as a legitimate form of work deserving of support by the state. Family leave policies, flex-time at work, and family and child allowances would be instituted to support caregiving as a parallel track of work needed to be done to promote family and societal well-being. Fraser, however, notes that caregiving would likely remain an inferior gendered track and its perpetuation of gender hierarchy will continue to favor male-identified breadwinning over female-identified caregiving. The welfare state would remain gendered.

Fraser therefore turns to her preferred "universal caregiver" model, where all citizens are seen as having caregiving responsibilities that need to be supported by the state. Fraser, however, does not think that this model will be adopted any time soon, but it provides a beacon lighting our way to a gender-fair welfare state in the post-industrial era after the decline of the family wage system and the demise of the traditional two-parent ideal. Fraser writes:

> A Universal Caregiver welfare state would promote gender equity by effectively dismantling the gendered opposition between breadwinning and caregiving. It would integrate activities that are currently separated from one another, eliminate their gender-coding, and encourage men to perform them too. This is, however, tantamount to a wholesale restructuring of the institution of gender. The construction of breadwinning and caregiving as separate codes, coded masculine and feminine respectively, is a principal under girding of the current gender order. To dismantle those roles and their cultural coding is in effect to overturn that order. It means subverting the existing gender division of labor and reducing the salience of gender as a structural principle of social organization. At the limit, it suggests deconstructing gender. By deconstructing the opposition between breadwinning and caregiving, moreover, Universal Caregiver would simultaneously deconstruct the associated opposition between

bureaucratized public institutional settings and intimate private domestic settings. Treating civil society as an additional site for carework, it would overcome both the "workerism" of Universal Breadwinner and the domestic privatism of Caregiver Parity....

The trick is to imagine a social world in which citizens' lives integrate wage earning, caregiving, community activism, political participation, and involvement in the associational life of civil society—while also leaving time for some fun. This world is not likely to come into being in the immediate future, but it is the only imaginable postindustrial world that promises true gender equity. And unless we are guided by this vision now, we will never get any closer to achieving it.[19]

The Gendered Welfare State

From these perspectives, it is evident that the welfare state is gendered in ways that devalue caregiving. The welfare state more often than not bases entitlement rights on whether a male breadwinner has earned benefits via participation in the labor market. Entitlement rights are much less frequently likely to accrue to families based on whether any caregiver, let alone a female caregiver, has provided needed care. Feminist theorists of the welfare state have noted that even the most prominent models for categorizing and classifying welfare states are gendered in not highlighting this gender bias.

The most prominent model for comparing welfare states in terms of their ability to protect families from the insecurities of the market has been provided by Gosta Esping-Andersen.[20] Esping-Andersen has offered the much-cited "Three Worlds of Welfare Capitalism" model based on his comparisons of the liberal market-centered regimes like the United States, the United Kingdom, Australia, Canada, and New Zealand; the conservative corporativist regimes like Austria, France, Germany, and Italy; and social democratic regimes like Sweden, Norway, and Denmark. The three worlds of welfare capitalism varied primarily along the axis of what Esping-Andersen called "decommodification." This is where the state provided protection to workers against the risks associated with their families' security being tied strictly to the workers' ability to commodify their labor and sell it in the labor market. Social welfare protections enabled workers to still be able to support their families even when they

---

19. Nancy Fraser, *Justice Interruptus: Critical Reflections on the "Postsocialist" Condition* (New York: Routledge, 1997), pp. 61–62.

20. Gosta Esping-Andersen, *Three Worlds of Welfare Capitalism* (Princeton: Princeton University Press, 1994).

could not commodify their labor sufficiently to meet their families' needs, due to unemployment, disability, retirement, death, etc.

Diane Sainsbury has noted that Esping-Andersen's tripartite model was gendered in ways that uncritically accepted the basing of entitlement rights on the breadwinner.[21] All "three worlds of welfare capitalism" were in this sense workerist, reinforcing the ideal worker model, the family wage logic, and the ideal of the traditional two-parent family; and Esping-Andersen's synoptic overview for understanding welfare state variation failed to highlight this. Sainsbury notes: "As many feminists have objected, decommodification scarcely addresses the situation of women who perform unpaid labor in the home and the conditions for their emancipation."[22] In addition, this oversight provided no way to begin to analyze how welfare states varied in their effectiveness in supporting caregiving, something on which they do vary quite a bit even if they all tend to have a workerist bias because their overriding theme is the degree to which labor is decommodified. For instance, Heidi Hartmann and Hsiao-ye Yi have noted:

> As Nancy Fraser has pointed out, the United States is nearly unique among advanced industrial countries in having no ongoing financial support for mothers, either in the form of paid maternity leave for workers (which is strictly voluntary in all but five states in the United States) or in the form of child allowances. While most industrial nations have both maternity/child rearing financial aid and poor relief, the United States rolls both programs into one, providing maternal support only for those women who are desperately poor and lack other resources. Consequently, there is a stigma attached to the poor stay-at-home mom, the only mom who is obviously subsidized by taxpayers.[23]

Sainsbury argues that Esping-Andersen's attempts to rectify the lack of consideration of gendered caregiving in his categorization of welfare states fails even if he came to include child care and other issues of central concern to women as workers.[24] Esping-Andersen's model does not go beyond analyzing state-market relations in terms of the decommodifying effects of social welfare benefits for workers. Women are introduced into the equation but as workers instead of as caregivers. Care remains the

21. Sainsbury, *Gender Equality and Welfare States*, pp. 33–40.
22. Sainsbury, *Gender Equality and Welfare States*, p. 36.
23. Heidi Hartmann and Hsiao-ye Yi, "The Rhetoric and Reality of Welfare Reform," in *Women and Welfare: Theory and Practice in the United States and Europe*, Nancy J. Hirschmann and Ulrike Liebert, eds. (New Brunswick: Rutgers University Press, 2001), pp. 160–76.
24. Sainsbury, *Gender Equality and Welfare States*, pp. 37–38.

missing ingredient in the analysis of welfare states. The preoccupation remains workerist.

Sainsbury notes that there is a significant difference of opinion about how to get beyond the workerist bias that comes from evaluating welfare states strictly in terms of decommodification. She writes:

> Ann Orloff has argued that decommodification as a measure of the quality of social rights needs to be complemented by two additional dimensions: "access to paid work;" and "the capacity to form and maintain an autonomous household." The capacity to form and maintain an autonomous household underscores women's freedom to enter and exit from marriage and cohabitation. As Ruth Lister notes, however, this formulation glosses over the ability to achieve financial autonomy within marriage. Drawing a parallel with decommodification, she suggests defamilialization as "the degree to which individual adults can uphold a socially acceptable standard of living, independently of family relationships, either through paid work or social security provision."[25]

It is at this juncture that the political economy, the welfare state, the state-market-family triad operating at the base of society, and the underlying family wage logic to the whole set of arrangements that arise from these social formations and relationships must be seen as involving more than issues of economics, class relations, and exploitation. In addition, consideration must be given to the gendered nature of this complex system as well. Defamilialization must be joined to decommodification as standards for evaluating the extent to which public policies are helping to address the ways in which the existing system operates to oppress, as well as exploit, caregivers and workers, citizens all in their various positioning in the social order.

The United States Is Not a Model

The United States, however, is of course the last place to look to see if there has been any advance by welfare states on this effort to tie defamilialization with decommodification. This is sadly the case even though the United States in many ways has been a leader in the advancement of women's rights and had seen a rapid increase of women into the paid labor market, beginning in the 1960s and 1970s. That increase has led to some economic advances for women, but it has also seen women predominate in the low-wage labor market, often taking jobs associated with devalued

---

25. Sainsbury, *Gender Equality and Welfare States*, p. 39. Also see Orloff, "Gender and the Social Rights of Citizenship," pp. 303–28; and Lister, "Dilemmas in Engendering Citizenship."

"women's work" from cleaning to clerical positions. Women's entrance into the paid labor market has many virtues but it has also further devalued caregiving. Women have often taken low-wage work associated with caregiving, and a sad irony is that it has forced women to have to balance paid work and caregiving in ways that undermine their status in both roles.

Vicky Lovell and Heidi Hartmann[26] have noted this problem and have highlighted the particular barriers facing women in the low-wage labor market. Lovell and Hartmann also emphasize that women experience the labor market very differently than do men. They often work in different occupations and for a different number of hours per week and take more time out of the workforce to care for their families. These gendered differences exist even among low-wage workers such that women in low-wage jobs earn less than do men in comparable positions during the course of their working lives, and as a result, their incomes are lower when they retire.

Lowell and Hartmann underscore how far the United States has to go in addressing this problem. They recommend a number of serious policy changes that would make it easier for low-wage female workers to begin to benefit from the opportunity to work. First, they recommend policies that support workers with caregiving responsibilities so that they are able to increase their work hours. Then they add policies that would increase women's wages through skill development and through changes in wage-setting mechanisms. These policies would be enhanced with income supplement policies, such as the Earned Income Tax Credit, which subsidizes low wages, and paid family leave. Last, Lovell and Hartmann look to policies designed to change labor and equal employment opportunity laws that would help strengthen women's bargaining power in the labor market.

In other words, the United States has a long way to go before it can be said that it is doing what it needs to do to support women who are trying to balance work and care responsibilities on their own or in a partnered relationship. For Ann Orloff, this means that advocates must promote policies that support women in both caregiving and breadwinning.[27] Emphasizing

---

26. Vicky Lovell and Heidi Hartmann, "Increasing Economic Security for Low-Wage Women Workers," in *Low-Wage Workers in the New Economy*, Richard Kazis and Marc S. Miller, eds. (Washington, DC: Urban Institute Press, 2001), pp. 205–22.

27. Ann Shola Orloff, "Ending the Entitlements of Poor Single Mothers: Changing Social Policies, Women's Employment, and Caregiving in the Contemporary United States," in *Women and Welfare: Theory and Practice in the United States and Europe*, Nancy J. Hirschmann and Ulrike Liebert, eds. (New Brunswick: Rutgers University Press, 2001), pp. 133–50.

one and not the other will not suffice. Otherwise, in the American context, women leaving welfare will be expected most often to take whatever low-wage work is available while still being expected to shoulder caregiving responsibilities largely on their own. This is a recipe for an acceleration of the feminization of poverty. Even if jobs are available, if there are no policies that ensure support for both breadwinning and caregiving responsibilities, the result will likely be what we have seen: a shift from the welfare poor to the working poor.

The reality is that the United States as a liberal capitalist welfare regime does not support either care or work very effectively, leaving it to women exiting welfare, and many other women as well, to scrap together on their own the resources to balance these dual responsibilities. Rebecca Blank thoughtfully writes:

> Hence, a key "lesson" from the U.S. is that job availability is NOT the only requirement for a successful transition to work. European nations that provide substantial support to working mothers (such as Sweden) are in a better situation than the U.S. to deal effectively with job-holding problems that relate to the availability of child care and/or health care. Even if some of these nations may face more difficulties in helping women locate jobs, they have an advantage in having other work supports already in place. Hence, they may be able to concentrate more of their program resources on the job creation and location issue, while in the U.S. more program resources have had to go into other work supports. European nations that provide little support to working mothers (such as Germany) need to worry about this lack of support if they want to provide more work incentives within social assistance programs. Both the U.S. and Europe, however, need to be more aware of the barriers.[28]

Yet, it is really an open question not so much whether Europe does better than the United States in addressing gender bias in social welfare policy as it is whether it does as much as it needs to. If we examine the leaders in building an inclusive social welfare state, Sweden and Norway, we can see that things are perhaps not as simple as we would like. It turns out that this issue is one that highlights just how deeply entrenched gender is in the broader society, the market, and the family. Gender-sensitive or gender-neutral social welfare policies that do not address this are doomed to have limited impact. Gender in social welfare is nested in a larger complex system of gender relations deeply embedded in interrelated discursive practices lived and experienced across the domains of social life from the family to the market to civil society in broader terms.

---

28. See Rebecca Blank, "U.S. Welfare Reform: What's Relevant for Europe?" *CESinfo Economic Studies* 49, 1 (2003): 68.

Sweden and Norway highlight that degendering welfare policy is a beginning, but the struggle to realize gender justice involves much more. Sweden and Norway each provides an example of attempts to balance the tradeoffs of gender-neutral and gender-sensitive policies that seek to address the persistence of gender inequality even with the introduction of policies designed to support caregiving by workers. Both have tremendous advantages over the gender-insensitive policies of U.S. welfare reform, as Blank effectively notes. Yet, both highlight the issue of just how deeply embedded gender is in society, the market, and the family. Any social welfare reform designed to promote gender fairness will have to address this embeddedness, or the truth of social policy reform will continue to be that leaving issues of caregiving to the side will mean the persistence of gender inequities.

Gender-Neutral Versus Gender-Sensitive Leave Policy: The Case of Sweden

Sweden in many ways continues to be an innovator in welfare state development. Sweden has demonstrated its innovativeness by being responsive to demographic changes in society that pose new risks for families. As Jacob Hacker reminds us, welfare state retrenchment can occur not only through overt actions to reduce or eliminate a particular program or policy.[29] Instead, welfare state retrenchment can also occur through non-actions that result in a country not responding to new developments that pose social and economic risks to citizens. The growing numbers of women, especially mothers, entering the paid workforce outside the home is just one such, particularly noteworthy, demographic change that poses significant risks to families.

Both two-parent families in which both parents are working and lone mothers who must dual-shift between breadwinning and homemaking are at increased risk for not being able to handle their child-rearing responsibilities when mothers begin working more hours, take full-time jobs, or even pursue professional careers. A welfare state that fails to develop new policies to compensate for these developments, particularly policies that support caregiving, is allowing caregiving to become a more fragile part of the social fabric. A welfare state that fails to respond to these developments

---

29. Jacob Hacker, "Privatizing Risk without Privatizing the Welfare State: The Hidden Politics of Social Policy Retrenchment in the United States," *American Political Science Review* 98, 2 (May 2004): 243–60.

with new policies that support caregiving is actually undergoing retrenchment relative to the social and economic risks facing families even though no overt actions to retrench policies has been initiated. Retrenchment by default, in fact, is what is happening in a number of welfare states as more mothers work more outside the home and policies fail to keep pace. Sweden is among the countries that have been willing to face this problem and develop responses in the form of policies designed to support caregiving while an increasing number of mothers take paid work outside the home.

Examining this problem as a question of discourse enables us to extend Hacker's insight about the covert power of inaction. Discourse inevitably privileges some identities over others, and welfare policy discourse is no exception.[30] Across welfare states throughout the modern era, welfare policy, more often than not, has privileged the enduring identity of the male breadwinner of the traditional two-parent family. Even the most progressive welfare states, including Sweden, have been founded on an ideal worker model, which assumes the welfare state's primary responsibility is to ensure the family of the male breadwinner against risks associated with the loss of income from that male working in paid employment for reasons related to unemployment, disability, retirement, and death. Welfare policy discourse therefore operates as a form of covert power by virtue of its failure to act on behalf of other identities other than the privileged one of the male breadwinner. It is already a powerful form of inaction even before social changes, like women increasingly taking paid employment, put it at risk of falling behind because it fails to take action to compensate families for those changes.

Sweden has for years been much more willing than most countries to confront the embedded gender biases of its political economy. In recent years, it has increasingly given more attention to emphasizing a gender-neutral approach seeking to denaturalize the work/care divide and de-gender the breadwinning and homemaking roles. Part of the context that has allowed this to happen is that marriage is no longer as strong an institution in Swedish society; Sweden has very high rates of children born outside of marriage. Nonetheless, parents often co-habited if they did not marry. As more and more women took paid employment outside the home, more couples became dual wage-earning families. With time, pressures to challenge the embedded biases of the ideal worker model developed in Sweden. Finally, this led to significant policy changes,

---

30. Sanford F. Schram, "Postmodern Policy Analysis: Discourse and Identity Welfare Policy," *Policy Sciences* 26, 3 (August 1993): 249–70.

starting with the repeal of tax advantages for breadwinners with stay-at-home spouses in the 1970s, when the wife's earnings were no longer "added on to the husband's and taxed at the highest possible rate. Under the new system, which treated spouses as individuals, only the most economically irrational men would seek to keep their wives out of the labor market. The last residue of the male breadwinner wage was the widows' pensions, which were phased out in 1989."[31]

Helena Bergman and Barbara Hobson note that eventually Sweden went beyond creating disincentives to the male monopoly on breadwinning and moved on to creating incentives for men to share caregiving responsibilities. Reflecting this paradigm shift, child leave policy was eventually over time revised to allow parents to share leave. "By 1989, parents could take up to one year and were compensated with 90 percent of their salaries up to a very high ceiling (about 32,000 American 1989 dollars per year) and a further three months with a flat benefit of 8 dollars a day."[32] Yet, despite these dramatic policy changes, embedded gender coding of family roles remained operative in Swedish society, even as increasing numbers of women, including mothers, took paid employment outside the home, and dual–wage-earning couples, married and unmarried, grew in numbers. "Researchers from around the world who came to Sweden to study the dual-earner family model concluded that, while women had changed, men had not."[33] Gender-neutral public policy was increasingly seen as inadequate for addressing embedded gender discourse in the broader society.

By the 1990s, various political interests were pushing for more explicit policies to support men in fulfilling their responsibilities as fathers. Women's rights groups joined with groups concerned about the family and others to move to a more gender-sensitive policy that would get men to take leave and care for their children. In 1994, the "Daddy's Month" provision was included in the parental leave so as to intentionally increase men's use of the parental leave policy. "Though the policy was couched in gender-neutral terms, it was understood that it was a policy for fathers.

31. Helena Bergman and Barbara Hobson, "Compulsory Fatherhood: The Coding of Fatherhood in the Swedish Welfare State," *Making Men into Fathers: Men, Masculinities and the Social Politics of Fatherhood* (New York: Cambridge University Press, 2002), p. 105.

32. Bergman and Hobson, "Compulsory Fatherhood: The Coding of Fatherhood in the Swedish Welfare State," p. 105.

33. Bergman and Hobson, "Compulsory Fatherhood: The Coding of Fatherhood in the Swedish Welfare State," p. 108.

Two months of the leave would be set aside for each parent at the highest benefit rate (now at 80 percent of one's salary) and the rest could be divided according to the preferences of individual family members."[34] Males who earned more than their spouses now had leave time specifically reserved for them as a greater incentive to take time off from work and care for their children. I would argue that even the Daddy's Month provision is consistent with the effort to achieve a degendering of parental roles, therefore making this but an extension of the gender-neutral approach to attacking the embedded gender biases of the Swedish political economy.

In fact, it was widely thought in Sweden at the time that this targeted approach to degendering caregiving would be more effective in overcoming embedded gender coding of parental roles in the broader society.[35] And men's use of parental leave increased from less than 20 percent of fathers having taken leave in the early 1980s to over 50 percent indicating that they had done so in the years after the enactment of the Daddy's Month change in policy. Yet, the policy has not been as successful in overcoming the gendered nature of care as these numbers imply. Caregiving is still mostly done by mothers; most of the leaves are taken by women, and women continue use most of the leave days taken. Since the 1980s, men have increased their proportion of all leave days taken from 1987 to 1997 from approximately 6 to 10 percent. The overwhelming number of leave days taken under the current policy are still used by women. Further, women concentrate much of their leave taking during the critical formative years of children up to about the age of 14, after which their rate of taken leave drops dramatically. Men, however, remain steady across the entire age range of their children, suggesting that their leave is not as focused on the essential responsibilities of child rearing but are associated with ancillary activities like long weekends and vacations. "The division of the parental leave suggests that men are still expected to be the main breadwinners and that interruptions in male careers are perceived as most costly.... In fact, studies show that men who take advantage of their rights as parents are penalized more in their careers than women."[36] It seems that Sweden's predominately, gender-neutral

---

34. Bergman and Hobson, "Compulsory Fatherhood: The Coding of Fatherhood in the Swedish Welfare State," p. 109.

35. The figures reported in this paragraph are from Bergman and Hobson, "Compulsory Fatherhood: The Coding of Fatherhood in the Swedish Welfare State," pp. 113–15.

36. Bergman and Hobson, "Compulsory Fatherhood: The Coding of Fatherhood in the Swedish Welfare State," pp. 115, 124.

approach has not really been that successful in overcoming embedded
gender roles in the broader society.

Now, one could argue that the shifts in policy have not gone far enough
or have not had enough time to contribute to revision of gender roles in
the broader society. Yet, the Swedish experience with attempts to dis-
mantle the family wage system and the emphasis on the male breadwinner
raises questions about how policy needs to be framed, as well as how far it
must go to decode gender in the political economy. Perhaps, Sweden
should return to giving more emphasis to a more gender-sensitive approach that supports women in fulfilling their care responsibilities. In fact,
given the relatively generous nature of Sweden's parental leave policy, it
might want to simply admit defeat in trying to degender the work/care
divide, declare victory in creating a women-friendly welfare state, and
happily go on as if this is what it intended all along.

The Case of Norway

Yet, whether a gender-sensitive approach supporting women in fulfilling
their care responsibilities is the ideal approach is also subject to question.
Next door to Sweden, Norway provides a noteworthy counterpoint.[37] In
Norway, for most of its modern history, welfare was not stigmatized like
in the United States, but was seen as an entitlement right earned by
citizenship as opposed to one's contributions via paid employment. This
has included transitional allowances to lone mothers with children under
the age of 10, which were initially enacted in 1964 until changed in 1998
to limit aid to mothers with children under the age of 4 so as to encourage
single parents to rely at least in part on paid employment for their support.
Until 1998, there were no work requirements, but with the changes enacted that year, aid to any family beyond three years was accompanied by
requirements that mothers be involved in education, training, or employment. These dramatic revisions in assistance were in good part in
response to the globalizing discourse of welfare dependency and the
model that the U.S. welfare reforms of 1996 produced. The changes in
Norway's transitional allowance enacted in 1998 halved the number of
recipients by 2001 and resulted in about four of five of those continuing to
receive assistance to be involved in education or work of some kind.

37. The analysis of Norway's recent changes in care policy draws heavily on Nina
Berven, *National Politics and Global Ideas? Welfare, Work and Legitimacy in Norway and
the United States* (Bergen, Norway: Stein Rokkan Centre for Social Studies, University of Bergen, Working Paper 12–2002, September 2002).

The retrenchment of Norwegian transitional allowances was not received with much opposition compared with changes in the United States, where welfare rights groups have continued to criticize the 1996 welfare reforms and their emphasis on time limits, work requirements, and sanctions for single mothers receiving public assistance. Part of the reason for the lack of opposition in Norway is perhaps due to the fact that Norway has been working harder than the United States to help women balance the dual responsibilities of work and care. Norway has not been content to go totally over to the neo-liberal market-based approach to insisting that single- or dual-parent families provide for themselves via paid employment without significant support for caregiving from the state. Instead, at the same time that Norway retrenched transitional allowances, it initiated a new policy of Cash-for-Care. Cash-for-Care is not limited to lone mothers but instead allows all families with children to support a parent who stays at home with a child or to cover the costs of child care while they are working. From 1998 to 2003, the amount of support per family was 3000 kroners (or $430) a month. In 2003, the sum was increased to 3600 kroners (or $514) a month. The aid is available, however, only when children are 1 to 3 years of age. The only limitation is a prohibition on using publicly funded child care centers to provide the care, thereby stimulating more private provision of the care. Lone mothers on transitional allowance remain eligible for Cash-for-Care and are expected to make use of this aid in making the transition to taking on the dual responsibilities of work and care by themselves. While this can remain a major challenge not sufficiently addressed by this limited policy, it is indeed a major improvement over what the United States has put in place to as part of its effort to move single mothers from welfare to paid employment as the primary source for supporting their families.

While Cash-for-Care can be paid to either parent, it is most often seen as a benefit being paid to mothers to support their caregiving. In Norway, like Sweden, it is not controversial that a growing number of children are born outside of marriage, and Cash-for-Care follows this trend to help mothers balance the dual responsibilities of work and care. In this sense, it is primarily a policy designed to help women fulfill their caregiving policies even as they increased their hours of paid employment. As such, Cash-for-Care can be categorized as a gender-sensitive policy that Norway has enacted in order to buffer the effects of promoting more employment by women, especially lone mothers. Debate has not surprisingly ensued as to whether this sort of emendation of globalized welfare-to-work reform is at risk of reinscribing women's natural status as primarily caregivers and only secondarily as breadwinners. Nina Berven has written:

The value of [women] being able to combine wage and family work is another aspect continuously stressed in policy and media debates, as well as in the general public. Norwegian women are characterized as "superwomen" in this matter: they are ranking at the top of international statistics over fertility as well as employment. That most of them are part-time workers, still performing the largest bulk of unpaid house- and care-work as well, clearly highlights the ambivalence in this matter—and one can ask whether Norwegian equality of gender is more of a myth than a fact. . . . Likewise, one of the major objections to cash-for-care is its potential weakening of women's connections to the labour market by creating increased options for retreating or reducing wage work for a limited period of time.[38]

In other words, when compared with Sweden's largely gender-neutral care reforms, Norway's pronounced gender-sensitive Cash-for-Care reforms suggest that welfare policy that seeks to address women's needs is damned if it does and damned if it doesn't take women's distinctive position in society into account. Either way may not be sufficient to overcome embedded gender bias in the broader society.

This is especially the case once we take account of the fact that Norway, like Sweden, had already in 1994 revised paid family leave to introduce time off specifically for fathers. The results have been similar to those in Sweden. And Norway, like Sweden, continues to have debate about the persistence of gender bias in leave policy.[39] In 1994, Norway introduced a father's quota to the country's one-year parental leave scheme. In Norway, parents can choose between 52 weeks of 80 percent wage compensation or 42 weeks of 100 percent compensation for family leave. There is a gender-sensitive dimension to their leave policy: for each family, three weeks before and six weeks after giving birth are exclusively for the mother, and 4 weeks of the total are exclusively for the father. The rest is in principle up to the parents to decide how to use it between them. The father quota was intended to get fathers to participate more in care as something that ought be done rather than simply a choice. Before implementation of the father quota, only 8 percent of Norwegian fathers took leave to be with their children, but in 2003, the share of fathers using the father quota was 87 percent. Nonetheless, only 15 percent took more leave than the quota, meaning that the typical father left the remaining leave time that he could split with the mother of his children to her. Care has remained in Norway, as in Sweden, primarily a women's responsibility.

---

38. Berven, *National Politics and Global Ideas? Welfare, Work and Legitimacy in Norway and the United States*, pp. 16–17.

39. Nina Berven, personal correspondence, October 4, 2004.

Nonetheless, the role of fathers in care is increasingly stressed in public debates about this issue. Family leave reforms that are being debated include expanding leave to 15 months and making four of these exclusively for fathers. There are concerns that being away from one's career this long will affect future advancement, especially in the case of women. Another option being discussed is to increase the father quota to two or three months, but *within* the current leave scheme. Parental leave, the proponents say, is not a *mothers'* right—it is a *parental* right. Yet, if past results of policy changes in this area are any indication, then it is likely that regardless of whether it is a gender-neutral or gender-sensitive approach, gender bias in issues of work and care will continue if the structural biases of gender in the broader society are not addressed.

It therefore may be harder than we suggested at the outset to overturn the embedded gender biases of the family wage logic (Fraser), the ideal worker model (Williams), and the discourse of dependency (Fineman). Neither gender-neutral policy nor gender-sensitive policy in itself will be sufficient to deconstruct embedded gender biases in the broader society. Each in its own way can lead to a limited policy that might help women up to a point but will inevitably end up reinscribing those gender biases.

Each welfare state may indeed have its own "path dependency" where established ways of making policy in that country create a precedent for continuing to make policy in that way.[40] Yet, unless the embedded structural bias associated with gender relations is addressed, then the persistence of gender bias will continue to occur regardless of which policy approach is stressed.

The Double Bind: Reinscribed in Discourse

For a long time, feminists have noted the importance of a particularly troubling double bind: women's caregiving work at home is devalued; as a result, when they do that work outside the home, it is undervalued, thereby reinforcing the lack of value attached to their efforts at home. In other words, until we value care work as work, it will be seen as inferior. This is why Orloff and others emphasize the need to support both simultaneously; otherwise, the double bind will continue.

---

40. Paul Pierson, "Increasing Returns, Path Dependence, and the Study of Politics," *American Political Science Review* 94, 2 (June 2000): 251–67.

The double bind implies something other than a simple linear causality and instead points to gender as a complex system of circular causality.[41] Gender is as gender does, at least within the confines of the system. Women can act like men and take paid employment, but then they risk of being seen as deviant women, still women, only trying to be men, especially if their male partners are earning decent wages then the women are vulnerable to being criticized as failing to be good mothers who should stay at home with their children. In a system of linear causality, work might determine how gender is seen, but the experience of gender in any culture is not so straightforward or, in that sense, linear. In its own circular way, gender becomes its own self-fulfilling prophecy that operates in a number of ways. Jeanne Schroeder notes that "in patriarchal thought, a thing is privileged not because it is male, but is called 'male' when it is privileged."[42] It is not what is female that is seen as impoverished but what is impoverished comes to be seen as female and what is of value, even if it is what has been associated with women, whether it is cooking, home crafts, or, most important, caregiving, then becomes open to being appropriated by men as male.

One way of seeing this is that gender is a complex system that is in a sense always already there, held in reserve, available to be invoked as necessary to reassert male privilege, perhaps each time as social roles change, and therefore not always in ways that are entirely complete at any one point in time. Women get to work outside the home; but if their work is valued by the broader gendered society, then they are at risk of being seen as doing a man's job, not acting feminine, transgressing their pre-defined role, as a deviant, who is a source of trouble. It is as if gendered identities migrate even as we change gendered roles, thereby reinscribing gender even as it changes its location and comes to be embedded in new practices.

For J. M. Balkin, gender is a complex system of circular causality because it is embedded in a set of nested oppositions such as implied by the following homology of nature : culture :: absence : presence :: active : passive :: male : female.[43] For Balkin, each of these dichotomies refers not so much to the physical or objective world as they do to each other. The ultimate

---

41. It is important for my argument to note that the concept of a double bind was most profoundly developed by the anthropologist and systems theorist Gregory Bateson. See Gregory Bateson, et al., "Toward a Theory of Schizophrenia," *Behavioral Science* 1 (1956): 251–64.

42. Jeanne L. Schroeder, "Abduction from the Seraglio: Feminist Methodologies and the Logic of Imagination," *Texas Law Review* 70 (1991): 109–210, *as quoted by J. M. Balkin, Cultural Software: A Theory of Ideology* (New Haven: Yale University Press, 1998), p. 229.

43. Balkin, *Cultural Software*, pp. 216–41.

reference point that anchors the whole system is infinitely deferred and never accessed. Instead, we distinguish male from female by pointing to the other dichotomies, which in turn point back to each other and ultimately back to male : female. This is what is meant by the aphorism "real men eat quiche." To wit, real men are what real women are not. We know a man by distinguishing him from a woman and we know a woman by referencing another of the dichotomies, each nested and embedded in the other in circular fashion serving to reinforce each other. Men are not women, who are passive because they are tied to nature and therefore naturally born to be dependent because they lack what it takes to be a real man, who is active, independent due to his being less tied to nature; if he were, he would be more like a woman, which he is, as we have already shown, not. Such circular reasoning is not only exhausting, it is the acquired sensibility of any specific culture. Balkin sees an entire culture as fabricated by a constant reinvoking and reworking of the nested oppositions of class, race, and gender, as well as other distinctions. He calls it our "cultural software," and we make our world from it.

The issue of gender then is not so much that women are passive or dependent but that they are to be passive or dependent in ways that the culture finds logical given how we engage in social practices by invoking and reworking the nested set of oppositions. Therefore, women on welfare are stigmatized not so much because they are allegedly passive and dependent but because they have manifested their passivity and dependency in ways that are inconsistent with the dominant culture's understanding of the appropriate way for woman to practice their passivity and dependency: namely, by being homemakers in a traditional role of dependency on a husband who heads their family has a breadwinner. Women demonstrate an important cultural competence not when they become active and independent but when they are passive and dependent in the ways society has come to consider acceptable. As the culture evolves, these distinctions are recreated and transformed, say as when increasing paid employment outside the home. Nonetheless, the distinctions can be recreated in part or even strengthened in new ways as when women go to work but largely to take jobs consistent with their "true natures" as caregivers and related roles in offices, schools, human service agencies, and elsewhere. Women are denigrated for largely working in subordinate positions, but they work in subordinate positions because of their prior denigration as women being seen as inferior to men. The causal chain becomes circular. In the case of welfare recipients, it becomes unclear whether single mothers on welfare are denigrated for taking welfare or whether their denigration for being women increases the chances that they will need to rely on welfare.

Gender as a complex system of circular causality therefore creates the double bind. If women continue to act consistent with the acquired sensibility of our culture, they increase their chances of subordination as women. But if they transgress the gendered distinctions operative in society, they risk being stigmatized as deviant. They are damned if they do, damned if they don't. The double bind is an artifact of the embedded nature of a nested set of gendered distinctions and how they serve to reinforce gender hierarchy.

Gender therefore is a complex system where simply deemphasizing gender or trying to stress it will in neither case be sufficient to compensate for how gender distinctions thrive on their relationship to other cultural oppositions. In this sense, gender, as a complex system of circular causality, is like a virtual conspiracy of discourses where one discourse trades on distinctions made by another. Gender in this sense is a problem of intertextuality.

This conspiracy of intertextual discourse operates as a complex system where there is circular causality because there are seamless connections. Women's work inside the home is not valued, so when women go to work outside the home, they are devalued in the market, further reinforcing their subordination at home. Chicken and egg both serve as pretext for each other in a complex system of gender privilege and subordination.

The promise of gender justice in any one domain of social life is then arguably mortgaged to the gendered discourses operating in related arenas. Therefore, simply making social welfare policies gender neutral or gender sensitive will not be sufficient. The litmus tests are Sweden and Norway, the two most generous social-democratic workerist welfare states in existence in the capitalist world today. Even there, attempts to address the embedded gender distinctions operating in the practices of work and care flounder on the shoals of such intertextuality. The dream of gender justice remains deferred because simply degendering or regendering social welfare policy in and of itself is not sufficient to cut the ties to gendered relations in society writ large. Gender in social welfare policy is embedded in the broader society. It is nested in a set of interrelated dichotomies operating in allied discourses in the society, the market, and the family. Cutting through this Gordian knot of intertextual distinctions is what is needed if social welfare policy is to help articulate gender-fair practices in work and family relations. Neither gender-neutral nor gender-sensitive welfare policies will be effective in achieving gender justice unless they appreciate the double bind created by the conspiracy of gendered discourses that rely on each other to reinforce gender privilege and subordination in society overall. Effective public policy in service of gender justice must transcend the limits of welfare policy and be joined to larger efforts to deconstruct gender discourse as it reinscribes privilege in the broader political economy.

Relatedly, this necessarily entails that policies go beyond what we have reviewed here so that we are simultaneously promoting gender neutrality by being gender sensitive. When it comes to the issues of work and care, we must first push for gender-sensitive policies that better support women in fulfilling their current caregiving responsibilities, but we must do so in ways that create opportunities for building more gender-neutral practices so that women are not sequestered in caregiving, stuck in the inferior "mommy track" at work, or denied the necessary social supports to pursue the same work opportunities as men. Until that happens, both types of gender policies will continue to fall short even as they grapple with the issues of gender justice in work and care.

Conclusion

What it would take the welfare state to be gender fair? Challenging the workerist biases of the welfare state is a good place to start. Sweden and Norway each in their own way have for some time now done a good job of it. In recent years, Sweden and Norway have employed both gender-neutral and gender-sensitive approaches to helping mothers balance care and work responsibilities. Policies reflecting either of these emphases are quite laudable, have been a boon to women, and have led to improvements in support for caregiving. Yet, in both countries, embedded gender biases in the broader society remain intact and are even being reinforced by these policies.

Regardless of whether public policy is gender-neutral or gender-sensitive, it will only contribute significantly to building a welfare state that promotes gender justice if it accounts for the relationship to deeply embedded distinctions that operate in the broader society. Otherwise, policy ends up reinforcing existing hierarchies of gender privilege. The debate about gender-neutral versus gender-sensitive policy must be transcended by attending to the issue of discourse and how gender codes are nested in the broader political economy. Neither gender-neutral nor gender-sensitive public policy will be sufficient to obtain gender justice if it is not tied to more ambitious efforts to deconstruct gender as embedded in society writ large.

Only by calling out the embedded biases of gender discourse in the broader society can we begin to hope for gender justice from the welfare state. Once we make those embedded biases explicit, we can see the truth of the globalizing discourse of welfare dependency. The truth is that the discourse of dependency fails to attend to issues of care that are likely to only become more important as work is emphasized. The truth of the globalizing discourse of dependency is a woman and care is the real absence present in the globalization of welfare policy discourse.

4 Welfare as Racemaking

Contextualizing Racial Disparities in Welfare Reform

Welfare in the United States was dramatically reformed in 1996 in ways that I would argue are highly racialized but that Europe has yet to fully emulate.[1] Yet, American welfare reform's racial subtext remains understudied by mainstream policy analysis. And that is the focus of this chapter: given the way it is most normally conducted these days, conventional public policy research is incapable of addressing the major political questions, such as what is the racial character of welfare reform. Only when we place welfare reform in historical and cultural context so as to highlight in particular the role of discourse can we begin to see just how racialized welfare reform really is.

Welfare reform was indeed dramatic. The Personal Responsibility and Work Opportunity Reconciliation Act of 1996 abolished the long-standing Aid to Families with Dependent Children (AFDC) program originally enacted as part of the Social Security Act of 1935 and replaced it with the Temporary Assistance for Needy Families (TANF) block grant. Many procedural safeguards to accessing assistance were repealed. The TANF program has emphasized time limits and work requirements and allowed states to set stricter options than specified in the federal law. It has given states greater latitude to use sanctions to reduce benefits and terminate families from assistance. It has given birth to a "work first" welfare reform regime that puts in place a series of "get-tough" policies designed to reduce the problem of "welfare dependency."[2] Welfare has been reformed to have as its main purpose the promotion of self-sufficiency by enforcing work and family values among the poor.

---

1. On the critical role of race in distinctively shaping the welfare state in the United States compared with Europe, see Alberto Alesina and Edward L. Glaeser, *Fighting Poverty in the US and Europe: A World of Difference* (Oxford, UK: Oxford University Press, 2004).

2. Thomas Gais and R. Kent Weaver, *State Policy Choices Under Welfare Reform*, Welfare Reform & Beyond: Brief No. #21 (Washington, DC: Brookings Institution, April 2002).

As a result, the number of recipients receiving what is now called TANF fell from 13,242,000 in 1995 to 5,334,000 in 2002—a decline of 59.7 percent.[3] Largely for this reason alone, welfare reform has been widely heralded a "success" by policymakers, the media, and researchers.[4] Less attention, however, has been given to a growing body of research indicating a number of racial disparities in client treatment and outcomes under welfare reform. For instance: (1) whites are leaving welfare faster than blacks,[5] (2) among those leaving, blacks are more likely to be forced off welfare,[6] (3) blacks are more likely to exhaust their time allowed on welfare,[7] and (4) blacks are more likely to cycle back onto welfare after having left.[8] In addition, there is research indicating that black recipients are treated less favorably than whites when it comes to being referred for education and training.[9] Still other research indicates that the higher the percentage of the recipients who are nonwhite, the greater is the probability that a state will adopt stricter welfare reform options.[10]

3. *Statistical Abstract of the United States* (Washington, DC: U.S. Bureau of the Census, 2002), p. 354.

4. See Sanford F. Schram and Joe Soss, "Success Stories: Welfare Reform, Policy Discourse, and the Politics of Research," in *Lost Ground: Welfare, Reform, Poverty, and Beyond*, Randy Albelda and Ann Withorn, eds. (Boston: South End Press, 2002), pp. 57–78.

5. Elizabeth Lower-Basch, *"Leavers" and Diversion Studies: Preliminary Analysis of Racial Differences in Caseload Trends and Leaver Outcomes* (Washington, DC: U.S. Department of Health and Human Services, 2002) http://aspe.hhs.gov/hsp/leavers 99/race.htm; and Kenneth Finegold and Sarah Staveteig, "Race, Ethnicity, and Welfare Reform," *Welfare Reform: The Next Act*, Alan Weil and Kenneth Finegold, eds. (Washington, DC: Urban Institute Press, 2002), pp. 203–24.

6. Ariel Kalil, Kristin S. Seefeldt, and Hui-chen Wang, "Sanctions and Material Hardship under TANF," *Social Service Review* 76, 4 (December 2002): 642–62.

7. Greg J. Duncan, Kathleen Mullan Harris, and Johanne Boisjoly, "Time Limits and Welfare Reform: New Estimates of the Number and Characteristics of Affected Families," *Social Service Review* 74, 1 (March 2000): 55–75.

8. Pamela J. Loprest, *Who Returns to Welfare?* (Washington, DC: Urban Institute, Assessing the New Federalism, 2002), http://www.urban.org.

9. Susan Gooden, "Contemporary Approaches to Enduring Challenges: Using Performance Measures to Promote Racial Equality under TANF," in *Race and the Politics of Welfare Reform*, Sanford F. Schram, Joe Soss, and Richard C. Fording, eds. (Ann Arbor: University of Michigan Press), pp. 254–75.

10. Matthew C. Fellowes and Grethen Rowe, "The Politics of Welfare Reform(ed): How TANF Changed and Did Not Change Redistribution Politics," *American Journal of Political Science* 48, 2 (April 2004): 362–73; Gais and Weaver, *State Policy Choices Under Welfare Reform*; and Joe Soss, Sanford F. Schram, Thomas P. Vartanian, and Erin O'Brien, "Setting the Terms of Relief: Explaining State Policy Choices in the Devolution Revolution," *American Journal of Political Science* 45, 2 (April 2001): 378–403.

These findings have inaugurated a debate about how we should interpret racial disparities under welfare reform and what should be done about them. The U.S. Commission on Civil Rights has issued a report reviewing the available research and concluding that the growing number of statistical disparities being uncovered pointed to a need to revise welfare policy to prevent discriminatory practices.[11] And legislation has been proposed in Congress to ensure racial fairness in the administration of welfare reform.[12]

Yet, there are analysts who contend that welfare reform, as a post–Civil Rights era, racially neutral public policy, can legitimately have differential outcomes for different racial groups.[13] For these observers, the racial disparities found are merely epiphenomenal indicators associated with other factors, such as nonwhite recipients having on average less education making them less employable.[14] Lawrence Mead in particular has argued that, in a post–Civil Rights society where racial discrimination has diminished, the "paternalism" of a get-tough approach to welfare reform neither reflects nor perpetuates racial disadvantage. Instead, in the current era, it is actually just what low-income blacks in particular need in order to overcome the personal pathologies associated with poverty. Mead writes:

> [W]hen poverty was "rediscovered" in the 1960s, it was at first widely seen as a byproduct of the historical disadvantage suffered by black Americans. It was believed that by passing civil-rights laws, the social problems linked to blacks, such as welfare and crime, would abate. Unfortunately, this did not happen.... And although racial bias remains in America, it has declined, and at the very same time that poverty has increased in the inner city. Racism no longer accounts for poverty in the way it once seemed to. ... [I]t is difficult today for policy makers to keep arguing that the public demand for order reflects prejudice and that some further social reform must be achieved first. ... The idea is

---

11. U.S. Commission on Civil Rights, *A New Paradigm for Welfare Reform: The Need for Civil Rights Enforcement* (Washington, DC: 2002).

12. On April 3, 2003, U.S. Senator Russell Feingold (D-WI) reintroduced the Fair Treatment and Due Process Protection Act of 2003 (S. 770) designed to monitor the implementation of welfare reform to ensure racial fairness for applicants and clients.

13. Lawrence M. Mead, *The New Politics of Poverty: The Nonworking Poor in America* (New York: Basic Books, 1992), pp. 111–15.

14. Lawrence M. Mead, "Welfare Reform and the Family," *Family Matters* 54 (1999): 12–17; and Douglas J. Besharov, "The Past and Future of Welfare Reform," *Public Interest* 150 (2003): 4–21. Robert Rector et al. emphasize relatively high rates of female-headed families among blacks as the main reason for higher rates of welfare dependence, lower levels of education, lower employment rates, and lower incomes. See Robert Rector, Kirk A. Johnson, and Patrick F. Fagan, *Understanding Differences in Black and White Child Poverty Rates* (Washington, DC: Heritage Foundation, Center for Data Analysis Report #01–04, 2001).

that the poor need support, but they also require structure—a combination of help and hassle.... The implications are particularly momentous for racial minorities, who are overrepresented among the poor. Understandably, federal policy toward these groups has emphasized the dismantling of barriers, because past denials of equal opportunity are central to their disadvantages. Paternalism applied to the black poor can easily seem like a return to slavery or Jim Crow, at least to critics. But although racism undoubtedly helped demoralize the ghetto, discrimination in the old sense is too minor a cause of poverty today to justify further anti-bias measures.[15]

In what follows, I review the research on racial disparities under welfare reform to try to answer the question of whether welfare reform is racially biased and, if so, in what ways and what should be done about it. First, I frame the issue in terms of the different meanings of the term "race bias" and the different ways in which welfare reform may in fact be race biased.[16] I offer three major interpretations regarding race bias in welfare reform. These contrasting interpretations focus on how welfare reform is a policy regime that is therefore actively engaged in reordering society.[17] Each of these interpretations suggests that welfare reform, as a policy regime, should be characterized as implicated in promoting a particular form of racial relations. Each interpretation offers a characterization of welfare reform as a particular type of what we can call a "racial policy regime." By a racial policy regime, I do not mean to limit it to only the implementation of a policy that governs race relations, such as anti–employment discrimination laws. Instead, I construe a racial policy regime more broadly to mean the implementation of any policy that actively affects racial hierarchy in society.

The first interpretation is that welfare reform is race neutral in intent and effect and should be characterized as a policy that is contributing to a racially fair society. The second interpretation is that welfare reform is an explicitly race-biased policy that is actively reordering society in ways that intensify racial hierarchy. The third interpretation goes beyond the polar

15. Lawrence M. Mead, "Telling the Poor What to Do," *The Public Interest* 103 (1998): 104–9.
16. I use the term "race bias" rather than "racism" in order to explore the variety of practices that lead to producing racial disadvantage, including those practices that do not involve intentional acts by individuals. "Racism," it seems to me, is better reserved for the latter. A noteworthy attempt to address this issue was when Stokely Carmichael and Charles Hamilton coined the term "institutionalized racism" in their 1967 book *Black Power*. See Kwame Ture and Charles V. Hamilton, *Black Power: The Politics of Liberation*, Reissue Edition (New York: Vintage Books, 1992), pp. 4–6.
17. Gosta Esping-Andersen, *Three Worlds of Welfare Capitalism* (Princeton, NJ: Princeton University Press, 1994).

types of race bias offered by the first two interpretations and suggests that welfare reform reflects an ostensibly race-neutral discourse that nonetheless operates to actively reproduce racial disadvantage in society.

Next, I turn to examining the available data to assess these different interpretations of welfare reform as a racial policy regime. This review allows me to demonstrate that the same data can be used to support different conclusions about the racial character of welfare reform. The analysis, therefore, most significantly underscores the importance of interpretation in all data analysis, something that is generally accepted in discussions about social science methodology but nonetheless tends to be minimized in conventional public policy analysis.[18] This analysis, however, is not designed to suggest that the issue of race bias in welfare reform cannot be resolved; instead, I argue that it is only remains indefinite if we confine ourselves to conventional welfare policy research that deemphasizes the role of interpretation in statistical research and focuses on isolated empirical findings, such as the demographic composition of the welfare population, the rates at which different groups leave welfare, employment rates, sanction rates, rates of returning to welfare, etc.

My analysis responds to the call of Sandra Morgen, Alice O'Connor, and others for a "new poverty research."[19] Such an approach goes beyond the limitations of mainstream welfare policy research and develops more robust interpretations by recognizing the normative standards implicit in statistical measurements.[20] A "new poverty research" enables us to see, for instance, that different poverty measures each provide a baseline that implies a different understanding of the purpose of welfare and which population should be represented. Such an orientation encourages us to give greater emphasis to the normative implications of using different statistics and therefore provides a way to break the impasse that mute statistical disparities create regarding the question of whether welfare reform is racially biased. This "new poverty research" breaks that impasse

18. Deborah Stone, *Policy Paradox: The Art of Political Decision Making*, Revised Edition (New York: W. W. Norton & Company, 2002).

19. Sandra Morgen, "The Politics of Welfare and of Poverty Research," *Anthropological Quarterly* 75, 4 (2002): 745–57; Alice O'Connor, *Poverty Knowledge: Social Science, Social Policy, and the Poor in Twentieth-Century U.S. History* (Princeton: Princeton University Press, 2001); and Sanford F. Schram, *Words of Welfare: The Poverty of Social Science and the Social Science of Poverty* (Minneapolis: University of Minnesota Press, 1995). Also see Judith Goode and Jeffrey Maskovsky, *The New Poverty Studies: The Ethnography of Power, Politics, and Impoverished People in the United States* (New York: New York University Press, 2001).

20. Stone, *Policy Paradox*, pp. 163–87.

by emphasizing the importance of placing welfare reform in historical and social context. Placing policy in context helps decide which statistics should be given stress so as to improve our ability to make nor-mative assessments. In this way, we can better interpret the data, judge whether welfare reform is race biased, and decide what actions need to be taken.[21]

By practicing my brand of the "new poverty research," we can offer an alternative to Mead's account of the racial character of welfare reform in a post–Civil Rights society. We can see how the available data support an interpretation that welfare reform is ostensibly neutral, stated in a euphemistic discourse, but operating in a way that actively recreates racial disadvantage among the poor. By placing the available data in this discursive context, we can begin to see how welfare reform is its own form of what Loïc Wacquant calls "racemaking."[22]

This approach enables us to see how the racial policy regime of welfare reform has evolved out of past policy and is reflective of the social conditions of the current period. We are able to emphasize that welfare has always been an inferior program reserved for serving low-income families who are almost all headed by women.[23] It was structured in the Social Security Act of 1935 to afford states substantial discretion in determining eligibility and setting benefits, in no small part to placate southern congressmen who wanted to be sure the program could be tailored to their local social and economic practices, including treating African Americans in a discriminatory and arbitrary way.[24] As blacks began to gain rights to assistance in the 1960s, the program came to be seen as a "black program," making it more politically vulnerable and increasing calls for its retrenchment, which, after years of political gridlock, finally came in the 1990s.[25] From this perspective,

21. On the importance of accounting for context in assessing reform across welfare states, see Yuri Kazepov, "Cities in Europe," in *Cities in Europe: Changing Contexts, Local Arrangements and the Challenge to Social Cohesion*, Yuri Kazepov, ed. (Oxford, UK: Blackwell, 2004), pp. 3–42.

22. Loïc Wacquant, "From Slavery to Mass Incarceration: Rethinking the 'Race Question' in the US," *New Left Review* 13, 1 (2003): 41–60.

23. Frances Fox Piven and Richard A. Cloward, *Regulating the Poor: The Functions of Public Welfare* (New York: Vintage, 1971, updated edition, 1993).

24. Robert C. Lieberman, *Shifting the Color Line: Race and the American Welfare State* (Cambridge: Harvard University Press, 1998); and Michael K. Brown, *Race, Money, and the American Welfare State* (Ithaca, NY: Cornell University Press, 1999).

25. Jill Quadagno, *The Color of Welfare: How Racism Undermined the War on Poverty* (Oxford, UK: Oxford University Press, 1994); Martin Gilens, *Why Americans Hate Welfare: Race, Media, and the Politics of Antipoverty Policy* (Chicago: University of Chicago Press, 1999); and Kenneth J. Neubeck and Noel A. Cazenave, *Welfare Racism: Playing the Race Card Against America's Poor* (New York: Routledge, 2001).

it is unlikely that had welfare been seen as a "white program" for middle-class, traditional families that it would have been attacked as it was. Further, that the program's effects fall more harshly on nonwhites does not significantly undermine the general assessment of welfare reform as a success; however, this would probably not hold if it were whites who were more likely to be disadvantaged by welfare reform. Welfare's implicit association with blacks facilitates its retrenchment and its disproportionate negative impact on blacks leaves reform's reputation as a "success" unsullied.

The analysis that follows highlights how the very ways in which welfare policy is structured and implemented reflect the racial biases of the broader society and contribute to reproducing them. As a policy regime, welfare reform works actively to produce racial disadvantage through its treatment of black welfare recipients. From time limits to work requirements, sanctions policies, and limitations on benefits, welfare reform is administered in ways that make it less supportive of poor blacks who are concentrated in marginalized neighborhoods and confront distinctive barriers associated with race bias in the broader society. A welfare regime that punishes welfare recipients who fail to find work due to reasons associated with the historical legacies of race is a racial policy regime that is actively working to recreate racial disadvantage in society. If the ultimate purpose of welfare reform today is to promote self-sufficiency via the promotion of work and family, it is failing its black recipients before all others and doing so in ways that are reminiscent of the welfare's racially charged history.

This analysis is based on an appreciation of the fact that there can be a variety of forms of race bias.[26] As is often the case, the issue is not simply whether a policy is explicitly racist. We would think that welfare reform that was neither intended to explicitly discriminate against blacks nor is implemented in way that disadvantages blacks can hardly be called racist and should not been seen as involving race bias. The analysis that follows underscores that it is important to recognize that a welfare reform policy that fails to account for preexisting economic inequalities should not for that reason alone be called race biased. It is unreasonable to expect welfare reform expect to account for all of the racial inequalities existing in the society at large. Yet, my argument is that welfare reform not only fails to account for preexisting racial disparities but also uncritically reflects and incorporates those biases in the policy's structure and its implementation. A welfare reform policy regime that punishes blacks for failing to access

---

26. See Ture and Hamilton, *Black Power*, pp. 4–6.

jobs and create stable families as quickly as whites for reasons that lie largely in the society, and the job market in particular, is profoundly race biased. As a result, welfare policy ends up not just failing to account for preexisting racial inequities but reproduces them in its treatment of clients and the resulting outcomes it produces.

Welfare reform is therefore an ostensibly neutral public policy that is part of a vicious cycle of race bias: it is a policy that grows out of and reinforces racially biased institutions and practices in the broader society, concerning education, jobs, housing, and other factors affecting life chances.[27] The key to seeing this is in recognizing how welfare reform's ostensibly neutral, euphemistic discourse silences how it operates as a policy regime that actively participates in perpetuating pre-existing racial disadvantage in society. My brand of the "new poverty research" therefore allows for a more robust form of causal analysis that better highlights welfare reform's relationship to issues of race.[28] Such an approach provides a more nuanced way of attributing a causal role for race in structuring welfare reform, while also assigning a causal role for welfare reform in producing and reproducing racial disparities. Racial division in our society creates the conditions for reform that cracks down on a program that also just happens to be more important to nonwhites than to whites. At the same time, welfare reform is instrumental in perpetuating those very same social and economic racial inequalities that give rise to making welfare an inferior "black" program that is vulnerable to retrenchment.[29] Contextualizing racial character of welfare reform enables us to tell a better causal story with the available statistics.[30] It also enables us to move beyond simple models of linear causality that make conventional public policy research inadequate for addressing such questions.[31] It becomes possible to see welfare reform as enacting a vicious cycle where race-neutral public policy incorporates preexisting inequalities in its implementation of that

27. Frances Fox Piven, "Why Welfare Is Racist," in *Race and the Politics of Welfare Reform*, Sanford F. Schram, Joe Soss, and Richard C. Fording, eds. (Ann Arbor: University of Michigan Press, 2003), pp. 323–36.

28. Lieberman, *Shifting the Color Line*, pp. 3–9.

29. Wacquant, "From Slavery to Mass Incarceration: Rethinking the 'Race Question' in the US," pp. 41–60.

30. See Stone, *Policy Paradox*, pp. 188–209.

31. For a critique of linear models of causality, see Anne Norton, *95 Theses on Politics, Culture, and Method* (New Haven, CT: Yale University Press, 2003). Also see Andrew Abbott, *Time Matters: On Theory and Method* (Chicago: University of Chicago Press, 2001), who warns against allowing quantitative analysis to trap us into believing in a "general linear reality" that seriously mischaracterizes the way the social world works.

policy in ways that end up actively helping to reproduce them. Contextualizing the euphemistic, falsely neutral discourse of welfare reform in this way highlights how it is its own form of what Wacquant calls "race-making" that works to reinforce the idea that the race is a marker highlighting real, durable differences between blacks and whites regarding things like intelligence, ability, and effort.[32]

As a result, we can also develop a more sophisticated model regarding responsibility for the racial bias inherent in welfare reform that motivates more effective responses.[33] Rather than the retrospective "fault model" that focuses on whether individuals have been found to be at fault for discrete acts of racial discrimination that have already been perpetrated, contextualizing race bias in welfare reform creates the basis for appreciating a prospective model of collective responsibility that works to reduce such institutionalized bias from producing deleterious effects in the future.[34] Under this model, even if welfare reform is not explicitly race biased, citizens of the United States accept responsibility to revise welfare reform policies so that they do not recreate racial disadvantage. Rather than limiting our concern to policing individuals to hold them responsible for specific instances of discrimination, the collective responsibility model emphasizes interrogating ostensibly neutral institutions and policies to prevent them from perpetrating future racial disadvantageness. This model leads to the conclusion that congressional action to ensure racial fairness in welfare reform should involve more than prohibiting specific instances of disparate treatment of clients by caseworkers. Instead, the more appropriate policy response involves rethinking welfare reform more structurally so as to prevent this ostensibly neutral public policy from systematically creating racial disadvantage.

In the end, this analysis suggests it is critical to get beyond the interpretive and normative limitations of conventional public policy research. Once we do so, we are better able to interpret racial disparities under

---

32. See Wacquant, "From Slavery to Mass Incarceration: Rethinking the 'Race Question' in the US," pp. 41–60.

33. On the importance of developing a pragmatic black political theory that can infuse empirical analysis with a normative dimension that suggests what should be done to attack race bias, see Hawley Fogg-Davis, "The Racial Retreat of Contemporary Political Theory," *Perspectives on Politics* 1, 3 (September 2003): 555–64.

34. Iris Marion Young, "Responsibility and Structural Injustice" (prepared for presentation at the Political Theory Workshop, Princeton University, December 4, 2003). The idea that racial injustice is a collective responsibility stemming from its structural roots parallels Carmichael and Hamilton's original argument on what to do about "institutionalized racism." See Ture and Hamilton, *Black Power*, pp. 4–6.

welfare reform. Placing welfare reform in historical and social context enables us to see how it is an ostensibly race-neutral public policy, expressed in a euphemistic discourse, but nonetheless very much implicated in reinforcing racial disadvantage for low-income nonwhite families. Such an approach to studying welfare reform improves our understanding of how it is race biased and does so in a way that more effectively suggests what we should do about it.[35] By practicing a "new poverty research" that places welfare policy in a broader historical and social context and highlights the interpretive dimension of policy analysis,[36] we can go beyond the limitations of conventional quantitative policy research, make normative judgments, and decide the actions that need to be taken regarding important policy issues such as the role of race bias in welfare reform.

The Multiple Meanings of Race Bias and the Racial Character of Welfare Reform

Welfare reform can produce a race-biased policy regime in a number ways because there are multiple ways in which race bias can be practiced. Individuals can practice race bias that is *conscious* or *intentional*. They can also unconsciously or unintentionally be implicated in racially biased practices

---

35. Before proceeding with this analysis, it is important to address two related issues. First, most families receiving welfare are single mothers with children. There are profound issues regarding gender bias historically in U.S. welfare policy that should not be ignored. See Linda Gordon, *Pitied but Not Entitled: Single Mothers and the History of Welfare, 1890–1935* (Cambridge: Harvard University Press, 1994); Gwendolyn Mink, "Violating Women: Rights Abuses in the Welfare Police State," in *Lost Ground: Welfare, Reform, Poverty, and Beyond*, Randy Albelda and Ann Withorn, eds. (Boston: South End Press, 2002), pp. 95–112; and Martha F. Davis, "Legislating Patriarchy," in *From Poverty to Punishment*, Gary Delgado, ed. (Oakland, CA: Applied Research Center, 2002), pp. 147–54. An important related concern is the intersection of race and gender in welfare policy so as to double the disadvantage of nonwhite single mothers who rely on public assistance; see Kimberle Crenshaw, "Demarginalizing the Intersection of Race and Sex: A Black Feminist Critique of Antidiscrimination Doctrine, Feminist Theory and Antiracist Politics," *University of Chicago Legal Forum* (1989): 139–67. Second, I mainly focus on black-white differences under welfare reform, with a primary concern for effects on African-Americans. I also consider effects for Latinos, labeled in government statistics as Hispanics (who can be either white or nonwhite). I give some attention to the treatment of immigrants (who are disproportionately nonwhite) as well. While race is increasingly more than a black-white issue in the United States, the history of discrimination against African-Americans continues to haunt welfare today and creates an urgent basis for focusing on the effects of racial disparities for African-Americans.

36. Dvora Yanow, *Conducting Interpretive Policy Analysis* (Thousand Oaks, CA: SAGE, 1999).

depending on the institutional setting in which an individual is acting. Such acts involve what has been called "institutionalized racism."[37] Therefore, race bias can be more *institutional* than *individual*. Policy can also be race biased in different ways. It can explicitly invoke racial categories and make what the courts have called "invidious distinctions" based on race. But policy can avoid such distinctions and still lead to disparate effects in ways that suggest the policy is failing to account for how it is creating racial disadvantage.[38] Race bias in policy can be *explicit* or *implicit*.

In addition, the federal structure of the welfare policy regime makes it important to account for the levels of policymaking and implementation. The source of race bias can be *national, state,* or *local.* Further, its source may also be agency implementation more than policymaking deliberation.

Last, it is important to envision how these different dimensions of racial bias may interact. Welfare reform could be explicitly biased in its stated policy as enacted at the federal level. Then again, it could be implicitly biased by promulgating a national policy that will be detrimental to blacks rather than whites but without explicitly saying so. It could be biased in the way states implement the program in terms of what policies they adopt for which populations. It could be biased in the ways the program is administered, especially by caseworkers in their treatment of individual clients. Welfare reform could be biased in ways that involve all these dimensions. For instance, a caseworker without consciously intending to discriminate may neutrally implement state policy choices that actively reproduce social and economic disadvantages such that the needs of nonwhite recipients for assistance and support are systematically dismissed to point of undermining their quest to achieve self-sufficiency. These racially biased effects may not have been part of an intentional design by policymakers or caseworkers or anyone in between. Nonetheless, welfare reform discourse ends up reproducing racial disadvantageness in the form of less economic opportunity and less overall well-being for nonwhites.

---

37. Ture and Hamilton, *Black Power,* pp. 4–6.

38. A parallel to examining racial disparities in outcomes under welfare reform is employment litigation that examines hiring and firing patterns rather than simply looking to see if employers intentionally and explicitly used race as a criterion for favoring whites, males, and other privileged groups. See Michael K. Brown, Martin Carnoy, Elliot Currie, Troy Duster, David B. Oppenheimer, Marjorie B. Shultz, and David Wellman, *Whitewashing Race: The Myth of a Color-Blind Society* (Berkeley: University of California Press, 2003).

Given the multiple meanings of race bias and different ways it can be operating in welfare reform, a number of interpretations are possible. For purposes of analysis, I review the available evidence based on three distinct basic interpretations: (1) welfare reform is not race biased, (2) welfare reform is explicitly race biased, and (3) welfare reform is race-neutral but structured and operating in ways that actively work to reproduce racial disadvantage.

Evidence for the first hypothesis would include the absence of race-related categories in the stated policy, participation rates indicating equal access to the program by different racial groups (relative to need or some other pertinent standard), and other data suggesting that nonwhites are not being singled out for disadvantage. Even evidence of racial disparities in treatment and outcome would still be consistent with this interpretation if it can be shown that such disparities are interpreted as being more a result of differences between clients than differential treatment by federal policymakers or state administrators.

Evidence supporting the second hypothesis might be found in the language and structure of the federal welfare reform policy, in the way states choose program options to participate in the program, and in the way state agencies and their contractors are administering it. This interpretation would be credible if we were to find that the welfare reform law explicitly specified differential treatment for white and black recipients, if states were found to rely on race for deciding how to structure their programs, and if caseworkers and other administrators treated black recipients differently than whites. Data on differential outcomes for blacks and whites would provide evidence supporting evidence if it could be shown that these disparate outcomes result from race being invoked to structure welfare reform policy, state program choices, or agency administration.

Evidence for the third hypothesis would come from data indicating that the implementation of welfare reform treats black and white clients similarly but that this "equal" treatment results in blacks being systematically disadvantaged. Supporting evidence would show that welfare reform fails to ensure that its "equal" treatment of clients does not lead black families to be more likely to remain poor, be unemployed, to receive lower wages, to have a greater need to cycle back onto welfare, and to be less able to make improvements in their standard of living.

My thesis is that the data by themselves are never enough to answer big questions such as what is the racial character of welfare reform. Therefore, whether the data reviewed here should be seen as offering support for any of the three interpretations depends on how well the case could be made that the data and interpretation fit together. Part of the argument of this analysis is that placing welfare reform in historical and social context helps make this fit between the data and this interpretation. My main thesis is that when we do this, it enables us to appreciate how welfare reform discourse is ostensibly race-neutral post–Civil Rights but nonetheless actively operates to reproduce racial disadvantage in society.

I now turn to the three basic interpretations to examine how the data do or do not support them.

Welfare Reform Is a Race-Neutral Policy Regime

The first interpretation that welfare reform is a race-neutral policy regime is based in the idea that welfare reform is a post–Civil Rights public policy. The national legislation does not explicitly favor whites over blacks. Neither do the policies that states have put in place to implement welfare reform. Then again, what public policies say and what they do may very well be different things. Even before the Civil Rights era, racially discriminatory welfare policies often operated implicitly.[39] Probably the best data that welfare reform is not race biased can be found in examination of welfare participation rates. From the 1930s into the 1960s, states were able to discriminate against blacks receiving assistance with relative impunity. Southern states in particular did so, but they were not alone.[40] Civil Rights legislation and litigation attacked such practices. In the post–Civil Rights era, there has been less evidence that states erect barriers that are designed to systematically exclude nonwhites from receiving assistance. Welfare reform has focused on reducing the rolls, and states have used the increased latitude given them in the welfare reform period to establish "diversion" programs that are intended to discourage families from enrolling in the TANF program.[41] Yet, the available data do not provide evidence one way or another that indicates conclusively that welfare reform has led to blacks being systematically denied welfare at rates higher than whites.

One way to assess whether blacks are underrepresented on the welfare rolls in the welfare reform period is to compare poverty and welfare rates by race. Poverty is unevenly distributed across the U.S. population. Nonwhites are disproportionately over-represented in the poverty population,

---

39. Brown, et al., *Whitewashing Race*, pp. 1–33.

40. Robert C. Lieberman, and John Lapinski, "American Federalism, Race and the Administration of Welfare," *British Journal of Political Science* 31, 2 (2001): 303–29.

41. Matthew Diller, "The Revolution in Welfare Administration: Rules, Discretion, and Entrepreneurial Government," *New York University Law Review* 75, 5 (2000): 1121–220.

and therefore in a racially unbiased welfare system, we would expect nonwhites to comprise a relatively large number of welfare recipients. The poverty rate for the U.S. population overall in 2003 was 12.5 percent, up from 11.7 percent in 2001.[42] In 2003, people below the poverty thresholds numbered 35.9 million. For non-Hispanic whites, the poverty rate rose from 7.8 percent in 2001 to 8.2 percent in 2003. For African Americans, the poverty rate was much higher, increasing in 2003 to 24.4 percent up from 22.7 percent in 2001. For Hispanics, the rate increased from 21.8 percent in 2001 to 22.5 in 2003; and for Asians and Pacific Islanders, it increased from 10.0 to 11.8 percent. While African Americans have the highest poverty rate among these groups, their numbers were among the lowest they have been since the federal government began measuring poverty. Yet, these numbers still confirm that nonwhites—African Americans and Hispanics in particular—are much more likely to have incomes below the poverty line, and therefore we should not be surprised that nonwhites comprise a larger proportion of the welfare population than they do of the population overall. And in fact, that has been the case for several decades.[43]

Table 4–1 compares the racial breakdown of families with incomes below the poverty line to the racial composition of families receiving welfare. Forty-three percent of families with incomes below the poverty line in 2003 were non-Hispanic whites compared with only 32 percent of the families receiving TANF in 2002.[44] Only 27 percent of all poor families were black compared with 38 percent of TANF families. Twenty-five percent of all poor families were Hispanic and the same percent of families receiving TANF were Hispanic. It seems then that blacks were by no means under-represented in their receipt of welfare in the reform period.

Nonetheless, these data are hardly definitive. Welfare is a program largely for low-income female-headed families with children under 18. Therefore, the more relevant statistics concern the racial breakdown for these families with incomes below the poverty level. If we compare columns 2 through 4 with column 5, a different picture begins to emerge. Columns 2 through 4 indicate the racial breakdown for persons in families

42. Census data reported in this section are from U.S. Census Current Population Survey for 2003, the Annual Social and Economic Supplement, available at http://www.census.gov/hhe/www/poverty.html.

43. Sanford F. Schram, *Praxis for the Poor: Piven and Cloward and the Future of Social Science in Social Welfare* (New York: New York University Press, 2002), pp. 157–85.

44. The latest year for which there are available data on the racial composition of the welfare population is 2002.

TABLE 4-1. Comparison by Race of Families in Poverty and of Families on Welfare, 2003*

Racial/Ethnic Composition	100% of Poverty or Less		75% of Poverty or Less	50% Poverty or Less	
	Persons in Families		Persons in Female-Headed Families with Children <18		Persons Receiving Welfare
White (non-Hispanic)	43%	37%	36%	36%	32%
Black	27%	39%	41%	41%	38%
Hispanic	25%	21%	21%	20%	25%
Asian or Pacific Islander	4%	2%	2%	2%	2%
Other	1%	1%	<1%	1%	3%

*Welfare = Temporary Assistance for Needy Families (TANF). Poverty data are for 2003 and welfare data are for 2002 (i.e., the latest year available). Sources: Data on the poverty population are from the U.S. Census Current Population Survey for 2003, the Annual Social and Economic Supplement, formerly called the March Supplement, available at http:/www.census .gov/hhes/www/poverty.html. The data on the Welfare Population are from the U.S. Department of Health and Human Services, Office of Family Assistance, 2004.

with incomes below 100, 75, and 50 percent of the poverty level. These data show that the poorer the population, the greater is the proportion that is nonwhite. The percentage of whites families with children under 18 and incomes below 100 percent of the poverty level in 2003 was 37 percent, whereas it was 36 percent for 75 percent of the poverty level and 50 percent of the poverty level. The percentage such families that were black increased from 39 to 41 to 41 percent for 100, 75, and 50 percent of the poverty level, respectively.

In addition, when we compare these data with those in the last column indicating the racial breakdown of families receiving TANF, we find that perhaps blacks are underrepresented. Only 38 percent of families receiving welfare were black, whereas 39 percent of all poor families with children were black, but the figure rises to 41 percent at 75 percent of the poverty level and stays at 41 percent for 50 percent of the poverty level. Therefore, although there is reason to believe that in our post–Civil Rights era racial barriers to accessing welfare have been repealed, the available data do not definitively prove that black underrepresentation on welfare is a thing of the past. Instead, the available data suggest that blacks in fact may still be not receiving assistance at a rate comparable to their level of need.

These data, however, do not enable us to conclusively answer the question of whether blacks are underrepresented in welfare and, more important, whether this is a result of systematic bias in policy and program implementation. What the data do effectively highlight is that each measure of poverty implicitly indicates a standard for evaluating the welfare program.[45] For instance, if we were to focus on the overall poverty rate, we are suggesting welfare is about assisting all poor persons. Yet, if we were alternatively to use the proportion of all families with children below 50 percent of the poverty line, then we are implying that welfare is about assisting the very poorest of these particular families. Which statistic is used determines what normative standard is assumed. As the data in Table 4–1 suggest, blacks can be seen as underrepresented or overrepresented depending on the poverty standard that is referenced. The decision of which statistic and standard to use is a normative issue that depends on who we decide should be the primary target population of the welfare program, poor people in general or the poorest families. Until we decide that question, we cannot decide the issue of racial representation.

Other evidence, however, that can be used to suggest that welfare programs are open to nonwhites. There are available statistics indicating that poor nonwhites are more likely to receive a variety of forms of government assistance compared with whites. Table 4-2 presents the percentage of poor persons in 2003 who were living in households where at least one member received some form of government assistance. According to these data, 68 percent of the poor lived in a household where at least one member was receiving a means-tested benefit of any kind from the government and 62 percent were in households that received a means-tested benefit other than school lunches. Yet, only 23 percent of the poor in 2003 were in households where means-tested cash assistance was received. A slightly greater proportion of the poor—36 percent—lived in a household where someone was receiving Food Stamps, and 55 percent lived in households that received Medicaid. Yet, only 18 percent of the poor in 2003 were in a household that received subsidized public housing.

A similar pattern holds for blacks but the rates were higher, suggesting that they are not being systematically prevented from receiving assistance more than are whites. Approximately 81 percent of poor blacks lived in households that were receiving means-tested benefits of some kind, 76 percent received means-tested benefits other than school lunches, 32 percent

---

45. Stone, *Policy Paradox*, pp. 167–72.

TABLE 4-2. Percent of Poor Receiving Welfare, 2003

Type of Benefit	Total	Black	Hispanic	White	Asian
Means-tested benefits (MTB)	68%	81%	80%	55%	53%
MTB excluding school lunch	62%	76%	66%	52%	48%
Cash MTB	23%	32%	21%	18%	14%
Food Stamps	36%	51%	35%	28%	19%
Medicaid	55%	66%	64%	45%	41%
Subsidized public housing	18%	34%	15%	12%	11%

Source: Calculations from U.S. Census Current Population Survey, Annual Social and Economic Supplement for 2003.

received means-tested cash benefits, 51 received food stamps, 66 percent received Medicaid, and 32 percent received subsidized housing. The rates for poor Hispanics fell between those for blacks and those for the total poverty population for most means-tested benefits but lagged behind both for Food Stamps, Cash means-tested benefits and subsidized housing. Rates for whites and Asians consistently fell below the rates for the population overall.

Table 4-2 indicates that nonwhites in the post–Civil Rights era can receive public assistance benefits at rates even exceeding those for whites; therefore, one possible interpretation from these data is that there is less racial discrimination in welfare compared with several decades ago. Yet, these data are also less than definitive. The data presented in Table 4-1 show that the proportion of the poor who are black rises the further down the income scale we go. Poor black families have lower average incomes than poor white families; they are more likely to be among the poorest of the poor; and therefore they are more likely to have a greater need for public assistance. The higher public assistance participation rates for poor blacks may be nothing more than an artifact of their lower incomes compared with poor whites. This also suggests the possibility that once we account for their lower incomes, we might find that poor blacks actually participate in public assistance programs at rates below those of poor whites.

Yet, the issue of whether welfare reform policies enable eligible black families to access assistance at rates comparable to those of whites requires more refined measures than poverty and participation rates. To provide such data, we would need to measure whether *eligible* blacks participate at rates comparable to those of *eligible* whites and also whether differences in participation rates by race were due to policy and program administration, including, for instance, discrimination by intake workers. While there have been many studies on racial differences in welfare participation, only a few major studies are sufficiently refined to account for actual eligibility rates for blacks and whites;[46] and none measures racial differences in application, acceptance, and rejection rates, let alone whether these rates have changed under welfare reform.[47] Further, blacks' participation rates that are compatible to or better than those of whites may be attributable to racial bias operating in social welfare policy and the broader political economy producing their greater inability to access other, better social welfare programs or their greater inability to access decent paying jobs. It may be that the issue of whether blacks get to participate in welfare programs is now considered moot in the post–Civil Rights era, but nonetheless, without the further study it remains an open question.

Additional evidence regarding racial bias in accessing welfare can be gleaned from examining data on changes in the racial and ethnic composition of the welfare population. Table 4-3 indicates that under welfare reform since the mid-1990s, there has been a growth in the proportion of welfare recipients who are nonwhite. In 1992, 39 percent of welfare families were white; by 2002, that had fallen to 32 percent. The percentage of families who were black increased slightly over that same time period from 37 percent to 38 percent, while the percentage of families who were Hispanic increased along with its growing share of the overall population, rising from 18 percent in 1992 to 25 percent in 2002. The net effect of these changes is that the welfare rolls have become considerably less white during the years of welfare reform. In particular, the gap between the percentage of recipients who are non-Hispanic whites and non-Hispanic nonwhites has widened so that blacks are now a much larger percentage of the total welfare population: 38 percent versus 32 percent. If Hispanics were categorized as to whether they were white or not, it is

---

46. Rebecca Blank and Patricia Ruggles find that blacks are more likely than whites to be receiving welfare at the end of a spell of eligibility. Their study suggests that a number of risk factors, such as lack of access to informal sources of financial support, increase participation among eligible blacks. See Rebecca Blank and Patricia Ruggles, "When Do Women Use Aid to Families with Dependent Children and Food Stamps? The Dynamics of Eligibility Versus Participation," *Journal of Human Resources* 31, 1 (1996): 57–89. Also see Robert A. Moffitt and Peter T. Gottschalk, "Ethnic and Racial Differences in Welfare Receipt in the United States," in *America Becoming: Racial Trends and Their Consequences, Volume I*, Neil J. Smelser, William Julius Wilson, and Faith Mitchell, eds. (Washington, DC: National Academy Press, 2001), pp. 152–73.
47. See Moffitt and Gottschalk "Ethnic and Racial Differences in Welfare Receipt in the United States," pp. 152–73.

TABLE 4-3. Racial Composition of Welfare Families, 1992–2002

	1992	1994	1996	1998	1999	2000	2002
Families							
Total	4,769,000	5,046,000	4,553,000	3,176,000	2,648,000	2,269,000	2,060,300
Percent of Total							
White	39%	37%	36%	33%	31%	31%	32%
African-American	37%	36%	37%	39%	38%	39%	38%
Hispanic*	18%	20%	21%	22%	25%	25%	25%
Asian	3%	3%	3%	3%	4%	2%	2%
Native American	1%	1%	1%	2%	2%	2%	1%
Other	-	-	-	1%	1%	1%	1%
Unknown	2%	2%	2%	1%	1%	1%	1%

*Can be of any race.
Source: U.S. Department of Health and Human Services, Office of Family Assistance, 2004.

likely that the proportion of recipient families who are nonwhite would exceed 50 percent.[48]

We might be tempted to read these data as suggesting a growing racial liberalism in social welfare policies of the post–Civil Rights era; however, that would be a mistake. There are good reasons to interpret these data as a sign that new welfare-to-work programs worked better for whites than for nonwhites, leaving the latter group to comprise a growing proportion of recipients left behind.[49]

Systematic racial barriers to accessing welfare and related government benefits have declined in the post–Civil Rights era, and no data available on participation rates suggest that barriers have been rebuilt in the reform

---

48. For a discussion of race differences among persons who are categorized by the government as Hispanic, see Bernadette D. Proctor and Joseph Dalaker, *Poverty in the United States: 2002*, Series P60–222 (Washington, DC: U.S. Bureau of the Census, September 2003).

49. Loprest, *How Families that Left Welfare Are Doing: A National Picture* (Washington, DC: Urban Institute, Assessing the New Federalism, 1999). Also see Pamela J. Loprest, *Who Returns to Welfare?* (Washington, DC: Urban Institute, Assessing the New Federalism, 2002); Lower-Basch, *"Leavers" and Diversion Studies: Preliminary Analysis of Racial Differences in Caseload Trends and Leaver Outcomes*; and Duncan, Harris, and Boisjoly, "Time Limits and Welfare Reform: New Estimates of the Number and Characteristics of Affected Families," pp. 55–75.

era. For the years immediately before and after welfare reform, available data indicate high rates of participation for nonwhites and blacks in particular.[50] Yet, the data are by no means definitive in dismissing the possibility that blacks are underrepresented in welfare programs and in whether such underrepresentation is the result of systematic race bias in policy and program implementation. The available data offer an array of implicit normative standards and in the end are simply too porous to prevent multiple interpretations. Even data indicating that the growing proportion of welfare recipients who are nonwhite can be used to support competing interpretations. A further issue, which the data never even begin to reach, is that welfare is a very limited program and that even if all eligible families were receiving it, we would need to assess how it missed all those families who were not eligible but needed assistance. Such "target inefficiency" may itself be race related. Therefore, although there may be good reasons to believe that welfare as reformed does not perpetuate the race-biased practices of earlier periods, it will take more than available statistical data to make this question as moot as it is often treated in public policy deliberations.

Welfare Reform Is an Explicitly Race-Biased Regime

The available data on welfare participation do not prove that welfare in the reform period is either race neutral or race biased. To find evidence that supports the second interpretation that welfare reform is an explicitly race-biased policy regime, we will have to look elsewhere. At each level of government, federal, state, and local agency, there is empirical evidence of explicit race bias in welfare reform.

We can start with the national welfare reform legislation itself. As a post–Civil Rights era public policy, we would be hard put to find evidence that welfare reform explicitly makes a Jim Crow-era distinction between black and white recipients. Yet, there is evidence that the law explicitly invokes nationality and thereby indirectly reinscribes racial and ethnic otherness as a way of disqualifying whole categories of persons in need of assistance. The 1996 welfare reform law and the immigration reform law passed the same year both worked to restrict access to welfare by

50. Moffitt and Gottschalk, "Ethnic and Racial Differences in Welfare Receipt in the United States," pp. 152–73; and Blank and Ruggles, "When Do Women Use Aid to Families with Dependent Children and Food Stamps?" pp. 57–89.

immigrants. Immigrant single mothers with children who entered the United States after 1996 are most often ineligible for not only TANF but also food stamps and Medicaid. In those instances where immigrants are eligible for assistance, states welfare programs have reduced their access by not providing such crucial support as translation services. There is evidence that this occurs even when a significant proportion of the clientele were not proficient in English. Treating both English and non-English speakers the same way by not providing either of them with translation services is perhaps yet another way that "equal" treatment reinforces disparities in accessing services.[51]

The case of immigrants, however, is complicated by several issues. First, they are not citizens and the issue of whether noncitizens should be accorded the same rights as citizens does not necessarily involve the question of race. Second, immigrants may not necessarily be nonwhite, although increasingly they are Latino or Asian. Therefore, the question of whether restricting immigrant access to welfare is evidence of explicit race bias is still subject to interpretation.

Evidence of explicit race bias in welfare reform may exist at the state level. There is evidence that race is a salient factor in affecting state policy adoption. Elizabeth Lower-Basch notes: "Race may also affect the treatment received by recipients in a more indirect way, by affecting the policies chosen by policymakers at the state and local level. To the extent that welfare recipients are perceived as predominantly of a different racial or ethnic group than the majority of the taxpaying/voting citizens of a state, lawmakers may be more ready to impose stringent conditions on welfare receipt."[52] A number of recent studies find a strong statistical relationship between the racial composition of the welfare population and whether a state adopts an aggressive approach to imposing get-tough welfare reforms, including full family sanctions, relatively short time limits, and family cap policies.[53] (The family cap denies aid for any child born to a family already receiving welfare—thereby "capping" the family benefit at its current level.) This research suggests that race operates as a

---

51. See Ellen Shelton and Greg Owen, *The Issues Behind the Outcomes: For Somali, Hmong, African American, and American Indian Welfare Participants in Minnesota* (St. Paul: Wilder Foundation, 2003).

52. Lower-Basch, *"Leavers" and Diversion Studies: Preliminary Analysis of Racial Differences in Caseload Trends and Leaver Outcomes.*

53. Fellowes and Rowe, "The Politics of Welfare Reform(ed): How TANF Changed and did not Change Redistribution Politics," pp. 362–73; Gais and Weaver, *State Policy Choices under Welfare Reform*; and Soss, et al., "Setting the Terms of Relief," pp. 378–403.

contextual factor structuring how states go about implementing welfare reform.[54]

Figure 4–1 presents the results from one of these studies,[55] indicating the effect of an increase in the percentage of the state's welfare population that are black on the probability of adopting stringent reforms. The probability of adopting full family sanctions increases from 54 to 97 percent,

---

54. Prior research on AFDC has demonstrated the role of race in structuring state welfare policymaking and local agency administration. Earlier studies on AFDC found a negative correlation between the black population and black welfare participation rates on the one hand and welfare benefit levels on the other. On participation rates, see Lieberman and Lapinski, "American Federalism, Race and the Administration of Welfare," pp. 303–29. On benefit levels, see Larry L. Orr, "Income Transfers as a Public Good: An Application to AFDC," *American Economic Review* 66, 3 (1976): 359–71; Gerald C. Wright, "Racism and Welfare Policy in America," *Social Science Quarterly* 57, 4 (1976): 718–30; and Christopher Howard, "Field Essay: American Welfare State or States?" *Political Research Quarterly* 52, 2 (1999): 421–42. Lieberman and Lapinski, "American Federalism, Race and the Administration of Welfare," pp. 302–29, however, also find that at the county level, black population size interacts positively with political party organization to improve black welfare participation rates. More recent research by Lael R. Keiser, Peter Mueser, and Seung-Whan Choi also indicates that heavily black counties in which blacks increase their political power are likely to have lower welfare reform sanction rates. See Lael R. Keiser, Peter Mueser, and Seung-Whan Choi, "Race, Bureaucratic Discretion and the Implementation of Welfare Reform," *American Journal of Political Science* 48, 2 (2004): 314–27. Consistent with Lieberman and Lapinski and with Keiser et al., Richard Fording finds a curvilinear relationship at the state level for black population and state welfare reform waivers in the pre-welfare reform era of the early 1990s, indicating that a higher black population is correlated with more conservative welfare reform waivers up to a threshold above which higher black populations translate into greater political power and less likelihood of the adoption of conservative waivers. See Richard C Fording, "Laboratories of Democracy or Symbolic Politics? The Racial Origins of Welfare Reform," in *Race and the Politics of Welfare Reform*, Sanford F. Schram, Joe Soss, and Richard C. Fording, eds. (Ann Arbor: University of Michigan Press, 2003), pp. 78–100.

55. The probability curves reported in Figure 4–1 are derived from the data used originally in Soss, et al., "Setting the Terms of Relief," pp. 378–403. The graphs report the predicted probabilities for a state in adopting "get-tough" policy options under welfare reform (the family cap, time limits, and immediate, full-family sanctions), given the state's proportion of welfare recipients who are black and controlling for other state factors by holding them at their means. (The other major state policy option under welfare reform—work requirements—was not related to race.) In other words, the curves trace changes in the probability of the "average" state adopting "get-tough" policy options associated with changes in the percentage of the welfare population that is black. In addition to the percentage of recipients who are African-American, the other factors accounted for are the percentage of recipients who are Latino, the unemployment rate, the rate of increase in the incarceration rate, the ideology of state-elected officials, interparty competition, low-income voter turnout, the recipient/population ratio, the out-of-marriage birth rate, and state initiation of program waivers from the federal government. See Soss, et al., "Setting the Terms of Relief," pp. 378–403.

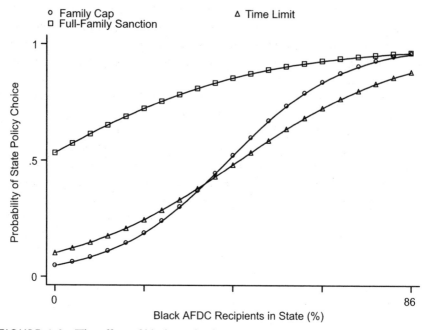

FIGURE 4-1. The effect of black caseload percentage on welfare policy choices in a hypothetical "average" state.
Source: Joe Soss, Sanford F. Schram, Thomas P. Vartanian, and Erin O'Brien, "Welfare Policy Choices in the States: Does the Hard Line Follow the Color Line?" *Focus* 23, 1 (Winter 2004): 9–15.

the probability of adopting a family cap rises from 5 percent to 96 percent, and the probability of adopting a time limit shorter than five years increases from 10 percent to 88 percent.

In addition, nonwhites are more likely to live in states that adopt tough welfare policies.[56] Therefore, one reason national studies have found that blacks are more likely to be sanctioned may be because they live in states with tougher policies.[57] As Figure 4-1 suggests, this correlation may be the result of its own circular causality; the prevalence of nonwhites on the rolls increases the chances that a state will choose to impose an extreme form of get-tough reforms which in turn results in nonwhites facing a greater chance that they will be affected by the most draconian policies.

---

56. Soss, et al., "Setting the Terms of Relief," p. 245.

57. Lower-Basch, *"Leavers" and Diversion Studies: Preliminary Analysis of Racial Differences in Caseload Trends and Leaver Outcomes*, notes that even within states with a uniform sanction policy, blacks are more likely to be sanctioned than are whites. Also see Kalil, Seefeldt, and Wang, "Sanctions and Material Hardship under TANF," pp. 642–62.

Yet, whether the relationship between the racial composition of the welfare population and the state's welfare reform policy choices is evidence of what we would call explicit race bias is undoubtedly subject to interpretation. In one sense, that the racial composition of a state's welfare population is related to how tough a state chooses to be can itself be interpreted as a form of race bias. Yet, white recipients in states where blacks comprise a relatively large proportion of the recipients are subject to the same get-tough policies, making it harder to characterize states' structuring of welfare reform policy choices as explicit race bias. In this sense, it might be better to suggest that the get-tough state policy choices are race-neutral public policies triggered by racial considerations.

Even this interpretation needs further exploration, because, while race is correlated with state welfare reform policy choices, it is not clear that that necessarily means state policymakers are intentionally acting in a racially biased way. A more contextual understanding of the role of race bias in welfare reform may better explain the correlation.

Bureaucratic encounters between clients and caseworkers suggest additional evidence of explicit race bias. Race-neutral rules can be applied unevenly by caseworkers. Here the available research has focused on how race bias is being enacted more individually than institutionally. The main work in this area is by Susan Gooden, who has published a series of studies on racial discrimination in the administration of welfare reform.[58] Gooden's research suggests that it is unlikely that the differential rates at which clients of different races access education and training under welfare reform are the result of coincidence or differences in the backgrounds and attitudes of the clients. Her research suggests that the more likely cause is the different treatment caseworkers give to clients of different races and ethnicities. In one study of the administration of welfare in Virginia, Gooden finds a bias in favor of extending education to white recipients compared with blacks. She writes: "Although it is well documented that earnings are positively correlated with increased education, in two Virginia counties 41 percent of white clients reported their caseworker continued to promote education, compared to none of the black clients."[59] In the same study, Gooden also examined the degree to which

58. For an overview of her major findings, see Gooden, "Contemporary Approaches to Enduring Challenges: Using Performance Measures to Promote Racial Equality under TANF," pp. 254–75.
59. Susan Gooden, "All Things Not Being Equal: Difference in Caseworker Support toward Black and White Welfare Clients," *Harvard Journal of African American Public Policy* 4, 1 (1998): 23–33.

caseworkers provided assistance to clients in securing child care and transportation assistance. These are, as Gooden reminds us, key factors affecting a client's ability to get and keep a job. While Gooden did not find differentials in accessing child care, she did report: "Forty-seven percent of the white respondents reported that their caseworker expressed a willingness to provide additional transportation assistance including helping them obtain a driver's license, a vehicle or vehicle repairs. None of the African-American respondents reported any offers of transportation assistance aside from the standard issuance of gas vouchers." Gooden's research is suggestive but also indicates that race bias might exist on some dimensions more than others.

Thus, at each level of government, federal, state, and local agency, there is evidence of explicit race bias. Yet in each case, the data allow for multiple interpretations and therefore fail to provide a definitive evidentiary base that welfare reform is an explicitly race-biased policy regime.

A New Policy Regime: Ostensibly Race Neutral but Producing Racial Disadvantage

While there is evidence at each level of the government suggesting that explicit race bias is operating in welfare reform, the inconclusiveness of the data presents the need to consider the third interpretation—welfare reform is a race-neutral policy that operates in ways that actively reproduce racial disadvantage. Much of the data we have already reviewed to consider the first two interpretations can be considered along with other data in support of the third interpretation.

For instance, the growing preponderance of nonwhites on welfare that is reported in Table 4–3 can be read to suggest that nonwhites needing public assistance are more vulnerable under an ostensibly neutral welfare reform regime that fails to address the specific barriers they confront in leaving welfare. As result, blacks on welfare might be treated as equally as white welfare recipients in terms of work requirements, time limits, the imposition of sanctions, referrals for education and training, etc., but given their relative disadvantages in average education, readiness for employment, access to other sources of financial support, and other confounding factors such as residential isolation and employer discrimination, such "equal" treatment ends up producing more racial disadvantage.

Other data can be similarly interpreted. Blacks are more likely to be sanctioned off welfare than are whites. Concern about the racial disparity in sanction rates is heightened by other research indicating that families forced off welfare fare relatively poorly compared with families who leave for other reasons.[60] Recent research suggests that recipients who are forced off welfare have higher rates of welfare recidivism.[61] This is especially true for blacks.[62] One possible reading of these data is that sanctions are forcing off nonwhites who are not as prepared to secure jobs as are other recipients because on average they have less education, less work experience, fewer skills, greater personal problems, more need to care for young children, and greater likelihood of confronting social barriers, including employer discrimination.[63] Additional research indicates that blacks are more likely to be forced off because they have exhausted their time allowed to receive welfare.[64] In these cases, the option to cycle back onto welfare is not available, suggesting that blacks are more likely than whites to face serious economic jeopardy due to time limits under welfare reform.

The data indicating that blacks are more likely to be forced off welfare due to sanctions or time limits might be read by some as indicating that blacks do not try as hard as whites to succeed in the world of work.[65] Yet, Lower-Basch notes that while blacks do not leave welfare as quickly as whites and are more likely to be forced off, blacks are nonetheless more likely to be working when leaving welfare and working more hours at increased earnings compared with whites who leave, even though blacks who leave tend to have on average less education than white leavers.[66]

Another possible interpretation is that white single mothers are more likely to marry or take up living arrangements with an employed male than are black single mothers who leave welfare. This interpretation points to disparities in employment rates between white and black low-income men. Low-income black males are much more likely than low-income white males to not be able to support their families for a variety of reasons

---

60. Robert Moffitt and Jennifer Roff, *The Diversity of Welfare Leavers. Welfare, Children, and Families: A Three-City Study*, Working Paper No. 00–01 (Baltimore: Johns Hopkins University, 2003).

61. Loprest, *Who Returns to Welfare?*

62. Loprest, *Who Returns to Welfare?*

63. Kalil, Seefeldt and Wang, "Sanctions and Material Hardship under TANF," pp. 642–62.

64. Duncan, Harris, and Boisjoly, "Time Limits and Welfare Reform: New Estimates of the Number and Characteristics of Affected Families," pp. 55–75.

65. Mead, *The New Politics of Poverty*, p. 65.

66. Lower-Basch, *"Leavers" and Diversion Studies: Preliminary Analysis of Racial Differences in Caseload Trends and Leaver Outcomes*.

ranging from incarceration to employer discrimination.[67] Therefore, both the higher employment rate and the lower marriage and cohabitation rates for black women who leave welfare can be read as being associated with barriers to employment that confront poor black men. The failure of welfare reform to account for the dire employment situation confronting low-income black men contributes to its failure to better support low-income black women who may require added assistance in order to leave welfare successfully.

Those who leave, black or white, and return to welfare form a group who by definition has difficulty making the transition off welfare. Studies indicate between a fifth and a third of leavers return to welfare within a year. Parents who return have significantly less education and work experience, as well as poorer health, compared with parents who do not return.[68] They also were less likely to have used transitional support services—such as child care, health insurance, and help with expenses. As mentioned earlier, an additional reason for returning was being sanctioned off welfare. One possible interpretation for this finding is that the punitive approach reflected in sanctions policy is frequently applied to families who have continued to need assistance.

As mentioned, under welfare reform, blacks are more likely than whites to return to the rolls. Pamela Loprest found that nationwide, although 21.9 percent of all leavers returned within a year of leaving welfare, the same was true for 32.2 percent of black leavers and 24.1 percent of Hispanic leavers.[69] Only 12.7 percent of white leavers returned within a year's time.[70] More

---

67. On the relationship of welfare retrenchment to increased imprisonment of the poor population, see Richard C Fording, "The Political Response to Black Insurgency: A Critical Test of Competing Theories of the State," *American Political Science Review* 95, 1 (2001): 115–31; and Wacquant, "From Slavery to Mass Incarceration," pp. 41–60.

68. Loprest, *Who Returns to Welfare?*

69. Loprest, *Who Returns to Welfare?*

70. An understudied population potentially important to understanding racial disparities is the "diverted," applicants who have been shunted away from receiving welfare. For instance, it is questionable to what extent the massive declines in the rolls from the mid-1990s through 2001 were due strictly to people leaving welfare. The rolls may have gone down in good part because large numbers of people did not come onto the rolls. Some of this decline in new entrants might have been due to good reasons of a relatively strong economy in the 1990s making welfare less needed. Yet, some of the decline in new entrants might have been due to bad reasons such as welfare reform ending the entitlement nature of welfare under AFDC and replacing it with a more discretionary program that allows for active "diverts" of families from needed assistance. Whether diversion is race related has yet to be studied. See Schram and Soss, "Success Stories," pp. 57–78; and Diller, "The Revolution in Welfare Administration," pp. 1121–220.

research is needed to specify the reasons for racial disparities related to welfare recidivism and whether discriminatory treatment in welfare agencies, labor markets, and elsewhere is involved in blacks being more likely to return to welfare; however, these disparities indicate a national policy that is insensitive to addressing those factors that make it harder for nonwhite recipients to succeed under welfare reform's "work-first" regime.[71]

There is evidence that black welfare recipients have on average a harder time leaving welfare for work due to employer discrimination. Harry Holzer and Michael Stoll note that: "Minority welfare recipients are hired somewhat less frequently than their representation in the population of poor female-headed households would lead us to predict. Conditional on hiring welfare recipients, the relative tendencies of establishments to hire minorities (especially African Americans) appear to be less closely related to overall demand conditions or employer skill needs than to location, and possibly to discriminatory employer preferences as well."[72] Jared Bernstein and Heidi Hartmann add: "Informal hiring networks account for between 25 and 60 percent of hires and are a particularly important hiring mechanism for entry-level employment, jobs that do not require college education, blue-collar jobs, and jobs with small employers. Such networks tend to be tightly knit and ethnically homogeneous. African American workers, in particular, tend to be excluded from them.... Discrimination negatively affects employment rates of African Americans, even when differences in skills have been taken into account."[73]

---

71. Most of the research on the effects of welfare reform on leavers was done while the economy was strong. Further research is needed to assess whether the racial disparities in leaving and returning to welfare are exacerbated during economic downturn.

72. Harry J. Holzer and Michael A. Stoll, *Employer Demand for Welfare Recipients by Race* (Washington, DC: Urban Institute, Assessing the New Federalism Report 01–07, 2002). Also see Devah Pager, "The Mark of a Criminal Record," *American Journal of Sociology* 108, 5 (2003): 937–75; and Marianne Bertrand and Sendhil Mullainathan, "Are Emily and Greg More Employable than Lakisha and Jamal? A Field Experiment on Labor Market Discrimination," Working Paper 9873 (Boston: National Bureau of Economic Research, 2003). In experiments, Pager found that being black reduces a job applicant's chances of being called back to that of a white applicant who served 18 months for drug possession with an intent to sell, whereas Bertrand and Mullainathan found that applicants were 50 percent more likely to be called for an interview if they had a white-sounding as opposed to a black-sounding name.

73. Jared Bernstein and Heidi Hartmann, "Defining and Characterizing the Low-Wage Labor Market," in *The Low-Wage Labor Market: Challenges and Opportunities for Economic Self-Sufficiency*, Kelleen Kaye and Demetra Smith Nightingale, eds. (Washington, DC: U.S. Department of Health and Human Services, Office of the Secretary Assistant Secretary for Planning and Evaluation, 2000). Also see Pager, "Mark of a Criminal Record," pp. 937–75; and Bertrand and Mullainathan, "Are Emily and Greg More Employable than Lakisha and Jamal?" pp. 23–24.

Overall, the data on racial disparities in outcomes under welfare reform point to an ostensibly race-neutral policy that fails to account for racial disadvantage operating in the broader society and the labor market in particular. As a result, blacks are more likely to be left behind in programs designed to move recipients off welfare and out of poverty. It might be argued that a race-neutral public policy should not be labeled race biased for its failure to account for preexisting racial disadvantageness or a failure to address program results that perpetuate those disadvantages. Yet, if neglect of preexisting conditions and program outcomes operates to recreate a consistent pattern of racial disparities in outcomes as found in the data on welfare reform, it becomes more plausible to label such a policy ostensibly race neutral but actually actively involved in reproducing racial disadvantage.

Support for this third interpretation is most effectively buttressed once we go beyond the limits of conventional public policy research and place welfare reform in historical and social context. Once we do that, the case can be better made that welfare reform reflects a post–Civil Rights discourse that turns a blind eye to how its own race neutrality ends up reinscribing racial subordination.

Contextualizing Welfare Reform: Post–Civil Rights Policy as Malign Neglect

The third interpretation finds the best support in the data but it takes on even greater plausibility once we move beyond the consideration of isolated statistics and place them in historical and social context.[74] Welfare historically has been an orphan in liberal-capitalist America. As Frances Fox Piven and Richard A. Cloward have noted, welfare historically has been a secondary institution calibrated to serve the primary needs of the state and the market in the United States. It was always structured to serve two potentially conflicting goals: (1) to reinforce the work ethic so that the poor would take whatever low-paying jobs the market provided and (2) to offer support to low-income families so as to recreate the conditions for maintaining the state's political legitimacy.[75] Welfare's status as a sec-

74. For arguments on behalf of the importance of taking the historical institutional context into account for explaining social welfare policy, see Theda. Skocpol, *Protecting Soldiers and Mothers: The Political Origins of Social Policy in the United States* (Cambridge: The Belknap Press of Harvard University Press, 1992), pp. 1–62; and Ira Katznelson, "The Doleful Dance of Politics and Policy: Can Historical Institutionalism Make a Difference?" *American Political Science Review* 92, 1 (1998): 191–97.
75. Piven and Cloward, *Regulating the Poor*, pp. xv–xvi.

ondary institution also meant that historically it operated in ways that did not undermine the racial regime of white-dominated America.

Mothers' Pensions programs were the precursor of AFDC and were developed to reduce the numbers of children being placed in orphanages because their mothers could not care for them.[76] Yet, the many reformers who championed these pensions explicitly did so in the name of safeguarding "republican motherhood" and fighting back the "race death" that was threatened by growing numbers of immigrant families who were then considered nonwhite.[77] In addition, Mothers' Pensions operated more to Americanize immigrant mothers than to assist indigenous blacks who were largely considered not deserving of such aid.[78]

AFDC was added to the Social Security Act of 1935. The Social Security Act was actually titled the Economic Security Act but rather quickly came to take on the name of its most popular program of old age insurance for retirees that was commonly referred to as Social Security.[79] The legislation is still seen as forging the cornerstone of the contemporary welfare state in the U.S. federal system of governance. And its being called the Social Security Act underscores the important, if troubling, role that federalism has played in that welfare state. The Social Security Act gave rise to a two-tiered welfare state that privileges national social insurance over state public assistance programs.[80] In addition, this tiered system tends to reinforce differences in society along class, race, and gender lines with the upper tier social insurance programs disproportionately benefiting families who were associated with more economically privileged white male workers and the lower tier public assistance programs being relied on by poorer female-headed families who were disproportionately nonwhite.

As Robert Lieberman has amply demonstrated, the system developed in accord with the role of federalism in our policymaking system.[81] Southern congressmen in particular lobbied hard to ensure that public

76. Matthew A. Crenson, *The Invisible Orphanage: A Prehistory of The American Welfare System* (Cambridge: Harvard University Press, 1998).

77. Allison Berg, *Mothering the Race: Women's Narratives of Reproduction, 1890–1930* (Chicago: University of Illinois Press, 2002).

78. Gordon, *Pitied but Not Entitled*, p. 48. Also see Deborah E. Ward, *Mothers' Pensions: The Institutional Legacy of the American Welfare State* (New York: Ph.D. Dissertation at Columbia University, 2000).

79. Michael Katz, *The Price of Citizenship*, p. 234.

80. Lieberman, *Shifting the Color Line*, pp. 216–19.

81. Lieberman, *Shifting the Color Line*, p. 122.

assistance titles be federal programs that gave the states substantial discretion in determining eligibility and setting benefits. They most especially wanted to ensure that public assistance to the poor families could be calibrated to the needs of the still powerful sharecropping system, which relied on impoverished black families to work the fields. With substantial discretion, southern states could ensure that these families could be moved on and off the welfare rolls with the beginning and end of the planting and harvesting seasons. Public assistance, as a second-tier program administered by the states, could therefore take its place in the political economy of the *ancien regime* that arose in the apartheid of the south. As a result, the main public assistance program that would come to be called AFDC was little more than a federal program that standardized and upgraded the limited Mothers' Pensions programs already in existence in many states. In addition, the top-tier social security program was originally structured to exclude coverage of certain occupations, such as agricultural workers and domestics, which disproportionately employed nonwhites and therefore provided access to this privileged program in a way that favored whites. Though revised many times, both tiers of the Social Security Act still perpetuate class, race, and gender bias.

As blacks began to gain rights to assistance in the 1960s, AFDC came to be seen as a "black program," making it more politically vulnerable and increasing calls for its retrenchment, which, after years of political gridlock, finally came in the 1990s.[82] The current context, however, is what I have been calling the "post–Civil Rights" era.[83] This is a time after concern about civil rights and the righting of racial injustices. On the one hand, it is a time for imagining that we as a country are done with the Civil Rights struggle, that the battle to defeat racial injustice was won, and that the nation no longer need to consider race in making public policy. This is a period when it is politically incorrect for public policy to explicitly invoke race to legislate either privileges for whites or disadvantages for blacks. In this era of "race-blind" public policy, racial hierarchy is recreated more by stealth. The encoded discourse of the welfare reform law is larded with euphemisms of "personal responsibility" and "self-sufficiency" that implicitly suggest the undeservingness of welfare mothers who just

82. Quadagno, *The Color of Welfare*; Gilens, *Why Americans Hate Welfare*; and Neubeck and Cazenave, *Welfare Racism*.

83. See Glenn C. Loury, *The Anatomy of Racial Inequality* (Cambridge: Harvard University Press, 2002); and Linda F. Williams, *The Constraint of Race: Legacies of White Skin Privilege in America* (University Park: Pennsylvania State University Press, 2003).

happen to be disproportionately black and are often mistakenly assumed to be overwhelmingly black. In addition, such euphemisms encourage the idea that everyone must conform to the same standards in the same ways and therefore in the process erase consideration that black recipients are much more likely to confront societal barriers when making the transition from welfare to work.[84] Some of the major effects of welfare reform, therefore, arise from how its euphemistic discourse tends to be obtuse to the distinctive needs of low-income single mothers who happen to be disproportionately nonwhite. As a result, a vicious cycle of causality is enacted. The data I have reviewed in the foregoing analysis provide support for the argument that in failing to account for preexisting economic inequalities, race-neutral public policy ends up creating racial disparities in outcomes that themselves serve to reinforce those original inequalities.

Race-neutral policies in the context of our post–Civil Rights era are therefore at risk of being "socially obtuse" policies that fail to account for the disadvantages that all low-income persons confront and which non-white low-income persons are more likely to confront. The "work-first" regime of welfare reform overlooks that many low-income single mothers of all races and ethnicities have lacked access to adequate education, training, jobs, community support, and other resources that are needed to make "rapid attachment" to the workforce and end a life of "welfare dependency." A "work-first" regime that assumes all single mothers can leave welfare quickly, practice "personal responsibility," and achieve "self-sufficiency" by participating the labor market is destined to fail most single mothers; but it is also likely to recreate racial disadvantages simply because nonwhites are less likely to have access to the needed resources and confront more barriers to making such a transition without support.

The ostensibly race-neutral discourse of welfare reform operates to make race a self-fulfilling prophecy in the treatment of both blacks as clients and black recipients as a group.[85] At the level of the individual client, even the unbiased caseworkers who carry out ostensibly race-neutral policies are implicated in this self-defeating cycle of proving some recipients are less personally responsible than others. Without even saying so, they give welfare recipients an ultimatum: go to work or lose what little social support we offer you. The result is that nonwhites, who on average

---

84. Sanford F. Schram, *After Welfare: The Culture of Postindustrial Social Policy* (New York: New York University Press, 2000).

85. Loury, *The Anatomy of Racial Inequality*, pp. 23–33.

have less education and work experience, are less able to comply, are more likely to be sanctioned, are less likely to find a job before their time on welfare is exhausted, are more likely to have to cycle back on to welfare, are less likely to get out of poverty, and so on. Caseworkers practice a latent race-biased form of what Herbert Simon once called "bounded rationality," where they consider only certain factors and not others given the organizational context in which they find themselves.[86] At the level of black recipients as a group, all of these racial disparities operate in public discourse to demonstrate that nonwhites are less deserving. In this way, the stigma of race becomes its own self-fulfilling prophecy and we are encouraged to be suspicious of the very idea of race neutrality. Along with caseworkers, the public is encouraged to think the unthinkable: it was wrong to assume that blacks would do as well as whites. While conservatives claim such race-neutral social policies "assume the best" about blacks, that is, that they can compete with whites, policies like welfare reform, with their false neutrality that fails to account for black disadvantage that pre-existed welfare reform, end up justifying "assuming the worst" about low-income blacks who need to rely on welfare.[87] The race disparities occurring in welfare reform find their own way to reinscribe racial hierarchy.

The concrete practices of welfare-to-work programs starkly illustrate how these programs produce racial disadvantage. Increasingly, welfare policy has focused on targeting resources to address what are euphemistically called "barriers" that prevent recipients from leaving welfare to work.[88] Welfare-to-work programs concentrate substantial energy on screening, diagnosing, and treating clients for various personal deficiencies so that they can take jobs and reduce their reliance on public assistance. Yet, as the research reviewed has indicated, one of the most well-documented barriers that a growing number of welfare recipients confront is a racial one: racial discrimination in hiring.[89] This external

86. Herbert Simon, *Administrative Behavior: A Study of Decision-Making Processes in Administrative Organization*. Second Edition (New York: The Free Press, 1957), p. xxiv.
87. Schram, *Praxis for the Poor*, pp. 24–26.
88. Sandra Danziger, Mary Corcoran, Sheldon Danziger, Colleen Heflin, Ariel Kalil, Judith Levine, Daniel Rosen, Kristin Seefeldt, Kristine Siefert, and Richard Tolman, "Barriers to the Employment of Welfare Recipients," in *Prosperity for All? The Economic Boom and African Americans*, Robert Cherry and William M. Rodgers III, eds. (New York: Russell Sage Foundation, 2000), pp. 245–78.
89. In particular, see Bertrand and Mullainathan, "Are Emily and Greg More Employable than Lakisha and Jamal?" pp. 23–24.

barrier is not addressed by most welfare-to-work programs that concentrate on changing the individual client. At best, there are self-esteem and dress-for-success programs designed to get welfare recipients to ingratiate themselves with prospective employers. Recipients who complete these classes and still fail to secure paid employment risk being penalized and even terminated from assistance depending on their time spent on welfare. These programs could, therefore, be interpreted as a perversion of efforts to address the racial barrier confronting welfare recipients. To the extent that these programs can be interpreted as attempting to overcome the racial barrier to employment, they constitute yet another instance in which welfare reform blames individuals for the structural problems of society. These programs seek to solve structural problems by getting victims to change their behavior. We need to recognize that some barriers, maybe the most important ones affecting welfare recipients, are structural and not individual, and a welfare reform program that fails to address relevant structural race biases and then blames individual recipients for failing to overcome those barriers is therefore itself a race-biased policy. As the example of the use of "barriers" in welfare-to-work highlights, the failure of welfare reform to account for relevant preexisting racial inequalities makes it an ostensibly neutral public policy that incorporates the race biases of the broader society into its very operations and, as a result, ends up helping to produce racial disadvantage.

This vicious cycle that blames black recipients as individuals and as a group also operates at the level of policy. It is not just that the latent race bias of ostensibly race-neutral policies produces racial disadvantages, but as the welfare population increasingly comes to be seen as a largely nonwhite population, the entire program itself, just like its nonwhite recipients, is at risk of being marginalized to the point where program administrators could not help black recipients even if they recognized this problem. With nonwhites becoming a growing proportion of welfare recipients, welfare risks increasingly being seen as a "black program" for those "other" people who are not conforming to the work and family rules of white middle-class society. Jill Quadagno has effectively argued that once a program comes to be seen as a "black program," it loses public support.[90] Martin Gilens has provided extensive evidence of this from survey data regarding welfare.[91] Experiments, such as the one by James Avery and Mark Peffley, provide further evidence that when welfare is

90. Quadagno, *The Color of Welfare*, pp. 10–15.
91. Gilens, *Why Americans Hate Welfare*, pp. 60–79.

associated with blacks, it loses public support.[92] The vicious cycle that blames individuals for preexisting racial inequalities is replicated at the policy level.

The racialization of welfare provision may, therefore, be another way that welfare reform policy becomes its own racially biased self-fulfilling prophecy. As welfare reform leads to nonwhites increasingly making up a growing proportion of the families on welfare, welfare policy is becoming more steadily focused on recipients' behaviors. And as we have shown, welfare reform has intensified state discretion in the program, such that the more the welfare population is nonwhite, the more likely states are to impose a strict behavioral modification regime for implementing welfare reform. As a result, the most dramatic welfare reforms come to be imposed on populations that are disproportionately nonwhite. The cycle repeats itself: these changes simultaneously are rationalized by and reinforce the idea that welfare is a program for black people who do not adhere to white middle-class values. Evidence of blacks predominating the rolls becomes its own self-fulfilling justification that the problem must be with recipients and their behavior, not with the structure of society, the economy, or its labor markets.

In a more abstract register, Slavoj Žižek has seconded this assessment and pointed it toward how the myth of the "black welfare queen" has been constructed out of need for an "other" to legitimate the middle-class white man of virtue who practices personal responsibility and has no need for assistance from the government:

> [E]ach universal ideological notion is always hegemonized by some particular content which colours its very universality and accounts for its efficiency. In the rejection of the social welfare system by the New Right in the US, for example, the universal notion of the welfare system as inefficient is sustained by the pseudo-concrete representation of the notorious African-American single mother, as if, in the last resort, social welfare is a programme for black single mothers—the particular case of the 'single black mother' is silently conceived as 'typical' of social welfare and of what is wrong with it . . . . Another name for this short-circuit between the Universal and the Particular is, of course, 'suture': the operation of hegemony 'sutures' the empty Universal to a particular content.[93]

92. See James M. Avery and Mark Peffley, "Race Matters: The Impact of News Coverage of Welfare Reform on Public Opinion," in *Race and the Politics of Welfare Reform*, Sanford F. Schram, Joe Soss, and Richard C. Fording, eds. (Ann Arbor: University of Michigan Press, 2003), pp. 131–50.
93. Slavoj Žižek, "Multiculturalism, or, the Cultural Logic of Multinational Capitalism," *New Left Review* 225 (September/October 1997): 28–29.

The concrete universal of the black welfare queen helps create the idea that the poor are the cause of their poverty, which in turn reinforces the idea that it is not worth investing in fighting the problem of black poverty. Ultimately, it becomes possible that this cycle can keep spinning to the point that welfare reform's "success" in cracking down on the problem of "welfare dependency" becomes a rationalization for white neglect of what is seen as a "black" problem.[94] Welfare reform's popularity reflects what George Lipsetz calls the "possessive investment in whiteness."[95] Whites have an added reason, a surplus benefit, for supporting welfare reform: it highlights blacks' disproportionate reliance on welfare as a sign of both black inferiority and white superiority. Welfare therefore helps promote its own form of "racemaking," whereby a particular social condition like poverty or welfare reliance becomes a way of suggesting that the races are different.[96] Welfare today operates to make issues of economic need out to be problems associated with a particular race of people. Yet, it is the economic marginalization of low-income black families that helps to reinforce the myth of black inferiority.[97] Welfare helps invert the causal arrows and makes race seem to be a cause of economic destitution when in fact it is economic destitution that helps create the idea of race.[98]

Conclusion

The data on racial disparities in contemporary welfare reform are insufficient to be able to determine whether welfare reform is race biased and, if so, how. Yet, once we place welfare reform in historical and social context, a credible case can be made that the available data support a particular understanding of how welfare reform is race biased. It is an ostensibly neutral, post–Civil Rights policy that nonetheless actively works in ways that produce racial disadvantage. It does so by punishing black recipients for the systematic barriers operating in society that make it harder for black recipients to succeed under welfare reform. In this context, state

---

94. Welfare reform's effect on white attitudes about race and poverty represent an example of policy's feedback effects. See Suzanne Mettler and Joe Soss, "The Consequences of Public Policy for Democratic Citizenship: Bridging Policy Studies and Mass Politics," *Perspectives on Politics* 2, 1 (March 2004): 55–74.

95. George Lipsetz, *The Possessive Investment in Whiteness: How White People Profit from Identity Politics* (Philadelphia: Temple University Press, 1998).

96. Wacquant, "From Slavery to Mass Incarceration," pp. 41–60.

97. Brown et al., *Whitewashing Race*, pp. 1–33.

98. On reverse causality, see Norton, *95 Theses*, pp. 120–26.

policies significantly reinforce a process where welfare discourse becomes a self-fulfilling prophecy about the failure of black recipients to become self-sufficient.

Therefore, in order to understand the way in which welfare reform is indeed race biased, we need to get beyond the limitations of conventional public policy analysis and its penchant to focus on statistical findings divorced from historical and social context. We need to practice a "new poverty research" that puts the data on racial disparities under welfare reform in context. Then we can see how welfare is a secondary institution that is calibrated to the economic and political biases of the broader society and is, therefore, in many ways destined to work in ways that produce the racial disadvantages of that broader society.[99]

An important issue becomes whether due process guarantees designed to ensure equal treatment of clients will be sufficient to attack the systematic perpetuation of racial disparities by the varied means that have been described.[100] At a minimum, we may need to monitor state policies and administrative practices to ensure the enforcement of a race-neutral process; it may be necessary to systematically track racial disparities that are actively reproduced via the implementation of race-neutral policies and practices. We may need to go beyond taking responsibility for individual instances of discriminatory treatment and assume collective responsibility for the racial disadvantages that are being reproduced by the silences of an ostensibly neutral public policy.[101] Only then will we be addressing the racial bias of welfare reform, hidden as it is in the false neutrality of its post–Civil Rights discourse.

---

99. Piven, "Why Welfare Is Racist," pp. 323–36.

100. On the issue of whether to emphasize race in the context of an ostensibly neutral policy like welfare, see Naomi R. Cahn, "Representing Race Outside of Explicitly Racialized Contexts," *Michigan Law Review* 95, 4 (February 1997): 965–1004.

101. Young, "Responsibility and Structural Injustice."

5 Recommodified Discourse

The Limits of the Asset-Building Approach to Fighting Poverty

Given the limited alternatives to welfare reform in today's political climate, some very progressive thinkers have joined a growing number of analysts, activists, administrators, and policymakers who believe that the some of the most feasible progressive alternatives lie in promoting asset accumulation by the poor.[1]

Asset-building policy initiatives are touted as transcending political differences and offering something appealing to both the left and the right. For the right, asset-building discourse moves policy away from income redistribution across the classes and refocuses policy on supporting low-income individuals in becoming more self-sufficient by way of taking steps to enhance their own wealth production via acquiring assets, such as an owned home or the assets that come from developing one's own human capital, say via education or training. President George W. Bush made policies aimed at savings for assets the centerpiece of his "ownership society" that he detailed in his renomination acceptance speech in 2004.[2]

For the left, asset-building policy discourse provides a good approach to overcoming how persistent economic inequality translates over time into durable lines of social and economic stratification, often reinforced by racial segregation and discrimination, making mobility up and out of

---

1. For the book that jump-started the project to move welfare policy toward emphasizing asset building, see Michael W. Sherraden, *Assets and the Poor: A New American Welfare Policy* (Armonk, NY: M. E. Sharpe, 1991). For a symposium on the idea as it developed, see Thomas M. Shapiro and Edward N. Wolff, eds. *Assets for the Poor: The Benefits of Spreading Asset Ownership* (New York: Russell Sage Foundation, 2001). For a survey of the major programs in place that promote asset building, see Michelle Miller-Adams, *Owning Up: Poverty, Assets, and the American Dream* (Washington, DC: Brookings Institution Press, 2002). The last two books were commissioned by the Ford Foundation as part of its Asset Building and Community Development initiative—one of three major funding streams by the foundation.
2. Warren Vieth, "Bush Makes His Pitch for 'Ownership Society'," *Los Angeles Times*, September 5, 2004, p. 25.

poverty that much more difficult. Enabling the poor to acquire assets that enhance their economic and human capital provides a way to activate that mobility. In fact, one of the most appealing dimensions of asset-building policy discourse for the left is that it focuses on overcoming the discriminatory practices that deny to the poor opportunities that the middle and upper classes have for building assets and acquiring wealth. Such a focus therefore enables us to see that asset-building policy discourse is consistent with related discursive shifts across the welfare states of Europe and other Anglo-speaking countries as well as the United States in that it deemphasizes directly attacking poverty and instead focuses on overcoming "social exclusion" as the main barrier to improved well-being for low-income individuals and families.[3]

With asset-building policies in place, the poor can begin to take advantage of the tax breaks, the grants, the loans, and other public policies that support individuals and families in acquiring wealth-producing assets, whether it is the mortgage interest deduction for homes, the tax deductions for education spending, the low-interest loans for financing an education, or other policies. Asset-building policy discourse is geared to enable the poor to partake of these middle and upper class–oriented policies and become full members in the middle and upper class wealth-acquiring society.

The real appeal of asset-building policy discourse is that it moves debate away from what increasingly is seen as the unrealistic objective of trying to change social welfare policies so that they more directly focus on meeting the needs of the poor and shifts the debate to the more realistic objective of helping low-income families participate in the system of public policies that exist for the asset-oriented, wealth-acquiring middle and upper classes. Rather than trying to change the major orientation of the overall social welfare policy regime with its emphasis on promoting self-sufficiency and personal responsibility, asset-building policy discourse focuses on the more circumspect activity of tweaking those policies so that low-income individuals and families can more effectively participate in that regime. Rather than regime change, with asset-based policy discourse, we get a focus on a policy adjustment that is seen as more realistic, more feasible, more likely to be adopted, and more likely to produce opportunities for social and economic improvement for low-income individuals and families in the short run.

---

3. See Chapter 2 for an in-depth critique of exclusionary practices paradoxically operating at the heart of the inclusionary efforts associated with some of the more prominent versions of anti-"social exclusion" policies that have been adopted in a number of welfare states under the banner of "labor activation" welfare reform.

One of the growing number of progressive analysts interested in promoting asset-based policies is a former undergraduate student who took several courses from me and who has gone on to complete a doctorate in political science from a leading research university and to land a position of significance in the national welfare policy process. When I mentioned that I had doubts about what people have been calling "asset-building" antipoverty policy, I got a very seasoned and thoughtful reply from the frontlines of policymaking process:

> [I]n today's world of global capitalism (which isn't going away any time soon), I have trouble imagining why individual and family asset-building wouldn't be *part* of a strategy of moving toward greater security, equality, and freedom. As Christopher Howard's *The Hidden Welfare State* makes vivid, the majority of Americans (including both of us) receive substantial government support for asset-building. [I]s your argument that nobody should receive these supports (which clearly would make inequality even greater, since then only the wealthy could realistically build assets), or that public policy should not be broadened to include progressive, inclusive asset-building, in place of the current regressive and exclusive policies? I think your position runs the risk of wanting the poor to live their lives as full-fledged socialists while the rest of us continue being 401k-owning capitalists.[4]

This is an argument that needs to be taken seriously. It resonates with Michael Harrington's old quip that in the United States we have "socialism for the rich and free enterprise for the poor."[5] Our welfare state is geared toward subsidizing the middle and upper classes in acquiring assets and generating wealth, while low-income individuals and families are expected to scrap by on their own, often not being able to come up with enough of their own money to take advantage of the tax breaks, grants, and loans that the government offers for buying homes, getting an education, and doing other things to acquire assets, invest in capital, and generate personal wealth.

In this chapter, I offer a critique of asset-building antipoverty policy but with an eye toward separating the wheat from the chaff, retaining what would be good while jettisoning the bad. My argument is that what is particularly bad about asset-building policy is its cramped commodifying discourse that reinforces limiting social welfare policy initiatives to only those who are consistent with the imperatives of the market system and thus

---

4. See Christopher Howard, *The Hidden Welfare State: Tax Expenditures and Social Policy in The United States* (Princeton: Princeton University Press, 1997).

5. See Michael Harrington, *The Other America* (New York: The Macmillan Company, 1962), p. 161.

assumed to be more palatable to a broader audience. Asset-building policy discourse dooms social welfare policy to being limited to getting low-income families to try to succeed in capital markets that are systematically designed to ensure their failure. Such policies can only succeed if they were to supplement low-income families' savings at rates high enough for them to acquire appreciable assets like the nonpoor. Yet that would make asset policies redistributive policies, which is what they are not supposed to be. Therefore some folks will be able to make the most of the more limited support they gain from assets policies to the point that they may indeed be able to escape a life of poverty. Yet, for most others, the emphasis on assets will lead them to be left behind or left out in markets that will not enable them to translate their asset-building efforts into improved social and economic well-being, only to be blamed for this failure.

In the end, I return to the quotation from a former student and try to think through the ways in which asset building can be rescued from the American culture of poverty arguments that the poor's behavior keeps them in a cycle of poverty. I return to globalization and find solace in the ways in which asset building has crossed the Atlantic and found a place in more supportive policy proposals in England. I offer suggestions about a return "Atlantic crossing," where the improved asset-based policy initiatives of Great Britain would get a fair hearing in the United States.[6]

I conclude by asking whether a "capabilities" discourse, as championed by Amartya Sen and others, and which at times has been folded into asset-building proposals, should be given more prominence in its own right, for it might prove less vulnerable to the cooptation that seems likely with the emerging asset-building discourse.[7] Supporting individuals and families to be able to be capable participants in the market and civil society holds out the hope of supporting low-income families without limiting them to building assets in an economy that makes its so difficult for them to do so. Yet, in the end, none of these approaches will go very far without attention to the ways in which the existing political economy systematically works to devalue the efforts of low-income individuals by sequestering them in poor neighborhoods, confining them to inadequate housing, limiting their access to decent schools, and ensuring them a life of low-wage work.

---

6. On the idea of "Atlantic crossings" for sharing social welfare policy reforms, see Daniel T. Rodgers, *Atlantic Crossings: Social Politics in a Progressive Age* (Cambridge: The Belknap Press of Harvard University Press, 1998). Marlena Melhunek suggested the parallel of asset-based discourse to the "culture of poverty."

7. See Amartya Sen, "Capability and Well-being," in *The Quality of Life*, Martha Nussbaum and Amartya Sen, eds. (Oxford: Clarendon Press, 1993), pp. 30–53.

Everything else is just more cycles of poverty, not inflicted by the poor on themselves but as an artifact of discourse that is content to name things they are not and expects to get away with it.

A Capital Idea

A genealogy of the idea of asset building in social welfare policy is a good place to start to question this discursive practice. Any genealogy of asset building inevitably would have to involve denaturalizing the very idea of assets itself. We tend to see assets, like capital, as literally wealth that has an objective, material, economic value. Yet, any one who has tried to sell a home quickly finds that the assessed value of the asset is often not what it will bring in terms of hard cash when finally sold on what is misleadingly called in common parlance the "open market." This is in part because no market, especially housing markets, is entirely open, with various restrictions as to who qualifies to buy. And housing markets have historically most often not been entirely open because they tend to be bounded by class, race, and related lines of privilege and disadvantageness. But another reason why the assessed value of assets is never an entirely reliable or objective indicator of their economic value is that assets are not entirely fungible or immediately convertible into capital, let alone into cash. Assets like owned homes, like all sources of wealth, are subjective in value: you may love your home and find comfort in that haven, but buyers may see it in less emotional terms and therefore put a lesser value on it, leading them to offer a lower price to complete a sale.

Yet, there is a third, even more subjective, dimension to assets. Assets, in social welfare policy, are seen as not just a form of wealth that you can cash out in order to increase your access to liquid economic resources. Instead, assets are often prized as not just a source of economic capital but also a source of "social capital." Families with assets get to network with other families with assets, increasing a family's ability to rely on social relationships for improving their well-being. Owning a home in particular puts a family in touch with other home-owning families and increases the networking possibilities.

Now, the idea of social capital has become quite popular in the social sciences in recent years.[8] Glenn Loury in economics, Pierre Bourdieu and James Coleman in sociology, and Robert Putnam in political science have

---

8. For a conceptual history of "social capital," see James Farr, "Social Capital: A Conceptual History," *Political Theory* 32, 1 (February 2004): 6–32.

all discussed its importance for economic advancement. Families who can access social capital improve the chances for economic success of their children in particular. Yet, the idea is actually older than Loury or Bourdieu, who are at times mentioned as scholars who coined the term. Instead, there is evidence that social capital is a very old idea and was championed by John Dewey in the late 19th century and other proponents of the philosophy of pragmatism. William James was fond of invoking economistic metaphors and asking what was the "cash value" of ideas.[9] For James, as a pragmatist, the truth of any idea was contingent upon its ability to be proved useful in the world of action. That was where its cash value was determined and where we found out the real worth of any truth claim.

Dewey himself was fond of combining the social and economic metaphors to underscore his pragmatism and its orientation toward creating possibilities for doing things in the world of action that would translate into improved living conditions for ordinary people. Dewey referred to books as "banks" that had received the investments of social intelligence from past generations. Social capital is but a short distance metaphorically from cash value and banking on the wisdom of ancestors, and Dewey made that leap. Just as Dewey emphasized that intelligence was social and something we partook of as members of a community, he saw capital in broad social terms as something we gained access to by virtue of our membership in a community. Being a member of a community provided intellectual and social resources that we could "cash in" in order to make a better life for ourselves and our fellow members of the community. Dewey's theories of education for which he became justly famous involved rethinking schooling as a collective process of learning. Students' natural interest in learning was considered a resource of uninvested capital to be activated by tapping into that wealth of preexisting social capital in ways that would cycle back and add to the community's collective intelligence, thereby producing more social capital from which all could benefit. Dewey was quite explicit about this as a process of building collective intelligence for the good of all:

> All points of skill are represented in every race, from the inferior individual to the superior individual, and a society that does not furnish the environment and education and the opportunity of all kinds which will bring out and make effective

---

9. See William James, *Pragmatism* (Cambridge: Harvard University Press, 1975), pp. 43–44. It is interesting to consider this chapter as a meditation on the negative cash value of "assets" in welfare policy discourse.

the superior ability wherever it is born, is not merely doing an injustice to that particular race and to those particular individuals, but it is doing an injustice to itself for it is depriving itself of just that much of social capital.[10]

According to James Farr, Dewey was in many ways following in the tradition of 19th-century political economists, including Marx, who were seeking to find a way to talk about capital in social ways so that individualistic, competitive capitalism could be countered with a more socially responsible alternative. Farr contrasts this with the proponents of "social capital" today who do more the reverse in seeking to highlight not so much the social in capital as the capital in social. Farr fears that this linguistic inversion has conceptual consequences of political import when he writes:

The political economists of the nineteenth century—from Marx to Marshall to Bellamy—took capital from the social point of view. Today's social capitalists, apparently, take "the social" from capital's point of view. The one reflected an age coming to terms with capital, the other an age coming to capital for its terms. Then, "social capital" expressed an explicit antithesis to an unsocial perspective upon capital, now, an implicit antithesis to a noncapitalist perspective on society. "Social capital" was once a category of political economy in a period of its transformation, now one of economized politics, expressing the general dominance of economic modes of analysis in society and social science. But, in the long view, these perspectives may not be logical antinomies so much as two sides of the same coin. Both, surely, sought or seek to comprehend the social relations constitutive of modern capitalist societies, and to position capital as their governing asset. And both, significantly, did so in the very terminology of "social capital." Thus a pathway that leads to the contemporary family of conceptions has now restored to it an even earlier discourse, in the same terms, than before we knew. This is historically instructive and genealogically important, I believe. The nineteenth century political economists may thus be as deserving as Tocqueville to be remembered, in Putnam's words, as "the patron saints of contemporary social capitalists." If not, they certainly deserve historical remembrance for having provided the terminological, temporal, and thematic point of departure for subsequent conceptual change. They used the term, sought its conceptual constituents, and hailed the associations of the cooperative movement.[11]

Farr asks that we consider this conceptual history not because it should be used to enforce some supposed original meaning of social capital on

10. "Address," in *Proceedings of the National Negro Conference* (New York: National Negro Conference, 1909), pp. 71–73, as quoted in Farr, "Social Capital," p. 18. Farr notes that subsequent to this speech Dewey worked with W. E. B. DuBois and the Committee of Forty to found the National Association for the Advancement of Colored People.
11. Farr, "Social Capital," p. 25.

contemporary policy debates. Instead, he offers it as a basis for re-considering the political limitations that arise from social capital discourse as it is practiced in contemporary parlance. This genealogy can be its own form of social capital, investing the contemporary generation with the wisdom of prior generations and creating a space for us to resist the commodification of social life for individual gain and to challenge ourselves to work for the socialization of economic life for collective benefit.

Asset-building policy discourse is not there yet. Instead, it is still best seen as a child of the contemporary social capital discourse that commodifies social life so as to imagine social relations, social networks, social community membership, etc., as possessing resources that the individual can tap into to extract benefit for themselves on the basis of who they know, how they are connected, what memberships they possess, etc.[12] Assets themselves are seen in this discourse as providing a way to better connect to sources of social capital as in purchasing a home increasing your likelihood of living in a better neighborhood of other homeowners who are, compared with renters, not just better off financially but more invested in their community and more committed to that community serving as a resource center for its member families. The circular reasoning of asset-building policy discourse promises a road out of poverty by accessing social capital that comes with possessing greater assets. Asset-building discourse reinforces the commodifying orientation of social capital and does so by way of promising more access to such social capital. As such, asset-building discourse becomes its own self-fulfilling prophecy: you need economic assets to get social capital that gets you more economic assets.

It may well be, as Farr suggests, that in the current period, when the hegemony of the market is unchallenged, the idea of commodifying social relations is looked upon less critically and, relatedly, the idea that low-income individuals can compete in the competition to extract wealth from assets is also treated less skeptically. Today, the hegemony of the market leads to both an increasing interest in commodifying social life and an increased willingness to assume that low-income individuals ought to be expected to act like those in the middle class and to compete with everyone in acquiring wealth. With the hegemony of the market, asset building becomes a capital idea not to be dismissed as positioning the poor to lose out in an economic competition that is rigged against them.

---

12. See Steven Durlauf, "The Case 'Against' Social Capital," *Focus* 20, 3 (Fall 1999): 1–5, for the critique that most concepts of social capital overlook that social community membership often produces increased access to economic advantages through various practices that we would call reprehensible, such as racial segregation.

Yet, an asset-building discourse that risks intensifying the commod-ifying effects of social capital is a problem for the poor at a profoundly political level. Such an individualistic discourse that looks at resources as things to be acquired and consumed exclusively by individuals and their families makes it more difficult to build over time a public philosophy oriented toward collective solidarity that is committed to ensuring we do not blame the poor for the poverty they were left by our individualistic, capitalistic society. In the long run, asset-building discourse makes it harder to develop policies that counter market principles and prevent the poverty that a market-centered society creates in the first place. One long-run consequence of assets-building policy discourse is that it is corrosive to the idea that we need to act collectively through the state to counteract the commodifying practices of the market that leave out so many low-income individuals in the rush to find the greatest sources of profit. In such a market-centered society, the relatively less attractive personal assets of the poor will go begging, while others with more attractive homes or brighter, shinier credentials will see their assets appreciate.

Once everyone is expected to be able to acquire appreciable assets, the risk grows in a market-centered society that the poor will once again be blamed for their poverty.[13] This time they will be blamed for bad in-vestment decisions, bad economic planning, bad capital management, etc. With a strong emphasis on the poor being able to be expected to compete in capital markets, we risk reinscribing the old culture of poverty argu-ments that the poor are different; that they lack middle-class values of discipline, hard work, savings, and delaying gratification; and that instead they are too impulsive, too present oriented, and too fixated on gratifying immediate wants to save, plan ahead, invest, and watch their assets ap-preciate. Expecting the poor to compete in housing markets and in efforts to improve their human capital through schooling are primary instances of what we can call the "assets trap." Investing in homes that most people will not want to buy risks saddling the poor with housing costs they cannot cover rather than increasing their families' wealth. And getting young people to borrow extensive amounts of money for community college coursework that often does not make them competitive in the various

---

13. For the classic rebuttal of the culture of poverty arguments that proliferated in the 1950s and 1960s, see William Ryan, *Blaming the Victim* (New York: Alfred A. Knopf, 1976). For a meticulous analysis of the evolution of culture of poverty ar-guments, see Alice O'Connor, *Poverty Knowledge* (Princeton: Princeton University Press, 2001), pp. 99–210.

occupational fields and career paths they are pursuing just saddles them with debt they may never be able to pay off, leaving them with a bad credit rating and less disposable income to meet basic needs. The idea that asset investments are the road out of poverty risks not only failing but also, when it fails, being turned back against the poor so that we end up blaming them all over again for their own poverty.

Saving the Poor by Getting the Poor to Save

Asset-building discourse was jump-started by the writings of Michael Sherraden, which took the social science and policy advocacy communities by storm with the idea that the poor are no different than the middle class, that they want to build for a better future just like everyone else, and that with help they could be taught to save, invest in capital, acquire assets, and grow wealth that they could pass on to their children.[14] In this way, both the Left's and the Right's criticism of the existing welfare system's emphasis on transferring income to the poor in ways that did not lead to escaping poverty could be addressed by shifting the basis for public policy away from income redistribution to asset development. The appeal of the idea of asset-building policy has been nothing less than a phenomenon itself spreading across the research and policy communities, energized in no small part by the enthusiasm of a number of private foundations for funding research and demonstration projects associated with testing out asset-building approaches: removing penalties for having assets like a car when applying for welfare or food stamps, individual development savings accounts (IDAs) for education, job training, and human capital investments, microenterprise initiatives to help low-income individuals save to develop their own businesses (often in their own homes), and policies designed to increase the ability of low-income families to own their own homes.[15]

But the popularity of the idea has not stopped at the water's edge, moving as it has in recent years first to Europe and now around the globe, migrating from the First to the Third World, finding fewer barriers to be sure with the collapse of communism and the growing interest everywhere of increasing participation in the global capitalist system and the oppor-

14. Fred M. Ssewamala and Michael Sherraden, "Integrating Saving into Micro-enterprise Programs for the Poor: Do Institutions Matter?" *Social Service Review* 78, 3 (September 2004): 404–29.
15. Miller-Adams, *Owning Up*, pp. 11–22.

tunity to gain wealth and improve personal well-being as a member of an "ownership society," as it is called by both advocates of the asset-building approach and the Bush administration.[16]

As much asset-building discourse involves resisting what George Bush called the "soft bigotry of low expectations" about the ability of the poor to act middle class, there is much to suggest that regardless of intentions, asset-building discourse ends up being too easily assimilated into the old culture of poverty arguments that William Ryan forcefully challenged years ago.[17] Asset-building discourse asserts an insistence that it is emphasizing how the poor are no different than everyone else, but then it ends up founding and justifying its approach on a psychological theory of the poor that sees them as trapped in an orientation to life that robs them of the motivation to save, plan for the future, and be interested in acquiring assets. The Organization for Economic Co-operation and Development in Europe (OECD) has emphasized this in documents extolling the virtues of asset-based approach in helping the poor think in more middle-class ways so that they will be better able to compete in various markets to get better jobs, start their own business, own their own property, etc. The OECD summarizes Sherraden's rationale for the asset-building approach in ways that highlight its focus on the psychology of the poor:

- *Assets improve household stability.* In the first instance, they function as precautionary savings to cushion income shocks that might otherwise throw people into income poverty.
- *Assets create an orientation toward the future.* A few assets create hope, and hope leads to future-oriented behaviour as opposed to entirely present-oriented survival strategies.
- *Assets promote development of human capital and other assets.* With a few means, people will begin to think about improving themselves. If they have physical assets, they will take care of them and try to improve them.
- *Assets enable focus and specialisation.* [S]pecialisation and the division of labour [are] the essence of participation in an organised social economy. Such behavior . . . would change with the end of exclusion and with focus and specialisation.

---

16. Ray Boshara and Michael Sherraden, *Status of Asset Building Worldwide* (New American Foundation, Assets Building Program, March 2004 (www.newamerica.net/Download_Docs/pdfs/Pub_File_1526_1.pdf).

17. See Ryan, *Blaming the Victim*, p. 3.

- *Assets provide a foundation for risk-taking.*...With more assets, the ability to take risks with a safety net is increased. The assertion also applies to entrepreneurship.
- *Assets increase personal efficacy.* To use a currently popular word, they become a source of empowerment.
- *Assets increase social influence.*...This point does not concern being rich. It concerns having enough to merit peer recognition.
- *Assets increase political participation.* With assets to protect, people pay attention to where their leaders lead them. They can no longer afford to live in "exclusion".... They join the system. This increases social cohesion.
- *Assets increase the welfare of offspring.* Children raised in households with sufficient assets to end preoccupation with immediate survival gain in myriad ways that provide them with human assets—beginning with better nutrition and health and ending with acculturation and education.[18]

"Improve household stability," "create an orientation to the future," "provide a foundation for risk-taking," "increase personal efficacy," and so on all underscore an approach to public policy that is firmly rooted in changing the psychology of the poor as the main way to attack poverty. It promotes the idea that asset building is an adjunct of clinical social work, requiring intensive counseling. Clinical social work's orientation, so popular in the United States, is to medicalize social problems and treat them as personal pathologies, and it is increasingly spreading around the developed world as part of globalization and the campaign to regiment populations to the new world order of low-wage work. Asset-building counseling is following in this clinical path. Disclaimers aside, this is a discourse that is deeply indebted to previous ideas about the culture of poverty. It risks setting the poor up to be blamed all over again for their own poverty. Whether we intend it or not, we may end up being asked, once again, to "assume the worst" about the poor, this time when they fail to convert assets into wealth.[19] Even when we do not mean it, such a vicious cycle is created when we get caught up in this conspiracy of dis-course.

---

18. OECD, *Asset Building and the Escape from Poverty: A New Welfare Policy Debate* (Paris: Organization for Economic Co-operation and Development, November 2003), p. 6–7.

19. See Chapter 6 for an analysis of how U.S. welfare policy discourse historically has tended to assume helping the poor makes them dependent.

Then again, the psychology of asset-based discourse is anything but unintentional. The focus on whether the poor will save is actually quite disturbing, given that what is appealing about asset-building discourse for progressives is that it supposedly would be a more politically feasible way to transfer wealth to the poor so as to overcome the inequities associated with the current socioeconomic structure and the way market-centered society works to marginalize low-income individuals living in poor neighborhoods, working in dead-end low-wage jobs, and going without access to the educational opportunities that would enable them and their children to escape poverty. Instead, Sherraden, with Ray Boshara, emphasizes the way in which asset policy will change the outlook of the poor more than the structure of society. In summarizing the developments in the field, Sherraden and Boshara emphasize research that shows that the poor can be taught to save:

> Perhaps most significantly, research (from both primary and secondary sources) suggests that (1) the poor can save and accumulate assets and (2) assets have positive social, psychological, and civic effects independent of the effects of income. Most notably, the "American Dream" Individual Development Account (IDA) Demonstration in the U.S. (organized by the Corporation for Enterprise Development and the Center for Social Development) and the Savings Gateway Pilot Project in the U.K. (sponsored by HM Treasury) produced evidence that participants could save in structured accounts.
>
> The idea that the poor should accumulate assets is now almost common, language such as "asset-based policy" is now mainstream, and research of many aspects of asset accumulation, distribution, and impacts is increasing.
>
> In 2003, OECD published *Asset Building and the Escape from Poverty*, probably the best report on the state of asset building worldwide. While directed primarily at a Western European audience, this report argues that asset policies hold the potential to transform "passive welfare states" into "active social investment states," through (a) the act of saving and the reciprocity it implies, and (b) the "asset effects" along with the greater return on scarce public dollars and better citizenship they may promote.
>
> Finally, other asset building projects and research are being pioneered around the world. In addition to primary and secondary research efforts connected to policies and projects in the U.S. and U.K., asset building projects and/or research efforts are underway by researchers in Hong Kong, Australia, Sweden, Taiwan, China, Singapore, Canada, Uganda, and Mexico, and research continues as well through various programs of the OECD.[20]

In other words, the emphasis of asset-building discourse on changing the psychology of the poor is helping it become part of the globalization of a new discourse of dependency, spreading around the world to buttress welfare state rollbacks with the shift toward labor activation policies that

---

20. Boshara and Sherraden, *Status of Asset Building Worldwide*, p. 1.

give priority to moving the poor into low-wage labor markets. So, then, we see here quite clearly that this is how one discourse trades on another, making each complicit in a conspiracy of discourse that reinscribes the otherness of the poor and intensifies the interest in studying, surveying, and treating the poor to become more active participants in the global order... even if it means their continued subordination at the bottom of competitive markets for housing, schooling, jobs, and the sources of well-being more generally. So it goes with the globalization of discourse in the emerging ownership society.

The Foundation of a Conspiracy

Asset-building policy discourse resonates with market principles and that makes it attractive to those who are seeking ways of promoting public policies to support low-income families within the limits of a market-centered society. Its consonance with market principles makes it an appealing discourse for private foundations which in recent years have prided themselves on promoting innovative ideas for social reform that are simultaneously feasible because they do not challenge the hegemony of market logic for structuring social relations. The Ford Foundation, like the Mott Foundation, the Annie E. Casey Foundation, the Schwab Foundation, and others, found asset-building policy a very appealing idea and has developed a major initiative to fund research and publishing projects designed to champion the idea. Asset building by individuals and communities is now one of three major funding streams for the Ford Foundation. In 2002, the Ford Foundations spent $143.0 million in grants to fund research and demonstration projects for this area compared with $239.9 million for peace and social justice and $134.1 million for knowledge, creativity, and freedom, its other two major areas for funding.[21] Asset building has become the main idea for organizing the Ford Foundation's efforts to fund projects designed to help attack the persistence of poverty in the United States and elsewhere.

Why is the Ford Foundation so willing to commit as much money as it has to promoting an asset-building policy discourse? While some have suggested that foundations unreflectively serve elite interests of their wealthy sponsors,[22] an even better explanation than a conspiracy of the

21. Ford Foundation, *Annual Report: 2003* (www.fordfound.org/about/program_approvals.cfm).
22. Joan Roelofs, *Foundations and Public Policy: The Mask of Pluralism* (Albany: State University of New York Press, 2003).

elite is a conspiracy of discourse. The latter I would argue is an even more insidious way of consolidating the power of capitalism.[23]

The Ford Foundation has over time built a sizeable staff and devoted large sums of money to promote work on asset building. It has in the process commissioned several books on the topic to further champion the idea.[24] Perhaps the most striking is Michelle Miller-Adams's *Owning Up: Poverty, Assets, and the American Dream*, published in 2002 by the Brookings Institution. As a foundation executive and political scientist, Miller-Adams was a logical person to be asked by the Ford Foundation to write a book that would introduce the idea of asset building for the poor to a broader audience. Her previous book had been about the World Bank.[25] Taking the books together suggests a focus more on how granting agencies are doing good works than on whether either the World Bank's policies or asset-building initiatives have a distinctive politics. Both books use stories from selected cases to emphasize what good is being done by those developing and funding these initiatives. As well-written and informative as they are, these are not critical works, nor are they intended to be a basis for serious assessment of the policies in either case. Instead, the emphasis is on letting a broader audience get to know about an area of assisting the poor that is assumed to be basically good.

In the case of asset building, it is clear the Ford Foundation wants more people to know about this way to frame social welfare policy reform. Now, this could be seen as indicating that a private elite foundation is committed to making social welfare policy change safe for capitalism. That it has that effect does not mean that it is the intentional result of elite planners, even if asset-building discourse seems overly focused on changing poor people's psychology and behavior. Instead, I would argue that the Ford Foundation is so keen to champion asset-building discourse for discursive reasons. The Ford Foundation is positioned in the institutional matrix of the globalizing capitalist social order to help make that system work more humanely. Its job is to find a way to talk about social

---

23. A good place to go for an analysis of how foundations are involved in a discourse that buttresses established power, see O'Connor, *Poverty Knowledge*, pp. 277–83, where O'Connor reviews the Rockefeller Foundation's five-year $6 million Program for Research on the Urban Underclass. "Underclass," to the dismay of program officers at Rockefeller, was eventually reputed by some researchers funded by the project as a thoroughly discredited concept lacking in empirical validity.

24. For example see Shapiro and Wolff, eds., *Assets for the Poor*; and Miller-Adams, *Owning Up*.

25. Michelle Miller-Adams, *World Bank: New Agendas in a Changing World* (New York: Routledge, 1999).

change without actually calling for social transformation. A discourse of amelioration is what the Ford Foundation needs to fulfill its own mission. I suspect it is for the Ford Foundation and other foundations the grantor's equivalent of a God-send that asset-building discourse came along, giving them a whole new terrain to work over, nurture, and support, for it affords multiple opportunities to talk about helping the poor fit into the existing structure of a market-centered society without having to question the fundamental principles of that society.

The Ford Foundation is at pains to note that it gives priority to proposed projects that will have as broad an impact as possible: "Because its funds are limited in relation to the great number of worthwhile proposals received, the Foundation directs its support to activities that are within its current interests and are likely to have wide effect."[26] At the same time, the foundation stresses that the initiative is designed to support largely research on this topic that will help the foundation further its overriding goals, which are to "strengthen democratic values; reduce poverty and injustice; promote international cooperation; and advance human achievement."

While the rhetoric is thick in human rights, democracy, and social justice, Ford's asset-building initiative is quintessential reformist politics, making it ideal for a private corporate foundation dedicated to improving the existing society and addressing its fundamental social and economic problems within the existing structure of that society. Asset-building discourse positions the poor as subpar consumers, investors, and wealth generators who need to be assisted to better participate in the existing system of wealth acquisition in ways that would mean acting more middle class so that they could actually become middle class. Now, there is nothing wrong with this tautology per se; but it is a quintessential re-formist discourse and it is one that risks reinscribing the idea that the poor need to learn to act middle class before they are to become middle class, when in fact there is at least as much evidence that the opposite is true—the poor will act middle class once they are given the resources to do so. Therefore, while imputing a cycle of poverty to the poor, asset-building discourse risks becoming its own vicious cycle where we saddle the poor with debts and diverted income streams that do not produce appreciable assets and only weigh them down in their struggle to escape poverty. All of this occurs because of a reluctance to articulate the need for public policies

---

26. Ford Foundation, *Annual Report: 2003* (www.fordfound.org/about/program_approvals.cfm).

that will override how profit-seeking behavior in the markets in which the poor participate will leave them behind in the competition to acquire wealth.

The Ford Foundation does support a wide variety of research and demonstration projects under the asset-building banner, and many are not reflective of the culture-of-poverty thesis. In some respects, this reflects the fact that the foundation has funded diverse projects in the past designed to address social and economic problems but in recent years has grouped them under the banner of asset building. Nonetheless, the banner is asset building and it is significant that this is what is being emphasized rather than more structural approaches to attacking poverty. In addition, the foundation underwrites a number of grants that are directly associated with the asset-building concept in ways that are reflective of a concern about asset-building being a tool for attacking the mentality associated with the culture of poverty.

Yet, my favorite example is from my own experience. Through a research center I co-direct, I have been associated with several Ford Foundation projects and have participated in a number of meetings in which more possible projects were discussed. By virtue of my institutional responsibilities, I too have become entangled in the world of asset building, if only a very little bit. One possible grant involves researching the extremely innovative idea of The Benefit Bank (TBB) developed by Robert Brand of Solutions for Progress in Philadelphia.[27] The idea of TBB is to work with congregations and community service centers all over the country to use computers, the Internet, and electronic communications to enable poor people to get their entitlements quickly and easily. In an age of disentitlement, where many low-income people are not being told about benefits such as the Earned Income Tax Credit (EITC) or educational grants and where they are finding barriers to accessing Food Stamps, Medicaid, child care, and other benefits, Bob Brand has sought to build a system where people can walk into a TBB location in their neighborhood and with the help of a trained counselor apply for everything for which they are eligible for right there, even to the point of sending in applications online. Still largely in development, Bob approached the Ford Foundation for funding for his brainchild. Ford program officers expressed interest and requested that there be a research component, about which Bob talked to me and several colleagues in a

---

27. Go to www.solfopro.com/sfp/Projects/thebenefitbank.htm to visit The Benefit Bank online.

number of conversations. What really struck me was how the culture-of-poverty outlook dressed up in asset-building rhetoric colored the Ford Foundation's framing of research questions. Although I wanted to study such things as to what extent did TBB overcome barriers to entitlement and increase the ability of particular racial and ethnic subcommunities to access benefits, and in which programs, the foundation staff instead emphasized studying what low-income individuals and families did with the benefits once they received them. For instance, they were interested in whether individuals who received a lump-sum benefit from the EITC used it to build savings, acquire assets, or spend it all at once in a frenzy of immediate self-gratification. I was horrified. It did not matter because to date we still have not received funding from the Ford Foundation. The conspiracy of discourse is insidious; even when reaching out to support efforts to help the poor get what the system will not give them, asset-based discourse redirects our attention to thinking about how to get the poor to think and behave differently. As a private foundation dedicated to helping the existing society better meet people's needs without seriously changing that society, the Ford Foundation, and other foundations as well, fall prey to the siren sounds of asset-based discourse, perhaps to the point of eventually getting caught up in the rolling retrenchment of the welfare state that globalization is encouraging. This is not so much a conscious conspiracy of the elite as it is the complicity of actors, institutions, and discourses in reproducing the limited horizons that the structure of power has set for us. Resisting the conspiracy of discourse therefore becomes a prime directive for progressive policy work. And it seems we need to begin with asset building as a primary case in point.

What Has Asset-Building Discourse Wrought?

In the formative years of the 1990s, asset-building initiatives were concentrated on reforming welfare policy to ease asset limits for qualifying for cash assistance, Food Stamps, and other programs, as well creating space in welfare policies for IDAs and support for microenterprise development by welfare recipients and other low-income persons. Eventually, more ambitious asset-building initiatives in the form of increasing the ability of low-income families to own their homes have become popular.

The easing of asset limits is noncontroversial, if not a major boon to the economic well-being of low-income individuals, because they increasingly do not qualify for welfare and related benefits for reasons such as time limits, work requirements, sanctions policies, and administrative barriers.

Microenterprise efforts have been more limited and flounder on the shoals of the risks associated with small business start-up. Most small businesses fail. The success of IDAs has been mixed at best. Jared Bernstein notes:

> The asset-building idea that has gone farthest politically and has the greatest bipartisan support is the Individual Development Account (IDA), a subsidized savings account. IDA demonstration projects currently going on around the country, funded by a 1998 federal pilot program and by nonprofit groups, work like this: Low-income persons make deposits to an IDA and their withdrawals—so long as they are for approved expenditures, such as education, housing or an independent business—are matched at a multiple, typically 2-to-1 or 3-to-1. The amount of dollars matched is capped to control program costs. The approach combines a savings incentive with a form of income distribution, in the hope of encouraging the poor to acquire the financial habits of the middle class. What could be wrong with that? A common objection from liberals is that IDAs are fine as far as they go, but the poor can't save enough to make much difference, even with the incentive of generous matches. This, by itself, wouldn't be so bad, critics say, but the effort that think tanks, advocates and policymakers are putting into asset development is taking energy and resources away from other activities that could make a difference. Research on IDAs does suggest, not surprisingly, that most of the poor are hard pressed to save much.[28]

Additionally, Bernstein notes concerns about the individualistic political consciousness in such an approach that seeks to get the poor to internalize the role as capitalists while distracting attention away from the more structural sources of poverty. Yet, more critically, Bernstein's major concern is not that IDAs are not in the end good policy in assisting the poor in the long run to escape poverty but that, ironically, they are not politically feasible. In order to make such an approach really effective in attacking poverty, the government would have spend much more money in matching savings. Further, if the necessary matching were done nationwide as a matter of national policy, it would pose a cost way beyond what the conservative champions of such an individualistic approach would be willing to even begin to think about supporting. In the end, according to Bernstein, IDAs are, for now at least, politically unrealistic. The discourse of what is politically feasible is often its opposite—utopian, at least in thinking that it can extract real resources from those who do not want to give them up simply by sugar-coating such demands in the

---

28. Jared Bernstein, "Savings Incentives for the Poor: Why the Scale Doesn't Match the Promise," *The American Prospect* 14, 5 (May 1, 2003) (www.prospect.org/print/V14/5/bernstein-j.html).

terminology preferred by the powerful. This form of "naïve cynicism" often leads to euphemistic politics that backfire.[29] Asset-based discourse is again a primary case in point.

When a House Is a Home . . . But Not an Asset

In recent years, a major area of policy development for asset building by the poor has been homeownership. It definitely is another asset-building idea that has merit up to a point. I found this out quickly when I embarked on a project working with two doctoral students to do research for a Philadelphia housing advocacy agency, the Women's Community Revitalization Project (WCRP) in the fall of 2003. Our research focused on low-income home repair policies in Philadelphia.[30]

Low-income homeownership is increasingly a very salient public policy objective in Philadelphia, as it is around the rest of the country. President George Bush has trumpeted the record levels of homeownership in the nation, reaching 68 percent of all households achieved during his first term in the White House. His administration has emphasized that homeownership is its major housing policy.[31] From this perspective, getting the poor to own homes is seen as a critical component in any asset-building approach to fighting poverty.[32] This makes sense given that the main asset that most families have is an owned home. So, the thinking goes, if the poor need to acquire wealth in the form of assets, it will logically be largely by owning homes, so they can begin to act as middle-class families and use the wealth acquired through homeownership to invest in their families and escape the culture of poverty that leads them to live from day-to-day without any prospect of building a better future.

Yet, a growing number of reports are indicating that the rush to increasing homeownership is saddling an increasing number of low-income families with dilapidated housing that is in need of costly repairs that they

---

29. See Sanford F. Schram, *Words of Welfare: The Poverty of Social Science and the Social Science of Poverty* (Minneapolis: University of Minnesota Press, 1995), pp. 20–37.

30. See Corey Shdaimah, Roland Stahl, and Sanford F. Schram, *When You Can See the Sky through Your Roof: Home Repair Policies in Philadelphia* (Philadelphia: Women's Community Revitalization Project, September 2004) (http://www.brynmawr.edu/Acads/GSSW/schram/wcrpreport.doc).

31. Amy Goldstein, "Bush Aims to Localize Rent Aid: Money-Saving Plan Would Relax Regulation of Section 8," *Washington Post*, April 13, 2004, p. A1.

32. See Michael Sherraden, ed., *Inclusion in the American Dream* (New York: Oxford University Press, 2004).

cannot afford.[33] As a result, with the rise in low-income homeownership, there has been a corresponding rise in foreclosures. Philadelphia is by no means exempt from these trends and in fact is a leader.[34] These troubling developments raised questions for our research project concerning the state of low-income homeownership in Philadelphia, what the city is doing about the problem, to what extent home repair policies are effectively addressing this problem, and what can be done differently to address the problem more effectively.

Our initial findings in the Philadelphia project were that it is a city with a very old housing stock, much of it in disrepair. As a result of the relatively old housing stock and other economic factors, the median value of owner-occupied homes in Philadelphia is relatively low according to the 2000 U.S. Census—$61,000 compared with $221,000 in New York, $210,000 in Boston, $153,500 in Washington, DC, $144,300 in Chicago, and $144,100 in Atlanta. Among the 15 cities we examined, only Pittsburgh has a lower median value than Philadelphia—$60,700. The median value for owner-occupied units in Detroit is $62,800, $63,500 in St. Louis, and $69,900 in Baltimore.

Much of the housing of the poor in Philadelphia is owned rather than rented. We found that Philadelphia had the highest rate of homeownership among poor families of any of 14 comparison cities according to the 2000 U.S. Census—38 percent compared with 8 percent in Newark, 9 percent in Boston and New Haven, 11 percent in New York, 16 percent in Miami and Washington, DC, and 18 percent in Atlanta and Chicago. The only other city with a homeownership rate among the poor over 30 percent was Detroit, at 33 percent. Baltimore was at 23 percent, Pittsburgh and St. Louis were at 22 percent, and Cleveland was at 21 percent.

Remarkably, many of the homes in Philadelphia owned by the poor are owned without mortgages, stemming in part from the low prices for many of these homes and their being passed along in families. Many of the low-income homeowners are elderly and nonwhite, and the homes were often

33. In particular, see Carolina Katz Reid, *Achieving the American Dream? A Longitudinal Analysis of the Homeownership Experiences of Low-Income Households* (Seattle: Center for Studies in Demography and Ecology, University of Washington, Working Paper 04–04, April, 2004). Also see Nicolas P. Retsinas and Eric S. Belsky, eds., *Low-Income Homeownership: Examining the Unexamined Goal* (Washington, DC: Brookings Institution Press, 2002).

34. Jason Straziuso, "As Volume of Foreclosures Swells, Some Want Moratorium," *Pocono Record*, February 9, 2004, p. 1.

of very low assessed values. That said, data from the 1999 American Housing Survey, conducted by the U.S. Census Bureau for the Department of Housing and Urban Development, suggest that for this population the options for renting affordable housing that is safe and in sound condition are also limited. Low-income renters often live in housing that is in no better condition than the homes owned by the poor. Therefore, helping low-income homeowners maintain their homes in livable condition becomes a major policy priority in Philadelphia. In fact, low-income home repair policies in Philadelphia have been demonstrated to reduce abandonment and homelessness.[35]

Yet, when we examine available data in detail we find that the repair and maintenance problems of low-income homeowners greatly exceed the city's current attempts to address them. In addition, many of the policies the city has developed have a number of limitations that further hamper the city's ability to address the problems of low-income homeownership and home repair. Timing is critical, as the city recently embarked on a major new Neighborhood Transformation Initiative (NTI) to demolish dilapidated housing and clear blocks for the possible development of new housing. At this time, much of this initiative is focused on attracting the development of housing that would bring more middle- and upper-class families back into the city. How much new affordable housing for low-income families will be built remains uncertain. Therefore, it is imperative that in the short run, expanding and revising Philadelphia's low-income home repair programs is critical. Given the severity of the problem and the limitations of current home repair policies, for the long run it is very important to also consider policies that develop more affordable rental housing for low-income families in Philadelphia.

Our research indicated:

> Philadelphia has a distinctive housing stock: disproportionately old, row houses, two-, three-stories, privately owned homes, with the poor owning at high rates, often without mortgages, at relatively low assessed values. In fact, Philadelphia has the highest homeownership rate among the poor of any comparable city in the country: a full 38 percent of Philadelphia households with incomes below the poverty line in 1999 owned their own homes. According to the 1999 American Housing Survey, about 23 percent of those home-owning households with incomes below the 150 percent of the poverty

---

35. *Blight Free Philadelphia: A Public-Private Strategy to Create and Enhance Neighborhood Value* (Philadelphia: Research for Democracy, a collaboration between the Eastern Pennsylvania Organizing Project and the Temple University Center for Public Policy, with Assistance from Diamond and Associates, October 2001), p. 31.

line had at least one significant home repair problem (29,371 of 125,703 homes). Further, about 11 percent of them (13,770) had homes that were rated as inadequate. Given these data, it is likely that other low-income homeowners had additional home repair problems not captured in these statistics. If the City were to fund its basic home repair program to begin to address all the low-income home repair needs in Philadelphia, we estimate that it would need to begin to spend significantly more money than it currently does on such efforts. For instance, if it were to extend the average amount of basic home repair services it currently spends on each house just to the estimated 11 percent of homes that are inadequate, it would have to increase its current fiscal year budget 10 times its current allotment upwards from about $8 million to $75 million. This, however, would neither eliminate the home repair problems of these homes that are rated inadequate, nor would it address the home repair problems of the remaining low-income households. But it would be a big improvement over the current dire situation.[36]

The Philadelphia project report highlighted what a number of other researchers have suggested about the complexities of emphasizing homeownership as an asset-building policy for the poor. Many poor families are able to own only the poorest of homes, which come with extensive repair and maintenance cost, often putting them at risk of being saddled with growing debts, leading at times to abandonment and re-possession. In addition, because these homes are often segregated by class and race in the poorest, least appealing neighborhoods, the market for these homes is very limited, decreasing the chances that the home, even if it is maintained, will appreciate in value so as to increase the family's wealth with time. "The only possible policy conclusion is that the evidence is mixed: the effects of home ownership will vary depending on the race of the low-income person and the neighborhood location of the home. It is also possible that for the poor, neighborhood location that improves their human capital through increased neighborhood use values will be as important as home ownership itself."[37]

Our Philadelphia study concluded that it was unassailable that, given the housing stock and the lack of alternatives, more had to be done to help low-income families continue to live in homes they owned; however, this was more a effort to prevent a bad situation from getting worse, not a program to help the poor acquire assets.

---

36. Shdaimah, Stahl and Schram, *When You Can See the Sky through Your Roof*, p. 8.
37. See Nancy A. Denton, "Housing as a Means of Asset Accumulation: A Good Strategy for the Poor?" in *Assets for the Poor: The Benefits of Spreading Asset Ownership*, Thomas M. Shapiro and Edward N. Wolff, eds. (New York: Russell Sage Foundation, 2001), p. 256.

Capabilities over Assets

Sherraden notes that an asset-building approach dovetails with or incorporates a capabilities approach as developed by the Nobel Prize–winning economist Amartya Sen: "the best policy alternatives move beyond the idea of consumption as well-being toward what Amartya Sen identifies as functionings or capabilities. Asset building is one policy pathway to increased capabilities."[38] Perhaps in theory, but in practice I would argue that asset-building discourse is as likely to reinforce Lawrence Mead's emphasis on competence as it is to lead to an emphasis on capabilities.[39] Sen emphasizes that we must first reallocate resources extensively so that all persons have the ability to develop their capabilities enough to participate as full members of society, but Mead argues that we must invert that logic by insisting that people first demonstrate their competence for being personally responsible, self-sufficient members of society before we agree to accord them entitlement rights.

In theory, asset-building discourse can go either way, depending, in part, on how well we support people in acquiring the capital (economic, human, social, and cultural) they need to sufficiently develop their capabilities. But I would say only in part because asset building ranges well beyond capabilities to issues of wealth accumulation and therefore risks being assimilated to a highly individualistic, capitalistic discourse of acquisition.

Capabilities discourse assiduously avoids couching its redistribution program in terms of wealth acquisition. This is crucial for safeguarding its own individualism from the more possessive forms of individualism to which asset-building discourse opens itself. Without such safeguards in place, asset-building discourse is free to be assimilated into the bribe of competence discourse, focusing more as it does on what people do first to show they are deserving. While Mead's competence discourse emphasizes people playing by the basic rules of work and family before qualifying, Sherraden's asset-building discourse looks to thrifty savings behavior to be the marker of one's deservingness. Both risk judging people as deficient and undeserving and thereby not to be given aid unless they meet the prerequisite implicit in their respective discourses.

---

38. Michael Sherraden, "Asset-Building Policy and Programs for the Poor," *Assets for the Poor: The Benefits of Spreading Asset Ownership*, in Thomas M. Shapiro and Edward N. Wolff, eds. (New York: Russell Sage Foundation, 2001), p. 305.
39. See Lawrence M. Mead, *The New Politics of Poverty: The Nonworking Poor in America* (New York: Basic Books, 1992), pp. 19–21.

Therefore, Sherraden is right to emphasize the important affinity between asset-building and capabilities discourses in shifting the locus of attention away from the short-run concern of consumption to the long-run concern of capabilities as the basis for determining well-being; however, there are important antinomies between asset-building and capabilities discourses. Asset building is much more vulnerable to being associated with a more capitalistic version of individualism that ends up emphasizing the need for people to demonstrate their personal responsibility before we deign to help them develop their capabilities. Asset building is far more judgmental than capabilities discourse in ways that are profoundly disconcerting. In this way, it risks judging the poor as deficient in terms of their thinking, behavior, culture, and lifestyle and thereby opens the door to them being othered, left out, denied full membership in society, and left without access to needed aid by virtue of their failure to meet threshold requirements, even when through no fault of their own, other than their being poor.

Asset building is even more vulnerable to being assimilated into a capitalistic discourse of exclusion because it can too easily be associated with the dirty little secret of social welfare policy discourse in a market-centered society. Asset building is very much like other proactive metaphors, including perhaps the most thoughtful one in social policy discourse—prevention. The prevention metaphor is most dramatically stated by William Julius Wilson when he states that one strategy for enlisting society's support in developing more generous social welfare policies is where we frame aid to children as investing for the long term in our most important resource—the next generation.[40] Pay me now, or pay later, said the mechanic in the old television advertisement for motor oil. Invest now in child well-being or wait and incur the greater costs at the other end in uneducated workers, more unemployed persons, more crime, more drug addiction, and more poverty. The preventive metaphor is compelling . . . but it almost never seems to work. The dirty little secret of prevention discourse is that those in power have no intentions of ever paying. They will just move to the suburbs or gated apartment complexes, or hire private security forces, or do whatever it is that they are now doing in droves given that they refuse to buy into the prevention metaphor. The prevention metaphor assumes that everyone shares a sense of collective responsibility for what will go wrong due to our failures to develop socially just policies in the present. But the truth is that

---

40. William Julius Wilson, *The Truly Disadvantaged: The Inner City, the Underclass, and Public Policy* (Chicago: University of Chicago Press, 1987), p. 164, as analyzed in Schram, *Words of Welfare*, p. 24.

almost no one does, at least not until they are forced to. It is almost always someone else's fault, and people who have the resources to avoid taking responsibility will often do just that, moving to the suburbs or whatever it takes. It will take more than appealing to their good sense by talking about prevention if we are to develop more just social welfare policies.

Asset building is a cousin of the prevention metaphor suggesting that if we help the poor save and acquire assets now they will be less likely to be poor in the future. Both could be proved in the right context to potentially be money-savers in the long run. This, however, is not just an empirical question regarding whether supporting individual savings now in the near term will reap savings for the society as a whole in the long term. Instead, it is a question of what kind of society we have. If helping people now means paying for something we would avoid paying for later, then it is not likely that we will be willing to pay very much. Further, even if we pay, if our society continues to work systematically to create an impoverished class whose property and human capital are not valued, then we will still need to be paying later regardless if we paid now. Any society that continues to marginalize the poor in highly stratified ways geographically, economically, socially, and culturally so that they and their possessions are systematically devalued is not a society where either the prevention or assets metaphor will work as much as we would like. Low-income families will still have a hard time acquiring wealth as they remain segregated in devalued neighborhoods and mired in low-wage work. Such are the limits of asset building as a prevention strategy in the United States today.

A More Robust Asset Building

The more ambitious forms of asset building do hold out some prospect of transferring needed wealth-generating ability to those poor families who can take advantage of them. Increasing the number of low-income families who can qualify for such support would seem to be of necessity a critical part of the asset-building agenda. Increasing the levels of public support for matching savings would be an equally important objective of those interested in promoting better asset-building policies. Even in the United Kingdom, which has followed the U.S. in welfare reform in a number of respects, the Savings Gateway and the Child Trust Fund programs reflect a number of important differences between asset-building policy development in the United States and the United Kingdom.[41] First, in the

---

41. *Asset-Building and the Escape from Poverty*, pp. 30–34.

United Kingdom, policy is being developed at the top and being implemented nationally in a much more ambitious way than in the United States, which tends to prefer limited experimentation focused on evaluating the initiatives for whether they will be exploited by the poor, who are looked at more suspiciously in America than in England. Second, programs in the United Kingdom receive greater financial backing and include greater incentives for the poor to participate. Third, the United Kingdom is explicitly redesigning its welfare reform system to have three pillars—income support, work, and savings—that are to work to reinforce each other rather than to replace one with any one of the others. The way welfare reform is going in the United States is that the discourse of dependency is creating a context where it is much more likely that work and savings, as manifestations of personal responsibility and self-sufficiency, are vulnerable to being incorporated into a campaign to replace income support. Fourth, in the United Kingdom, while the Savings Gateway program is limited to low-income individuals, it is far less paternalistic than American approaches to create incentives for the poor to save, because it does not seek to limit what the savings can be used for in some misguided effort to direct the poor to only those investments that have been approved by the state. Fifth, the Child Trust Fund is a form of what the British are calling progressive universalism and is open to all families, making it more likely to develop the necessary broad base of political support that it will need for it to grow in popularity and funding.

These developments in the United Kingdom suggest once again that the American context for welfare reform can be radically different than elsewhere and can make even good ideas more vulnerable to political subversion. Asset-building policy discourse would be again a primary case in point.

Conclusion

Context is then perhaps everything, or almost everything. And discourse invokes context, to the detriment of asset building in the United States. In theory, asset-building discourse in the United States is an incredibly innovative alternative that possesses the potential to get beyond the failures of public policy that make poverty seem intractable. It has become popular with advocates on both the Left and the Right, as well as with funders and policymakers, and not just in the United States, for now it is spreading around the world. Yet, all of this popularity is bound to raise suspicions. Perhaps it is, I dare say, too good an idea, at least in the sense of reinforcing some of the prejudices associated with the globalization of welfare reform and growing interest in rolling back the welfare state to make room for more profit seeking via the proliferation of low-wage labor markets filled by dispossessed former welfare recipients and others who have not been able to support themselves via the market system. But just as welfare reform is playing out differently in different welfare states, the same may become true of asset-building policies. In the United States, these policies are possibly tied too tightly to reinforcing an emphasis on personal responsibility and self-sufficiency, something that Americans in large numbers know all too well given how they have reacted with ambivalence, if not outright disappointment, to the proponents of privatization of social security couching their arguments in the terms of asset-building discourse. Asset-building initiatives in such a context risk having as their major consequence reinforcing the idea that the poor need to change their thinking and behavior and start demonstrating they are competent, before we are obligated to help them overcome their poverty.

In the end, Michael Sherraden's asset-building approach seems destined to suffer the same fate as the earlier culture of poverty argument. It is doomed to be assimilated into the structures of power in a liberal, individualistic, capitalistic society where the failure of the poor to do the impossible and pull themselves up by their bootstraps become the basis for blaming them for the poverty society forces them to endure. Researching the asset-building approach within the constraints of a positivistic research paradigm that focuses on individual behavior to the exclusion of structural considerations has undoubtedly reinforced this neglect of the original concerns of the asset-building perspective about the structural sources of wealth inequality. The victim-blaming logic of the culture of poverty argument dies hard in the land of rugged individualism. While the asset-building approach started out as a way to get social change within the society as structured, it ends in reinforcing that structure. This seems to be the case in the United States at least, where more progressive versions of state-subsidized asset building are not likely to be developed under the hyperindividualistic, capitalistic banner of an "ownership society."

We should therefore take heart from developments in Europe, even in the United Kingdom, which has gone the farthest in mimicking U.S. welfare reform. Their asset-building is much more supportive. Europeans, on the whole, are more skeptical, it seems, with the idea that we should repeal welfare altogether and replace it with a system for promoting personal responsibility. Europeans, on the whole, have a stronger commitment to the welfare state and a stronger sense that all citizens have, by virtue of their birthright, entitlement rights to be supported to live at some minimal level of decency. And you could argue that because of this, they have less poverty, less crime, less violence, longer life expectancy, and so on. You would think we could begin to learn from them. Starting with developing asset-building policies that reinforce solidaristic commitments to ensure all families can thrive rather than using these initiatives as a wedge to undermine what limited commitments our welfare state makes to its citizenry.

6 Deconstructing Dependency
Heading Toward a Counter-Discourse

Not too long ago, at the end of a somewhat rambling presentation on the rolling retrenchment in U.S. social welfare policy in the era of globalization, a member of my academic audience asked me the proverbial academic question: "What is your method?" I paused, having reluctantly to switch gears from policy analyst to methodologist, and then replied, "...Aphasia!"

A couple of thoughts inspired this response. I remembered reading Frederic Jameson's argument that postmodern political thought was a noncritical manifestation of the confusion of our postmodern times and the resulting indeterminacy.[1] Jameson in good part meant this as a criticism of how postmodernist thinking encourages emphasizing the undecidability of truth questions. I subsequently commented on Jameson's criticism in an article, saying that starting with the uncertainty wrought by the postmodern condition enabled us to appreciate the lack of objective foundations for all truth claims.[2] I also remembered reading Slavoj Žižek's suggestion that there is merit in the idea that we should enjoy our symptom, which I chose to interpret as allowing our uncertainty to be the beginning of insight into the impossibility of knowing the absolute truth of things.[3] For Žižek, enjoying our symptom applied most particularly in the paradigmatic case of the interpellated human subject. Žižek saw the self as an aftereffect that retroactively sutures the gap at the center of human existence, covering our indeterminacy with the illusion that there was a true self that was always there before we acted. The self was a symptom that did not point back to a preexisting reality but instead was a necessary illusion operating post hoc as a retroactive unifying structuring principle. It implied that all of these symptoms were not so much

1. Frederic Jameson, *Postmodernism: Or the Cultural Logic of Late Capitalism* (New York: Verso Press, 1991).
2. See Sanford F. Schram, "The Postmodern Presidency and the Grammar of Electronic Electioneering," *Critical Studies in Mass Communication* (June 1991): 210–16.
3. Slavoj Žižek, *The Sublime Object of Ideology* (New York: Verso Press, 1989).

ephemeral traces of our underlying true human nature but rather were as close as we could ever get to a true self that allegedly gave rise to the symptoms in the first place. Symptoms implied their own cause in circular fashion. The discourse of the self spoke us as much as we spoke it.

We might then want to argue that aphasia was a language dysfunction whose symptoms implied an underlying condition after the fact rather than being a condition that gave rise to the symptoms in the first place. If that were the case, then it might indeed be best to concentrate on studying the symptoms of aphasia rather than trying to first know aphasia as an underlying condition. One can suggest that in a similar way this is what Roman Jakobson decided should be done to understand the underlying structuring principles of language.[4] Jakobson pursued the topic of aphasia in great depth in his quest to understand how language operates. In his case, it could be argued that he believed that by studying what happens when language speaking breaks down, he could understand better how it operates when it works as it should.

Aphasia for Jakobson was the inability to say certain words due to some impairment, often caused by severe physical trauma such as a stroke, that resulted in impairment of the speaker's use of fundamental aspects of language. Jakobson saw aphasia operating along two axes: the paradigmatic, which involved metaphor, and the syntagmatic, which involved metonymy. Metaphors compared how what we were referencing were similar or different when choosing between categories, such as "cat" compared with "dog." Metaphors operated along the paradigmatic axis, where a signifier referenced a signified object. An aphasic who lost the ability to say when something was similar to something else suffered a similarity disorder and could not relate a signifier to what is being signified. Metonymies implied that contiguities that are associated with each other, such as "smokes" for "cigarettes," operated along the syntagmatic axis of language where a signifier pointed to another signifier, and an aphasic who suffered a contiguity disorder would not be able to follow one signifier to the next, often not being able to complete sentences.

---

4. Roman Jakobson, "Two Aspects of Language and Two Types of Aphasic Disturbances," *The Norton Anthology of Theory and Criticism*, Vincent B. Leitch, ed. (New York: Norton, 2001), pp. 1265–71. Also see Michael Issacharoff, "Roman Jakobson," in *Johns Hopkins Guide to Literary Theory and Criticism*, Michael Groden and Martin Kreiswirth, eds. (Baltimore: Johns Hopkins University Press, 1997) (http://www.press.jhu.edu/books/hopkins_guide_to_literary_theory/g-about_guide.html). It can be argued that Durkheim, Weber, Freud, and Foucault, like Jakobson, studied the abnormal in order to understand the underlying principles that formed the structure for what was taken to be normal for various aspects of the social order.

Metaphors involve substitution based on a transfer of meaning across categories. Metonymy involved the relation of objects within a domain of contiguous parts. For Jakobson, these two dimensions were suggestive of the fundamental uses of language: selection and substitution in the case of metaphor and combination in the case of metonymy. When the metaphoric function failed, speakers lost the ability to select one comparison for another; they could not, for example, initiate a conversation and had to fall back on the contiguity function, enabling them to respond to what was already said. When the metonymic function failed, speakers lost the ability to syntactically follow one word after another to make sentences grammatical. The trauma that induced aphasia necessitated the switch from one fundamental function of language to the other. While people who suffered aphasia experienced many forms of the illness, for Jakobson they all fell between two poles.

In this way, Jakobson came to understand the central roles that metaphor and metonymy play in normal language use even as he studied them as the different poles of aphasia. Jakobson showed that the metaphors and metonymies of aphasia are not so much aberrations of language as they are central to its very constitution. Metaphor involved the condensation of meaning, and metonymy, its displacement.

The discourse of welfare dependency is an example of metonymy. The trauma of confronting our society's complicity in perpetuating the destitution of low-income families is papered over with the shift from talking about poverty to focusing on the contiguous condition of welfare dependency. This simultaneously reorients our attention away from the structure of society to the behavior of the poor as the cause for the poverty of low-income families. The metonymy of welfare dependency has been the dominant way of discussing poverty in the United States, especially in recent years. There was the anomalous time of the presidency of Lyndon Baines Johnson, in the 1960s, when poverty was discussed more in metaphor as in the need to wage the moral equivalent of war in the form of a "war on poverty." Yet, while the war metaphor is less likely to displace the problem of poverty by relocating it in the personal deficiencies of the poor, it substituted confronting society's responsibility for poverty with the suggestion that the society must attack some alien source of the problem by going to war. Johnson called his administration the "Great Society," but a *great* society would never ever be the source of an inequity as profound as the poverty that afflicted as many as one fifth to one fourth of the country's population, as was estimated at the time. And like the war in Vietnam during this time, the war on poverty could be terminated simply by the government withdrawing without ever admitting it had lost the fight. The war on poverty metaphor was almost as much a form of denial as was the welfare dependency metonymy. Yet, with the end of the war on poverty, welfare policy discourse returned to the dependency metonymy and refocused its attack on the deficiencies of the poor, all the more so as to not examine society's responsibility for the injustices that created that poverty. The aphasias of poverty discourse were a symptom of the United States' continuing denial to take responsibility for the social injustice inflicted on the poor.

In this chapter, I examine dependency as a metonymy of welfare discourse historically and contemporarily to demonstrate how it is complicit in forging new forms of governance from old practices. By governance, I mean those forms of power that are emerging in the current era of globalization whereby the nation-state increasingly relies on civil society and the private sector to both provide social welfare and impose social control, while it is increasingly constrained by international links.[5] I hope to show how dependency discourse deconstructs to provide an opening for contextualizing, narrating, and understanding the problems of welfare policy differently.[6] I do this in the name of trying to create critical resources not just to resist the oppressions created by the new forms of welfare governance but also to create more supportive social policies for the most disadvantaged in society today.[7]

Dependency Discourse in Historical Perspective

Drawing on the work of Margaret Somers and Fred Block, we can see that the roots of the dependency metonymy in welfare discourse are deep, stretching back over two centuries.[8] From before Thomas Malthus wrote

---

5. See Mark Bevir, ed., Encyclopedia of Governance (http://igov.berkeley.edu/proj ects/encyclopedia.html). Governance is closely connected to the disciplinary practices that Michel Foucault associates with what he calls "governmentality." See Michel Foucault, "Governmentality," in *The Foucault Effect: Studies in Governmentality with Two Lectures by and an Interview with Michel Foucault*, Graham Burchell, Colin Gordon, and Peter Miller, eds. (Chicago: University of Chicago Press, 1991), pp. 87–104.

6. On deconstruction, see Niall Lucy, *A Derrida Dictionary* (Oxford, UK: Blackwell Publishing, 2004).

7. On discourse as creating new headings that allow us to go in new directions, see Jacques Derrida, *The Other Heading: Reflections on Today's Europe* (Bloomington: Indiana University Press, 1992).

8. For an excellent exposition of this theme, see Margaret Somers and Fred Block, "From Poverty to Perversity: Markets, States, and Institutions over Two Centuries of Welfare Debate," *American Sociological Review* 70, 2 (April 2005): 260–87.

his infamous *Essays on the Principles of Population* in 1798 to after Charles Murray reiterated those arguments in *Losing Ground* in 1984, social welfare policy discourse has been dominated by what Albert Hirschman has called the "perversity thesis."[9] The perversity thesis in Malthus's hands combined classic liberal economic theory and Christian morality to suggest that contrary to the apparent reality that offering financial aid to the poor was a kind and charitable act of assistance, such interventions actually undermined the natural order of things and corrupted individuals who took such succor that they lost the ability to practice self-discipline and exercise personal responsibility. Helping people in this way actually had perverse effects. The perversity thesis has proved resilient even in the face of secularization. For over two centuries, at varying points in time and to varying degrees, much success has come to the perversity thesis and its cousin, the futility thesis—"the poor will always be with us" no matter what we do.

This success testifies to the power of discourse. Arguments like the perversity thesis can be persuasive independent of historical circumstances. The facts of "welfare dependency" at any time seem far less significant than the enduring power of the perversity thesis to appeal to ingrained moralisms of western, liberal capitalist societies about public aid corrupting the individual and undermining self-discipline. The facts of welfare dependency in this sense are always already there, ready to be materialized in quotidian practices of welfare administration. All it takes is a less than active imagination willing to unreflectively interpret welfare participation as if it were without question a sign of personal deficiency. Sadly, the modern history of the western world, especially in the United States and England, is replete with such instances of how an underutilized imagination can place whatever facts were offered about welfare use in terms of this argument about an unchanging underlying moral order.

And the facts of welfare dependency are less than apparent. No amount of facts to refute the myths of the alleged welfare dependency crisis could undermine the ideological juggernaut the right had developed to impugn the already sullied image of welfare recipients as malingerers and

---

9. Albert O. Hirschman, *The Rhetoric of Reaction: Perversity, Futility, Jeopardy* (Cambridge: The Belknap Press of Harvard University Press, 1991), pp. 27–42. Thomas Malthus made his perversity argument about public assistance in *Essays on the Principles of Population* (London: Penguin Books, 1985) [1798 orig.]. These arguments were revisited in the 1980s by Charles Murray, *Losing Ground: American Social Policy 1950–1980* (New York: Basic Books, 1984). Murray's book proved influential in building opposition to welfare that led to the reforms of the 1990s.

no-counts, lazily living off of welfare.[10] By the 1990s, when welfare reform was hotly debated, the mere recitation of factual evidence about contemporary welfare recipients was to prove woefully inadequate in the face of an argument that had endured for over two centuries and had convincingly encouraged people to ignore empirical information to appreciate the underlying natural order of things.

Therefore, dependency discourse in the United States is arguably paradigmatic of discourse in general. It provides an exemplar of how discourse operates. Like all discourse, it takes symptoms as signs of some preexisting underlying condition that it retroactively imputes as always already being there. From Malthus on, dependency discourse with its perversity thesis imputes a preexisting condition to the poor as already being there, giving rise to the poverty and welfare dependency that we see in the contemporary scene.

In the American context, the dominance of the perversity thesis has been near total, making the development of social provision for low-income groups an uphill struggle, occurring only episodically in response to economic crisis and political instability. Various writers have challenged the thesis, from Jane Addams beginning in the late nineteenth century to Frances Fox Piven and Richard Cloward in the 1960s. Yet, the need to continue that challenge is apparent given the resurgence in influence of the perversity thesis with the welfare retrenchment of 1996.

Challenges to the perversity thesis can begin with questioning its assumptions—all of them—from how there is an underlying natural order to things that must not be tampered with to how giving aid corrupts and undermines commitment to work and family values. A good empirical base can be invoked by pointing to the experiences of other advanced industrial societies that have far more generous terms of social provision and do not see the deleterious effects predicted by the perversity thesis. However, this kind of factual base is never dispositive. For instance, in this case, countries with stronger welfare states tend to have higher levels of unemployment.[11] Instead, what is needed is a counterdiscourse that can provide an alternative basis for interpreting the facts.

---

10. For an example of the attempt to provide facts that could combat the myths surrounding welfare use, see *The Basics: Welfare Reform* (New York: Twentieth Century Fund, 1996) (http://www.tcf.org/Publications/Basics/welfare/index.html). Also see *Welfare Myths: Fact or Fiction? Exploring the Truth about Welfare* (New York: Welfare Law Center, 1996) (http://www.welfarelaw.org/mythtoc.html).

11. See Benjamin I. Page and James R. Simmons, *What Government Can Do: Reducing Poverty and Inequality* (Chicago: The University of Chicago Press, 2000).

Comparisons with other countries are also pertinent in the quest for a counterdiscourse because they show the extent to which our forms of social provision are distinctively vindictive, given the high degree to which they are structured by the perversity thesis.[12] In comparison with other advanced industrialized countries, U.S. social policies are to a far greater degree structured to treat welfare recipients with suspicion and end up producing a self-fulfilling prophecy. Programs are designed to emphasize suspicion, surveillance, and a reluctance to provide aid except under the most extreme circumstances when people demonstrate that they are in desperate need for assistance. Cash, food, housing, and health care assistance for low-income families all have operated under this suspicion. This leads to targeted, means-tested programs that are designed to covetously guard against providing aid to families with incomes above strict cut-off levels. As a result, recipients must of necessity restructure their identities, conform their behaviors, and fit themselves into the system of assistance to make it seem that they are the most desperate of all and therefore should be provided with aid. Ironically, the conservatives who most complain about how our welfare system creates dependency are in fact responsible for creating such a self-defeating mechanism that traps people in a system that forces them to prove their deservingness by keeping themselves poor so that they can tap much-needed aid.[13] Only when we begin to give the poor a sense of entitlement and offer the support they need will we start to break the cycle of dependency about which conservatives are so concerned. This means moving to systems of assistance that rely less on suspicion and surveillance, less on targeting and means-testing. Instead, we need more universal programs. But we need to move to them in ways that will not jeopardize the assistance that targeted programs provide to low-income families.[14]

This then is the beginning of a counterdiscourse that highlights how dependency discourse is the self-defeating motto of a welfare system thoroughly grounded in the perversity thesis. It provides the initial outline of an argument that not only points to the fallacious reasoning of the perversity thesis but also offers a counterdiscourse that explains the same phenomenon in terms that create the basis for supporting more generous forms of social provision. Such a counterdiscourse does not so much try to

---

12. See Stephen K. White, "Narratives of the Welfare State," *Theory & Event* 1 (1997) (http://muse.jhu.edu/journals/theory_and_event/v001/1.2white.html).
13. See Sanford F. Schram, *After Welfare: The Culture of Postindustrial Social Policy* (New York: New York University Press, 2000), pp. 80–81.
14. See Somers and Block, "From Poverty to Perversity," pp. 286–87.

convince by way of facts as it provides an alternative basis for explaining facts. And it arguably ends up creating a potentially more enduring basis for achieving the progressive agenda.

Medicalizing Welfare Dependency

Today, the age-old perversity thesis is being reincarnated in highly technocratic ways for the new forms of governance.[15] Today, welfare policy discourse understands reliance on public assistance in highly medicalized terms by borrowing metaphors from other service domains that end up locating the causes of poverty and welfare dependency in the individual and her or his personal deficiencies. Today, welfare policy discourse medicalizes welfare dependency in the name of facilitating the disciplining practices that Michel Foucault calls "governmentality," whereby state power is disseminated through the social institutions of civil society to further promoting practices of self-discipline as needed by the emerging social order.[16]

The medicalization of welfare dependency is fast becoming a major administrative focus under the new welfare reform regime instituted in the 1990s.[17] It is as if the aphasia of welfare discourse prevents us from confronting the trauma of poverty. We use euphemistic substitutes like welfare dependency to paper over our complicity in perpetuating other people's destitution, while simultaneously shifting the blame from the structure of society to the individual behavior of those who are forced to live in poverty. With this old aphasic shift taking new form, welfare dependency becomes the center of our discursive terrain about how in the contemporary parlance of our therapeutic culture to "treat" recipients for their diseased condition of dependence on welfare. Welfare use beyond the shortest periods of time as a form of transitional aid, as say when a single mother relies on welfare while working through a divorce, is now considered an abuse. In other words, welfare use beyond a few months is now welfare abuse, signaling the need to undergo treatment to overcome one's dependency on welfare. The dependency metonymy is a displacement for other terms that, for political reasons, people cannot use. So in aphasic fashion, "welfare use," "welfare receipt," and the especially

---

15. See Schram, *After Welfare*, pp. 59–88.
16. See Foucault, "Governmentality," pp. 87–104.
17. See Murray Edelman, *Political Language: Words that Succeed and Policies that Fail* (New York: Academic Press, 1977), pp. 57–76, for an analysis of therapeutic discourse.

verboten "welfare taking" are being replaced by "welfare dependency." As a result, reliance on welfare is articulated as a sign that a single mother suffers from welfare dependency, which like other dependencies is something from which the client needs to be weaned by way of the appropriate therapeutic treatment. Under welfare reform, all applicants for assistance are screened, diagnosed, assessed, and referred for the appropriate treatment so as to accelerate the process by which they can overcome their vulnerability for being dependent on welfare.

A major preoccupation in welfare reform as a new form of governance is assisting recipients to overcome "barriers" to self-sufficiency. "Barriers," contrary to the term's ostensible meaning, is most often construed under welfare reform as personal problems.[18] Further, more and more programming under welfare reform is concentrated on what are seen as the related conditions that give rise to welfare dependency, be they mental health issues, behavioral problems, addictions, etc.[19] Self-esteem classes and psychological counseling have become common features of welfare-to-work programs. And as more and more of the welfare population exits under welfare-to-work programs that require recipients to make "rapid attachment" to paid employment in the labor force, the remaining population is increasingly composed of recipients who do indeed incur certain personal problems at high rates. Rates for depression among the welfare reform population have been growing for some time. This ironically reinforces the medicalized character of welfare dependency as if it were a real phenomenon that was in fact always already there, as if most recipients were always suffering from the illness of welfare dependency and its related medicalized conditions. Just like any good discourse, "welfare dependency" becomes its own self-fulfilling prophecy, making itself real, manufacturing the reality that it claimed preexisted it. Reliance on welfare is then seen less as an economic problem and more as a mental health issue.

Borrowing the dependency metaphor from other medicalized discourses is, however, no historical accident.[20] The discourse of dependency grew out of an extensive campaign that began in the mid-1970s by

---

18. See Sandra Danziger, et al., "Barriers to the Employment of Welfare Recipients," *Prosperity for All? The Economic Boom and African Americans*, Robert Cherry and William M. Rodgers III, eds. (New York: Russell Sage Foundation, 2000), pp. 245–78.

19. See Sanford F. Schram, "In the Clinic: The Medicalization of Welfare," *Social Text* 62 (Spring 2000): 81–108.

20. The remainder of this chapter draws heavily on Sanford F. Schram and Joe Soss, "Success Stories: Welfare Reform, Policy Discourse, and the Politics of Research," *The Annals of the American Academy of Political and Social Science* 577 (September 2001): 49–65.

corporate interests to roll back the welfare state. Part of the campaign to discredit the welfare state was economic: the welfare state was seen as producing higher taxes, increased business regulation, heightened inflation, lower productivity, decreased work effort, and a growing government deficit. Welfare retrenchment was needed to increase the efficiency of local economies and to enable the United States to remain competitive globally. A major economic goal was to push the poor off welfare and into low-wage work so that employers could simultaneously lighten their tax burden and prevent the development of a labor force that could rely on the security of welfare state protections to more aggressively bargain for better wages.[21] Yet, the campaign was not strictly economic. Moral conservatives added a cultural dimension to the attack on the welfare state as part of a broader countermovement against changes in gender and race relations, consumption patterns, and sexual and familial norms that they saw as evidence of moral decline.[22]

In addition, starting in the 1980s, private foundations with extensive funding from corporations and selected wealthy families who had a morally conservative agenda supported the work of a number of critics whose writings reemphasized the age-old perversity thesis and its argument that helping the poor only mired them in a life of welfare dependency, passivity, and personal irresponsibility.[23] Government officials who saw political rewards to be gained in attacking federal welfare programs joined the chorus and emphasized devolving responsibility for welfare to states and localities. Advocates for low-income families were forced to defend an unpopular program that they perceived as inadequate but did so in ways that failed to establish a positive alternative to "dependency" as the frame for understanding welfare use by the poor.

Further, as more working- and middle-class mothers were able to find paid employment because it became more acceptable for women to work, single mothers who remained on welfare were increasingly at risk of being viewed as people who did not adhere to dominant work or family values. This perspective overlooked that many mothers were forced into the paid

21. See Frances Fox Piven, "Globalization, American Politics, and Welfare Policy," in *Lost Ground: Welfare Reform, Poverty and Beyond*, Randy Albelda and Ann Withorn, eds. (Cambridge: South End Press, 2002), pp. 27–42.

22. See Barbara Ehrenreich, "The New Right Attack on Social Welfare," in Frances Fox Piven, Richard A. Cloward, Barbara Ehrenreich, and Fred Block, *The Mean Season: The Attack on the Welfare State* (New York: Pantheon Books, 1987), pp. 161–93.

23. See Jean Stefancic and Richard Delgado, *No Mercy: How Conservative Think Tanks and Foundations Changed America's Social Agenda* (Philadelphia: Temple University Press, 1996).

labor force due to declines in the real value of their husbands' wages and that a significant minority of single mothers on welfare were already working, if most often part-time, as they supplemented their wages with welfare while assuming responsibility for breadwinning as well as home-making on their own. All of this was swept under the rug by a dependency discourse that redefined single mothers on welfare as pathologically de-pendent and in need of a paternalistic form of treatment to wean them from their irresponsible addiction to public aid.

This political campaign against welfare was strikingly successful in laying the groundwork for the eventual passage in the 1990s of welfare reform legislation that significantly retrenched public assistance to low-income families and individuals. Yet, the campaign's success was not because it changed fundamental attitudes about welfare, which remained ambivalent.[24] Even after the campaign ended, most Americans still did not in principle oppose government assistance for low-income families and in fact continued to believe that we have a collective obligation to help the poor. For instance, 70 to 90 percent of Americans indicate they support government assistance for the poor and believe the government has a responsibility to guarantee every citizen food to eat and a place to sleep.[25] At the same time, most Americans also continued to believe that those in need should receive assistance only if they maintain a commitment to personal responsibility and the work ethic.[26] The campaign against wel-fare dependency was successful not because it changed this mix of atti-tudes but rather because it reframed the issue to focus on welfare dependency as a problem that needed immediate treatment. The problem of dependency came to be seen as a major source of society's economic as well as social and cultural ills. It increasingly came to be seen as creating a significant drain on the economy even as it encouraged out-of-wedlock births, single-parent families, and a decline in the work ethic. The de-pendency frame saw public assistance not a hard-won protection *for* poor workers and their families; instead, it viewed welfare as a policy imposed *against* workers' values as well as their bank accounts.

---

24. See Jean Hardisty and Lucy A. Williams, "The Right's Campaign against Welfare," in *From Poverty to Punishment: How Welfare Reform Punishes the Poor* (Oakland: Applied Research Center, 2002), pp. 53–72.

25. See Martin Gilens, *Why Americans Hate Welfare: Race, Media, and the Politics of Antipoverty Policy* (Chicago: University of Chicago Press, 1999), p. 37.

26. See Stanley Feldman and John Zaller, "The Political Culture of Ambivalence: Ideological Responses to the Welfare State," *American Journal of Political Science* 36 (1992): 268–307.

This "us versus them" reframing of welfare was facilitated by the fact that welfare was at this time also increasingly being depicted in the mass media in highly misleading racial terms and imagery.[27] As a result, the public started to grossly exaggerate the extent to which blacks received public assistance and in turn became increasingly critical of welfare as a program for poor blacks who were not like most white middle-class families and were not adhering to work and family values. Racial resentments and old stereotypes of black laziness became more influential in spawning growing hostility toward welfare.

The reframing of the welfare issue as a problem of dependency concentrated in a black underclass involved the policy equivalent of a Gestalt switch whereby the same facts came to be seen through a new lens, leading to a different interpretation. In an earlier era, liberals had framed "troubling" behaviors among the poor as products of poverty and used images of social disorganization, especially among poor blacks, as evidence for the necessity of extending aid.[28] The conservative campaign against welfare dependency, however, reframed these same behaviors as products of "permissive" social programs that failed to limit program use, require work, and demand functional behavior. Long-term dependency became a keyword in welfare debates, usually treated as part of a broader syndrome of underclass pathologies that included drug use, violence, crime, teen pregnancy, single motherhood, and even poverty itself. Gradually, permissiveness and dependency displaced poverty and structural barriers to advancement as the central problems drawing attention from those who designed welfare policy.

The discursive turn to dependency had important political consequences. First, welfare dependency and its effects on the poor set the agenda for poverty research in the 1980s and 1990s.[29] To distinguish myths from realities, researchers expended great effort to identify the typical duration of participation spells and the individual-level correlates of long-term program use.[30] Structural questions received less attention as defenders responded to critics in a debate that focused on work effort, program use, and poor people's behaviors. Second, as dependency came to

---

27. See Gilens, *Why Americans Hate Welfare.*

28. See Daryl Michael Scott, *Contempt & Pity: Social Policy and the Image of the Damaged Black Psyche, 1880–1996* (Chapel Hill: University of North Carolina Press, 1997).

29. See Sanford F. Schram, *Words of Welfare: The Poverty of Social Science and the Social Science of Poverty* (Minneapolis: University of Minnesota Press, 1995), pp. 3–19.

30. For example, see Mary Jo Bane and David Ellwood, *Welfare Realities: From Rhetoric to Reform* (Cambridge: Harvard University Press, 1994).

be seen as a cause of intergenerational poverty, it became a kind of synecdoche—a single part used to represent the whole tangle of problems associated with the poor.[31] To fight dependency was, in essence, to fight a kind of substance abuse that led to unrestrained sexuality, drug problems, violent crime, civic irresponsibility, and even poverty itself.

As a synecdoche for diverse social ills, dependency became the basis for a powerful crisis narrative in the 1980s and 1990s. Critics spoke of a "crisis of dependency," often in conjunction with fellow travelers such as the "teen pregnancy crisis" and the "underclass crisis."[32] As Murray Edelman explains, such crisis language evokes perceptions of threat, conveys the need for immediate and extraordinary action, and suggests that "now is not the time" to air dissent or seek deliberation.[33] Claims about the prevalence of long-term program use were often overblown, and images of wholesale social disintegration depended on highly selective readings of poor people's attitudes and behaviors.[34] But by applying the label of *crisis*, critics turned ambiguous trends among the poor (many of which also existed in the rest of society) into a fearsome threat to the values of "middle America."

Just as the "drug crisis" seemed to require a tough, incarceration-minded "war on drugs," the crisis of dependency called for nothing short of an assault on permissiveness. In this environment, poverty advocates who tried to direct attention toward issues other than dependency were seen as fiddling while Rome burned. Long-term program use was a major social problem requiring a bold solution; it called for extraordinary measures, not tepid liberal palliatives. The only suitable response was to attack dependency at its root by imposing a new regime of welfare rules designed to dissuade and limit program use, enforce work, and curb unwanted behaviors. In 1996, that is exactly what welfare reform did.

---

31. Synecdoche is associated with metonymy, part to whole as opposed to part to related part, and as such constitutes a form of displacement diverting attention away from the other object not being referenced—in this case, poverty.

32. Kristin Luker, *Dubious Conceptions: The Politics of Teenage Pregnancy* (Cambridge: Harvard University Press, 1996).

33. Murray Edelman, *Political Language: Words that Succeed and Policies that Fail* (New York: Academic Press, 1977), Chapter 3. In the 1960s, liberals used such crisis language in tandem with the militaristic metaphor of a "war on poverty"—a construction that cued anxieties about the costs of inaction while also suggesting the state's capacity to use its arsenal of weapons to achieve victory. See Deborah Stone, *Policy Paradox: The Art of Political Decisionmaking* (New York: W. W. Norton, 2002).

34. See Mark R. Rank, *Living on the Edge: The Realities of Welfare in America* (New York: Columbia University Press, 1994).

This reframing of welfare dependency as a manifestation of the pathologies of the poor, and most especially black, underclass created the political climate that led to President Bill Clinton to join with a Republican Congress to "end welfare as we know it."[35] The result was the Personal Responsibility and Work Opportunity Reconciliation Act of 1996 that abolished the 61-year-old Aid to Families with Dependent Children (AFDC) program that had come to be an entitlement. In its place, states were given block grants under the Temporary Assistance for Needy Families program (TANF) that could be used to provide cash assistance as did AFDC but quotas must be met in moving recipients into paid employment. In addition, recipients face work requirements, time limits, caps on benefits, and the possibility of sanctions when they do not comply with contracts they sign in which they promise to take steps to leave welfare for work. The purging of the welfare rolls that had started in the early 1990s with waivers that allowed states to experiment with some of these new restrictions increased after 1996 until the economy slowed in 2001. As a result, the number of recipients receiving what is now called TANF fell from 13,242,000 in 1995 to 5,334,000 in 2002—a decline of 59.7 percent.[36] And while welfare reform has been widely heralded as a success for this reason alone, it led most single mothers leaving TANF to be mired in poverty, earning on average no more than $7.50 an hour, often without benefits and most often with increased out-of-pocket expenses associated with taking paid employment, most especially for child care. These hardships were more frequently visited on black single mothers, who were also more likely to be forced off welfare by sanctions and more likely to have to cycle back on if they had time-limited eligibility remaining.[37]

Make no mistake about it—welfare was retrenched in no small part because of the way welfare dependency discourse had reframed this policy issue in gendered and racialized ways that made welfare use out to be a pathology that had to be treated therapeutically. Borrowing metaphors from allied arenas of service provision laid the basis for a veritable medicalization of welfare dependency as a personal pathology that required individualized treatment as much as any other behavioral problem. With

35. See Sanford F. Schram, Joe Soss, and Richard C. Fording, eds., *Race and the Politics of Welfare Reform* (Ann Arbor: University of Michigan Press, 2003).
36. *Statistical Abstract of the United States* (Washington, DC: U.S. Department of Commerce, Bureau of the Census, 2002), p. 354.
37. See Sanford F. Schram, *Praxis for the Poor: Piven and Cloward and the Future of Social Science in Social Welfare* (New York: New York University Press, 2002), pp. 144–9.

such a reframing, it became all the more difficult to see reliance on welfare as a product of structural problems in the economy or society. Public opinion was not so much changed as it was mobilized to support the retrenchment of welfare as the primary means by which we as a society could attack not just the scourge of welfare dependency but also the cluster of pathological behaviors with which it was associated.

Now, with the medicalized discourse of dependency firmly entrenched in public deliberations about welfare use, welfare reform has increasingly turned into the social policy equivalent of a 12-step program.[38] Rather than being a program to redistribute needed income to poor families with children, it has become a behavioral-modification regime centered on getting the parents of these children to become self-disciplined so that they will become self-sufficient according to ascendant work and family values. Increasingly, this behavioral-modification regime is implemented via public-private partnerships in which state and local governments contract with private, often for-profit, providers to move single mothers with children off welfare and into jobs and marriages.[39] The medicalized discourse of dependency logically calls forth new forms of governance that can practice the governmentality needed to regiment low-income parents into the low-wage labor markets of the globalizing economy. The net result is that poverty is displaced as the persistent underlying problem that it is and welfare policy comes to be focused ever more so on reducing welfare dependency as an end itself.

One way of looking at welfare reform is through the lens of aphasia. The tendency to assume the worst about welfare recipients reinforced the denial of poverty as the underlying cause of their dependency. That most welfare recipients were idle when they could be working was the common assumption that was reinforced, and offering them aid was viewed as only perversely encouraging the bad habit of idleness. In today's medicalized parlance, doing that was "sick," as Newt Gingrich and others noted in the years just before welfare reform was adopted by Congress.[40] A "sick"

---

38. For a more in-depth examination of welfare reform's medicalization as related to globalization, see Schram, *Praxis for the Poor*, pp. 201–40.

39. For an analysis of welfare-to-work programs that emphasizes how globalization discourse encourages not so much a "hollowing out" of the national welfare state as a rescaling of nation-state labor regulation via decentralized contractual relations with private, local service providers, see Jamie Peck, "Political Economies of Scale: Fast Policy, Interscalar Relations, and Neoliberal Workfare," *Economic Geography* 78, 3 (July 2002): 331–60.

40. Sue O'Brien, "Outraged Watchers Eye Newt," *The Denver Post*, December 10, 1995, p. D-1.

society that coddled "sick" people was one that perversely would throw good money after bad. From this perspective, it became that much easier to believe that if welfare recipients were treated for their condition, they could then begin to take their place in the workforce and begin to work their way to self-sufficiency, if not quite out of poverty. And while the rolls have declined and the labor force participation rate and earnings of former welfare recipients are up, the underlying poverty persists. The "welfare poor" have been replaced by the "working poor." And the metonymy of dependency continues to leave us in denial about poverty.

Conclusion

Tracking the aphasia of a dependency discourse that avoids talking about poverty and focuses instead on the misleading issue of the extent to which low-income families rely on welfare demonstrates the important political work that is done by discourse analysis.[41] It is a way to remain vigilant in an age of governance where power increasingly operates at this most insidious discursive level. Discourse analysis in this form is the melding of intellectual and political work to create critical resources for resisting oppressive social and economic policies in an age of globalization. It is arguably one of the more effective ways to highlight how the age-old suspicion of the poor becomes a politically convenient resource for underwriting collective inaction and outright denial about the structural roots of poverty and inequality in the contemporary globalizing society.

Studying the aphasia of U.S. welfare policy discourse can help challenge the willful ignorance about poverty that it encourages. It can also help track the spread of the dependency talk around the developed world so as to resist the globalization of this sort of denial that displaces concern with economic subordination and replaces it with therapeutic concern for treating the poor as deficient people in need of paternalistic policies that will regiment them into the emerging low-wage labor markets of the globalizing economy. In the process, the laboring population in general is sent a large symbolic message about the implied standards for being considered a full citizen within the nation-state in an era of globalization.

---

41. For the opposite argument that discourse analysis needs to be independent of politics, see Stanley Fish, "Why Literary Theory Is Like Virtue," *London Review of Books* 15, 11 (June 10, 1993): 11–5; and for the same argument even when it comes to welfare policy research, see Stanley Fish, "Why We Built the Ivory Tower," *The New York Times*, May 21, 2004, p. 23.

While the power of discourse is never complete, the dominant readings of dependency discourse need to be challenged by pursuing alternative ones that highlight the dignity and earnest efforts of those who are being marginalized as allegedly passive dependents content to subsist on welfare payments. Alternative readings can highlight how all citizens in the globalizing work-first regime are subsidized in various ways by the welfare state. Studying the aphasia of dependency discourse can enable us to highlight how it makes the relative distinction of who is dependent versus independent into a naturalized, reified difference that it does not deserve to be but which capitalist society so desperately needs to make appear to be real. In this way, we can show that while discourse is not the only force for globalization, its contribution is significant and needs to be challenged. Attention to discourse can help strengthen efforts to challenge today's injustices of welfare policy both locally and globally.

7 Compassionate Liberalism

Harm Reduction as a Postmodern Ethic for the Welfare State

The discourse of globalization creates new ways of reinscribing privilege and subordination by calling forth new forms of governance for regimenting populations into the emerging social order.[1] How should people respond to the implicit understandings of self and other embedded in the globalization discourse's preoccupation with welfare dependency? They need to identify those embedded biases, call them out publicly, and propose alternative understandings about how they should practice relating each other, one-to-one and collectively. In so doing, they can make the welfare state less exclusionary and tap its latent possibilities for more compassionate policies. Failing to challenge the discourse of dependency means failing to challenge the disciplinary practices of the new forms of governance. Without the critical distance needed to question that discourse, people risk continuing to be caught in a vicious cycle that alternates from episodic charitable responses to poverty to cracking down on the poor as deviants who need to be punished for their poverty.[2] The U.S. response to the Katrina hurricane disaster is but one prominent example.

Thanks to a long pre-Katrina ride to the beach with my wife, the title of this chapter was changed to "Compassionate Liberalism." President George W. Bush, relying on the writings of Marvin Olasky, has championed the idea that public policies should reflect a "compassionate conservatism," where social welfare provision is provided on the basis of concern for helping the less privileged develop the self-discipline to be

---

1. For consideration of how globalization has accelerated the marginalization of the homeless as a special case of those who are seen as failing to conform to standards of the self-sufficient self, see Kathleen R. Arnold, *Homelessness, Citizenship and Identity* (Albany: SUNY Press, 2004).

2. Both compassionate charitable services and the more punitive policies that flow from compassion fatigue are united by an underlying logic that sees the poor as "other," lacking "the right to rights," and therefore unable to access entitlements from the welfare state. See Leonard C. Feldman, *Citizens without Shelter: Homelessness, Democracy, and Political Exclusion* (Ithaca, NY: Cornell University Press, 2004), p. 6.

able to adhere to moral standards.[3] Compassionate conservatism practices "tough love." My point in this chapter is that the president's compassionate conservatism is by no means the only or best way to express that sort of emotional commitment to helping those who are left behind by the changes wrought by the globalizing market-centered society. In fact, I will argue that compassionate conservatism is but a convenient discursive practice for rationalizing the discipline meted out by the new forms of governance emerging with the global order.

I like the idea that public policy should be compassionate. Liberalism, with its emphasis on a social contract and rational-legal logic, emphasizes rights to entitlement. Yet, it is just such a discourse that has led people away from thinking about compassion as a basis of social policy.[4] Legalistic rights discourse puts in the background alternative ways in which those who have been marginalized or subordinated have claims on other members of the political community. Yet, as is often the case, those left behind socially and economically have in any actually-existing liberal order less than the full complement of legal rights to entitlements to address all their needs. Therefore, insisting that legal rights to entitlement be the sole basis for their getting to make claims on collective resources can doom many families to a life of poverty. Western liberal individualistic culture, especially as experienced in the United States, has led people away from recognizing the critical roles of emotion, caring, and loving compassion in structuring people's relationships to each other. People need to recognize that they have emotional bonds to each other as members of a human, if politically constructed, community, whether they choose to act on those emotions through public or private actions, via the national welfare state or the local community.[5]

---

3. Marvin Olasky, *Compassionate Conservatism: What It Is, What It Does, and How It Can Transform America* (New York: Free Press, 2000).

4. Marc Stears, "Challenging Politics: Contention, Coercion and the Study of Political Theory" (paper presented at the Annual Meeting of the American Political Science Association, Chicago, September 2–5, 2004), notes that liberalism has sought to emphasize reason rather than compulsion as the basis for the state.

5. On the generosity that comes from an openness to enchantment with even the modern rational-legal order, see Jane Bennett, *The Enchantment of Modern Life: Attachments, Crossings, and Ethics* (Princeton: Princeton University Press, 2001). On the need for a greater exploration about the role of love in political thought, see Kennan Ferguson, "I Heart My Dog," *Political Theory* 32, 3 (June 2004): 373–95. For love's role in social welfare policy and social work more generally from a postmodern perspective, see Louise Morley and Jim Ife, "Social Work and a Love of Humanity," *Australian Social Work* 55, 1 (March 2002): 69–77.

While it is indeed very important to think about the role of compassion in social welfare policy as a way of getting beyond the limitations of the existing social welfare state, it is important to understand the varieties of compassion. And when we do, we may find compassionate conservatism to not be the best way to introduce more compassion into the welfare state. To understand what I mean by this, we need to take a short trip through some issues of political philosophy. When done, we may come out in a very different place than did the person in the White House. It might not make everyone a practitioner of compassionate liberalism, but it might help create resources for resisting the disciplinary practices of the new forms of governance.

Liberalism, Tolerance, and Multiculturalism

The popularity of the epithet "bleeding-heart liberal" implies that compassionate liberalism is a redundancy not needed as it is in the case of conservatism. Conservatives are more often vulnerable to the charge of not caring about society's problems, therefore making "compassionate conservatism" either an oxymoron or a distinctively new and hybrid form of conservatism that emphasizes the tough love of getting the less privileged to adhere to moral standards. Compassionate liberalism, however, risks not only being a redundancy but also a parody. Bleeding heart liberals are attacked by some on the Right as allowing emotion to overcome reason, leading them to support misguided projects to engage in government-run schemes of social engineering that are well intended to address fundamental social and economic problems but are doomed to fail. Bleeding-heart liberals are attacked by some on the Left as allowing emotion to overcome reason, leading them to naively think that ameliorist public policies will be sufficient for solving those problems even though those policies do not attack the way the existing structure of society manufactures those social and economic problems.

In other respects, compassionate conservatism seems redundant and compassionate liberalism the oxymoron. Conservatives emphasize values like family values, appeal to traditions, and engage in a politics of emotion; liberals are often posed as the ones who resist emotional appeals and rely on reason.[6] And compassion is a strong emotion, suggesting intense

---

6. For an example of reason's association with liberalism, see Robert Reich, *Reason: Why Liberals Will Win the Battle for America* (New York: Alfred A. Knopf, 2004). Reich's penultimate chapter is, however, entitled "It Will Take More than Reason."

commitment. It is in this sense a "thick" concept implying a deep level of meaning.[7] The historical commitment of liberalism to tolerance arises alongside the struggle for religious freedom in 17th-century Europe and implies a "thin" concept suggesting a reluctance to feel so strongly about any idea or value that you would ever express righteous indignation toward others who do not agree with you.[8] You would think the tolerance of liberalism would lead liberals to resist strong emotional reactions or intense commitments to any idea or value. The preoccupation of conservatism with upholding moral standards of good and evil readily lends itself to intense commitments and strong emotional reactions, but liberalism's tolerance for moral ambiguity should lead to tempering emotion and commitment, making compassion a word that liberals would not use.

Yet, as studies in neuroscience suggest, emotion and reason may be more entwined than past thinking has allowed.[9] Further, compassion as an

---

Regarding conservatism's emphasis more on values than on facts, it is noteworthy that the presidency of George W. Bush has been characterized at one point as a "faith-based presidency" because of his claims to rely on his "instincts" or what he feels in his guts to decide major policy issues like whether to go to war. In the 2004 presidential election campaign, George W. Bush lost all three debates to his opponent, John Kerry, according to the polls, but his support in those same polls went up shortly after the last debate. Bush maintained his popularity with many faith-based supporters because they believed he was right in his beliefs and that was all that counts, irrespective of facts or rational argument. His inability to offer factual justifications for his policies probably endeared him further to his faith-based supporters, who saw it as further proof that he acted based on faith, not on facts. John Kerry may not have improved his standing with Bush's faith-based supporters in part because he demonstrated that he was perhaps too enamored with facts and rational argument, making him someone they could not trust. On the "faith-based presidency" of George W. Bush, see Ron Suskind, "Without a Doubt," *The New York Times Magazine*, October 17, 2004, pp. 44–45. Suskind notes that after an earlier article was critical of President George W. Bush, a member of the Bush White House told him: "You people are in what we call the reality-based community that believe[s] that solutions emerge from your judicious study of discernible reality. [But] that's not the way the world really works anymore. We're an empire now, and when we act we create our own reality."

7. Roland Stahl suggested the distinction between "thick" and "thin" concepts. On the related distinction of "weak" and "strong" ontologies, see Stephen K. White, *Sustaining Affirmation: The Strengths of Weak Ontology in Political Theory* (Princeton: Princeton University Press, 2000).

8. On liberalism's Calvinist roots, see John Patrick Diggins, *The Lost Soul of American Politics: Virtue, Self-interest, and the Foundations of Modern Liberalism* (New York: Basic Books, 1984). Also see Jeremy Waldron, *God, Locke, and Equality: Christian Foundations of John Locke's Political Thought* (New York: Cambridge University Press, 2002).

9. See William E. Connolly, *Neuropolitics: Thinking, Culture, Speed* (Minneapolis: University of Minnesota Press, 2002).

emotion is a diffuse idea that lends itself to ambiguation. Compassion does not necessarily mean intense commitment or strong emotional reaction that is dedicated to caring about others based on explicit moral standards, as is the case with compassionate conservatives who express a tough love for the needy by holding them to moral standards for their own good and not practicing the "soft bigotry of low expectations" as President Bush often called liberal tolerance.[10] Compassion is more diffuse an idea than what is represented by the conservative emphasis on caring for people by insisting that they be helped to adhere to moral standards. Liberals therefore can be compassionate as well, and they do not have to give up their interest in promoting tolerance or recognizing moral ambiguity.

Today, however, it is not sufficient for compassionate liberalism to be founded on the rock of toleration, religious or otherwise. The 18th-century Quaker colonists of Pennsylvania could still espouse a commitment of religious tolerance that would lay the foundation for later abolitionism and participation in the Underground Railroad to usher slaves on their way to freedom in Canada. They could as late as 1883 erect a statue of William Penn in a remote section of Philadelphia's massive Fairmount Park simply labeled "Toleration," as if that expression of liberal compassion for the other in and of itself defined Penn and the other denizens of his woods. Yet today, toleration bespeaks of a paternalism that suggests "we" tolerate "you," simultaneously reinscribing the boundary between "us" and "them" and privileging the "us" in we over the "them" in you.

Rather than toleration, a compassionate liberalism looks to the discourse of multiculturalism. Multiculturalism can be defined as a philosophy of recognizing and appreciating cultural differences, not so as to tolerate others of different cultural backgrounds than ourselves but to affirm their equal worth. As things would have it, multiculturalism itself has been maligned as a cooptive discourse of global capitalism. Slavoj Žižek rejects multiculturalism as producing a false, postmodern dialectic which bypasses the more fundamental class antagonism still persisting in our very modern society.[11] Instead, postmodern multiculturalism leads to various forms of repressive tolerance, inverted racism, respect without real love, and actual fear of otherness in all of its problematic diversity. The idea of multiculturalism is, for Žižek, an empty gesture implying a desire

---

10. See Chuck Noe, "Bush Decries Democrats' Soft Bigotry of Low Expectations" *newsmax.com*, January 9, 2004. http://www.newsmax.com.

11. See Slavoj Žižek, "Multiculturalism, or, the Cultural Logic of Multinational Capitalism," *New Left Review* 225 (September/October 1997): 28–51.

to change things for the better while actually working within the system to keep things the same. This may well explain why multiculturalism is so popular with private corporate foundations as a topic for grant projects—because it is consistent with the foundations' general orientation to promote ameliorist projects that make the existing society less unjust without actually changing the fundamental structure of that society.[12] Ultimately, for Žižek, postmodern multiculturalism leads to denying our need to create a politically constructed universality that enables us to challenge the hegemonic power of capitalism. Žižek writes:

> How, then, is this multiculturalist ideological poetry embedded in today's global capitalism? The problem which lurks beneath it is that of universalism.... That is to say, the "real" universality of today's globalization through the global market involves its own hegemonic fiction (or even ideal) of multiculturalist tolerance, respect and protection of human rights, democracy, and so forth; it involves its own pseudo-Hegelian "concrete universality" of a world order whose universal features of the world market, human rights and democracy, allow each specific "life-style" to flourish in its particularity. So a tension inevitably emerges between this postmodern, post-nation state, "concrete universality," and the earlier "concrete universality" of the Nation-State.[13]

Additional criticism of a politics of multiculturalism comes from Nancy Fraser, who notes that it reinforces a politics of recognition at the expense of a politics of redistribution.[14] Cultural identities become naturalized, and a sort of tribal politics sets in that is focused on which group has been most victimized. With such an orientation in place, we risk becoming preoccupied with less-than-fundamental slights to our presumed natural identities at the expense of overcoming our differences enough to forge political coalitions that can challenge power that continues to manufacture privilege and disadvantageness. Fraser proposes a politics of deconstruction that would not naturalize but rather deconstruct identities as a way to making the necessary political coalition building possible.

So, perhaps, a compassionate liberalism today might be best associated with a postmodern deconstructive politics that allows us to care for each other in all our diversity without essentializing or naturalizing those differences to the point that we lose the political capacity to act in concert

---

12. See Joan Roelofs, *Foundations and Public Policy: The Mask of Pluralism* (Albany: State University of New York Press, 2003).

13. Žižek, "Multiculturalism," pp. 40–41.

14. Nancy Fraser, "From Redistribution to Recognition? Dilemmas of Justice in a 'Post-Socialist' Age," *New Left Review* 212 (July–August 1995): 68–95.

to challenge the hegemonic power that systematically works to create disadvantage among us. For Fraser, this kind of deconstructive politics could be in service of promoting a postnational sensibility that is increasingly needed in an era of globalization with its increasingly porous national boundaries. It would inform efforts that point a politics of recognition of differences toward promoting a politics of redistribution of material resources in an era of globalization.[15] In this way, we can exercise care for people of various identities who are marginalized by public and private institutions, by the state and by the market, by social relations and by cultural practices—not due to their true primordial identities but because these processes of marginalization make them out to be subjugated peoples.[16]

Fraser herself states that the recognition/redistribution dichotomy does not exhaust the sources of social justice and injustice.[17] Drawing on Max Weber's tripartite distinction of status, class, and power, Leonard Feldman argues that while recognition points to issues of status and redistribution to issues of class, there is a need to consider issues of power, especially when it comes to how the welfare state works to include marginalized populations in the social order in ways that ensure their status (and class) as second-class citizens. Using the writings of Giorgio Agamben, Feldman highlights how the state is involved in policies that amount to an "inclusive exclusion" of the socially and economically disadvantaged, such as the homeless. He suggests that attention needs to be given to how both the services that are based on a compassionate concern for the marginalized and the more punitive policies that flow from subsequent compassion fatigue share an underlying assumption that marginalized populations, like the homeless, are not full citizens with, in Hannah Arendt's phrase, the "right to have rights" before the state. Perhaps, then, we need to consider that only when we go beyond the

15. Nancy Fraser and Nancy A. Naples, "To Interpret the World and to Change It: An Interview with Nancy Fraser," *Signs* 29, 4 (Summer 2004): 1103–124.

16. The politics of compassionate liberalism as described in this chapter draws its theoretical sustenance from William Connolly's preference for a multidimensional pluralism. For Connolly, pluralism is grounded in an ethic of "critical responsiveness" that transgresses political boundaries, including between the public and private, to contest settled categories of the privileged self over the marginalized other. William E. Connolly, *Pluralism* (London: Duke University Press, 2005), pp. 1–67, 131–60. For an analysis of how such a politics of pluralism can help resist state practices that marginalize the poor, especially the homeless, see Feldman, *Citizens Without Shelter*, pp. 134–37.

17. Feldman, *Citizens Without Shelter*, pp. 86–103.

recognition/redistribution dichotomy and begin to attend to how state power includes marginal populations in ways that reinforce their subordinate status, will we then finally begin to get the kind of public policies called for by what I am calling compassionate liberalism.

Harm Reduction as Postmodern Liberalism

Metaphors can serve as cultural resources in this battle to make social welfare provision more compassionate. George Lakoff has suggested that conservatism's insistence on upholding clear moral standards appeals to our culture's understanding of the role of stern father while liberalism's call for toleration appeals, if less compellingly, to our need for a nurturing parent.[18] Lakoff fears that conservatism has an advantage because of an ingrained need for a dominant father; however, he hopes that a more active use of the nurturing parent metaphor will resonate with the public and increase the appeal of liberalism.

Metaphors of care actually are quite common across a variety of discursive venues, from common parlance to expert discourses. Many of these metaphors mask a care that is actually a form of surveillance and are therefore in service of a more oppressive, modern, biopolitical state that ends up regulating the conditions of life in ways that denies them to many. Welfare reform is indeed a major arena for these inverted metaphors, as country after country designates its labor activation policies as policies designed to help people overcome their "social exclusion." Here, the metaphor of care operates to perform Agamben's "inclusive exclusion" by which the sovereign state gets to decide who is a citizen and on what terms, and which, in the era of the modern welfare state, has come to include the conditions of "bare life," because, given the state's reach, the very terms of inclusion today affect one's basic ability to live.[19]

Agamben emphasizes that the state's sovereign power to ban can brand some as the modern equivalent of a bandit so as to make their needs illegitimate issues for the state, as the round up of those left behind in

---

18. George Lakoff, *Moral Politics: How Liberals and Conservatives Think* (Chicago: University of Chicago Press, 2002); and George Lakoff and Mark Johnson, *Metaphors We Live By* (Chicago: University of Chicago Press, 1980).
19. Giorgio Agamben, *Homo Sacer: Sovereign Power and Bare Life* (Stanford: Stanford University Press, 1998), p. 8. Also see Barbara Cruikshank, *The Will to Empower: Democratic Citizens and Other Subjects* (Ithaca: Cornell University Press, 1999); and William Corlett, "Remapping the Danger Zones: Privilege, Need, and Their Necessary Exclusions" (paper presented at the Annual Meeting of the American Political Science Association, Chicago, September 2–5, 2004).

Katrina eerily demonstrated. Yet, Agamben also notes that the same power to exclude can specify the terms of inclusion such that others can be considered members of the political community and have their needs addressed but only on terms that reinforce their subordination. The power to exclude and include each partakes of an underlying logic.[20] So some people might end up suffering the ill effects of being regimented into the low-wage labor markets of the globalizing economy, all in the name of helping them overcome their "social exclusion." Still others are left to become homeless and vulnerable to being regimented into the burgeoning system of providing inferior, if highly regulated, shelter for those on the very bottom of the globalizing socioeconomic order.[21] Care like this only strikes fear in the hearts of those being served and makes them the first to appreciate how the "inclusive exclusion" operates to make some people second-class citizens. In this way, metaphors of sovereign care are suspect. There is an underlying logic tying compassionate aid and punitive policies that should make us wary of state-regulated forms of care.

Yet some metaphors of care are more deconstructive than others, or at least are more open to a less-insistent reading about who should be cared for and how. One such metaphor of growing cachet in social work is that of "harm reduction." Harm reduction is most commonly associated with drug treatment programs, especially those addressing the problems with heroin use. One of the most popular uses of the term is for describing needle exchange programs that help heroin addicts access safe and clear ways to inject themselves. Harm reduction brackets the more ambitious attempts to intervene, to detoxify, to overcome addiction, and therefore to change behavior. The more ambitions interventions often involve passing judgment and insisting that the people being treated conform to particular standards of right and wrong. These are features associated with many abstinence-only drug treatment programs but especially with faith-based programs championed by proponents of compassionate conservatism.

Regarding harm reduction as an ethic for treatment, Samuel A. McMaster writes:

---

20. For analysis of the underlying affinity between a liberal's penchant for compassionate services for the homeless and a conservative's preferences for more punitive policies to regulate the homeless, see Feldman, *Citizens Without Shelter*, pp. 19–20.

21. For discussion that uses Agamben to explain the shift from policies of compassion for the homeless to punitive policies that reflect compassion fatigue, see Feldman, *Citizens Without Shelter*, pp. 22–24.

[As stated in the National Association of Social Workers' Code of Ethics,] social workers respect and promote the right of clients to self-determination and assist clients in their efforts to identify and clarify their goals. Social workers may limit clients' right to self-determination when, in the social workers' professional judgment, clients' actions or potential actions pose a serious, foreseeable, and imminent risk to themselves or others. An ethical concern about the use of harm-reduction strategies is related to the limits placed on self-determination, because it could be suggested that the use of harm reduction may cause risks for clients.... From a harm reduction perspective, the social workers' superseding the clients' rights to self-determination would be viewed as paternalistic. Harm reduction and social work ethics require that clients be met where they are and not where the social worker or agency believes they should be....

No ethical dilemma [for social workers] seems to be created by using a harm reduction perspective. It could be suggested that harm reduction provides a better fit than an abstinence-only perspective to social workers' mandates to maintain a commitment to clients' needs and to facilitate client self-determination.[22]

It is probably naïve to think that harm reduction poses no ethical dilemmas. In particular, harm reduction practice, especially in drug treatment programs, tends to shift the focus from structural, institutional, and contextual issues to the individual and their behavior, risking neglect of the extent to which forces beyond the individual need to be addressed to provide effective treatment. Further, harm reduction practice tends to be conducted as a stopgap measure with abstinence remaining as the long-term goal, thereby undercutting the extent to which it actually is suspending judgment as to what is right and wrong.[23]

Yet, even with these qualifications, there is reason to suggest that harm reduction reflects an ethical sensibility that is attuned to the play of power that comes with politicizing the conditions of bare life and placing them under the purview of the state, furthering the state's ability to decide who is excluded, included, or included in ways that perpetuate their exclusion within the social order and how. At a broader level beyond the arena of drug treatment, harm reduction can be defined as all interventions to help people who are practicing certain potentially harmful behaviors to be able to continue to practice them if they so choose in ways that will reduce their harm. Because harm reduction, therefore, reflects a willingness to help people live more safely without trying to change their behavior, it has

---

22. Samuel A. MacMaster, "Harm Reduction: A New Perspective on Substance Abuse Services," *Social Work* 49, 3 (July 2004): 356–63.
23. Thanks to Roland Stahl for suggesting these limitations in harm reduction practice.

in it a suspension, if temporary, of moral judgment, a respect for another's integrity as a human being to decide for herself or himself how to live. It bespeaks of a compassionate liberalism born of tolerance and dedicated to caring for others regardless of who they are, what they believe, or how they live. Harm reduction, as its own form of multiculturalism, does not fulfill the insistence that people being served be made safe in the ways that the state ordains for its purposes. It resists providing sovereign care and creates an alternative space by which those being served can get services on their own terms.

Once we see harm reduction in these terms as an ethic of service rather than a specific modality of treatment, we can begin to see how it is a new term for an old practice. This way of extending the arm of the state to care for those in need but in ways that resist the state's increased power over the basic terms of bare life has been a subversive practice a long time in coming. While much of social work has unreflectively served the sovereign power of the modern state to regulate the basic terms of bare life, it is possible to see how much good social work over the past 120 years has all the marks of being informed by an ethic of harm reduction. Jane Addams' work in Hull House from the 1890s until her death in 1935 was for much of that time informed by a similar ethic. Addams resisted judging the people she served; she was dedicated to helping them live more safely and to achieve greater well-being, most often regardless of what it was that their marginal position in the industrializing city led them to do in order to create a life for themselves.[24]

The idea of harm reduction has affinities with democracy that go beyond their shared commitments to self-determination. Žižek emphasizes that democracy is best seen as a wish that only makes sense until it is realized.[25] The same could be said of harm reduction. Both harm reduction and democracy lose their power if we insist on them too much. They risk becoming their opposites. Such is the nature of discourse: things often become their opposite, especially if we insist on them too

---

24. See Sanford F. Schram, *Praxis for the Poor: Piven and Cloward and the Future of Social Science in Social Welfare* (New York: New York University Press, 2002), Chapter 2. Also see Laura S. Abrams, "Guardians of Virtue: The Social Reformers and the 'Girl Problem,' 1890–1920," *Social Service Review* 74, 3 (September 2000): 436. For a counterperspective that emphasizes the extent to which Addams and others associated with early social work with urban youth were caught in a politically conservative form of social regulation, see Anthony M. Platt, *The Child Savers: The Invention of Delinquency* (Chicago: University of Chicago, 1969).
25. Slavoj Žižek, "The Ongoing 'Soft Revolution'," *Critical Inquiry* 30, 2 (Winter 2004): 292–323.

much. Democracy implies the mobilization of the collective will of the people, which when it is perfectly and completely realized becomes its opposite—totalitarianism. The very idea of the "will of the people" is undecidedly ambiguous, available to be mobilized as the manifestation of a crowd that can be all-inclusive to the point of being all-oppressive. The crowd can be mobilized for good or ill, for collective representation or suppression. Mobilizing the crowd poses the potential for the terror of the irrational mob to dominate as much as it creates the prospect for democratic self-expression to occur. The same thing could be said of harm reduction, which, if it taken to the extreme, would produce a totally sanitized and policed environment where dangerous practices would be totally eliminated.

In fact, a frightening thought in an age of the administered society is a democratically mandated, state-run system of total harm reduction that regulates our every behavior so that we can never be a threat to ourselves and others.[26] Such a medicalized system is perhaps one possible nightmarish future given the development of the modern, biopolitical, welfare state. Yet, it is a future we can resist by practicing a less insistent harm reduction. The beauty of harm reduction is that it is not harm elimination, only harm reduction. There is humility and a sense of prudence in the idea of only trying to reduce, as opposed to eliminate, harm. Harm reduction can help inform the ways in which we can care for each other without regimenting ourselves into an oppressive system of social engineering.

Perhaps this is what makes harm reduction an exemplar of what I am calling compassionate liberalism. It bespeaks of the liberal commitment to tolerance rather than the conservative commitment to insisting on strict standards for distinguishing good from bad in moral terms. Compassionate liberalism practices a tolerance that is informed by a kind of situational ethics, resisting the temptation to judge right and wrong for all time in clear terms of command ethics.[27] Compassionate conservatism wants to help the poor by teaching them the difference between good and evil and then getting them to practice what is good and resist what is evil. Compassionate conservatism is interested in abolishing poverty by saving one soul at a time, usually through charitable efforts in the private sector. Compassionate liberalism is interested in helping people live better

26. See Agamden, *Homo Sacer*, pp. 119–88.
27. See William E. Connolly, *Why I Am Not a Secularist* (Minneapolis: University of Minnesota Press, 1999), pp. 51–53, for a discussion of a "politics of becoming" that is open to reconsidering standards of judgment on the basis of continuing to encounter the other as other.

without judging whether they themselves are engaged in practices or behaviors that are good or bad in absolute moral terms.[28]

From Truth and Justice to Love and Mercy

Agamben has forcefully reminded us that the law's indifference to those in need stems from the law's relationship to violence.[29] This becomes its own vicious cycle where applications of the law reinvoke its relationship to the violence that brought the legal order into being in the first place. The law is founded on extrajuridical acts of violence that exist outside the system of law itself, are unregulated by it, and are reiterated by the state as the possessor of all legitimate means of violence.

Agamben states: "The production of bare life is the originating activity of sovereignty."[30] Bare life, like the state of nature, is less a preexisting reality as such than a threat of a dreaded future possibility. Both are an aftereffect of the state, constructed for the purposes of legitimating the state by force rather than by consent. With Hobbes, Agamben sees the ultimate source of state sovereignty arising from its ability to extract compliance based on its ability to punish more so than its ability to claim willful consent. The criteria for creating the excluded citizen are the basis for determining the terms of establishing the included citizen.

Agamben revisits the theoretical differences between Carl Schmitt and Walter Benjamin writing ominously during the Nazi period in Germany between 1928 and 1940, debating the relationship of violence to the legal power of the state. Agamben notes that Schmitt famously defined the

---

28. Compassionate liberalism is consistent with Christian ethics of *agape*, to turn the other cheek, break the cycle of vengeance, and let others be, rather than insisting that "they" must become like "us" before we acknowledge their right to live. See Slavoj Žižek, *The Fragile Absolute—Or, Why Is the Christian Legacy Worth Fighting For?* (New York: Verso, 2000). On Christianity, cycles, and violence, see Lisa Saltzman, "Gerhard Richter's Station of the Cross: On Martyrdom and Memory in Postwar German Art" (presentation at the Franke Institute for the Humanities, University of Chicago, November 14, 2002). The ultimate breaking of the cycle of violence is to choose to die to avoid perpetuating it and Richter's painting cycle or series titled *October 18, 1977* can be read to imply that suicide might have been what selected members of the Baader-Meinhof Group chose once their terrorists efforts had come to naught. Jacques Derrida questions Friedrich Nietzsche's overly strategic assessment of Christ's willingness to die for the sins of all humanity when Nietzsche referred to it as the "stroke of genius of Christianity." See Jacques Derrida, *The Gift of Death* (Chicago: University of Chicago Press, 1995), pp. 114–15.

29. Agamben, *Homo Sacer*, p. 26.

30. Agamben, *Homo Sacer*, p. 83.

sovereign power that gives rise to the law as the power to grant exceptions as in a state of emergency. Agamben uses Walter Benjamin's critique of "pure violence" to highlight the violence involved in a prejuridical constitutive power that gives rise to the right of state-sanctioned violence under the law and is used first and foremost to preserve that right, even to the point of suspending the law in a state of emergency. Many have noted that this is but a paradox of sovereignty whereby the state presupposes its origins, thereby giving it power to use violence to maintain itself, as if its extralegal foundation in violence is legitimate under the law that only came after.[31] This insight lay at the foundation of Max Weber's hope for a discipline of sociology that could explain how it is that we might come to accept the tragic reality that the state is born of violence and we must find some way to authorize it as legitimate despite that. This is also Jean Jacques Rousseau's insight that this may require that the basis of the social contract is not consent by all the parties to it but by the state "forcing men to be free."[32] Agamben writes: "Just as sovereign power is presupposed as state of nature, that is then maintained in a relation of exclusion with respect to the state of right, so does it separate itself into constituent and constitutive power and still relates to both by placing itself in their point of indifference."[33]

In this way, the constituted state is able to be above the law, can suspend the law, can declare a state of emergency, and in general can exercise its power to grant exception from the law to itself and whoever else it deems should not be subject to the law. The extralegality of the state lies

---

31. The paradox of sovereignty is Sieye's "vicious circle" as well as being a paradox noted by Jean Jacques Rousseau and many others who followed him. See Bonnie Honig, "Declarations of Independence: Arendt and Derrida on the Problem of Founding a Republic," *American Political Science Review* 85, 1 (March 1991): 99.

32. On Max Weber's tragic view of the state as a creature of violence that needed to be legitimated, see Peter Breiner, "Translating Max Weber: Exile Attempts to Forge a New Political Science," *European Journal of Political Theory* 3, 2 (April 2004): 133–49. On Jean Jacques Rousseau's similar concern, see Stears, "Challenging Politics: Contention, Coercion and the Study of Political Theory," p. 10.

33. Giorgio Agamben, "The State of Emergency" (http://www.generation-online .org/p/fpagambenschmitt.htm). Just as for Agamben, the violence of the law banishes us from having contact with the realities of bare life; for Jacques Lacan, so does our entrance into the world of language force us to have a mediated relationship to the real via a fantasy realm we call reality. "According to Lacan, our entrance into language and into the intersubjective network of laws and conventions that language makes possible forever severs us from the materiality of the real. Forever after, we can only see the world (and our own bodily drives) through the fantasy version of the real that we call reality." Desire cannot speak its right name but surfaces via metaphor. See Dino Franco Felluga, "Primer for Buffy, 'Restless' " (http://web.ics.purdue.edu/ ~felluga/sf/pop/PrimerRestless.html).

in its extralegal violent birth that gives rise to a constituent power that in turn enables the state to impose the law and suspend it with equal legitimacy, given its monopoly on the use of legitimate violence. It then becomes a point of indifference that extralegal state decrees have in fact the same force of law as the laws themselves. Even state decrees declaring a state of emergency and all subsequent decrees once law has been suspended have the same legal standing as the laws themselves.

Rejecting both Schmitt's attempt to rationalize the state's ability to suspend the law as an illegitimate act of violence and Benjamin's notion of pure violence that invalidates such actions, Agamben writes from a tragic Weberian perspective:

> The Western political system thus seems to be a double apparatus, founded in a dialectic between two heterogeneous and, as it were, antithetical elements; *nomos* and *anomy*, legal right and pure violence, the law and the forms of life whose articulation is to be guaranteed by the state of emergency. As long as these elements remain separated, their dialectic works, but when they tend toward a reciprocal indetermination and to a fusion into a unique power with two sides, when the state of emergency becomes the rule, the political system transforms into an apparatus of death.[34]

For Agamben, the state of emergency is today the normal state of affairs where those who suspend the basic civil liberties necessary for democracy or use state power to undermine democratic electoral processes can claim that exceptional circumstances necessitate that they do so in order to safeguard democracy.[35]

---

34. Giorgio Agamben, "The State of Emergency" (http://www.generation-online .org/p/fpagambenschmitt.htm).

35. A painful contemporary example of a state regime founded on and governed by the logic of a state of emergency is the presidency of George W. Bush. Bush's election was widely considered suspect in no small part due to the massive disenfranchisement of voters, especially low-income and nonwhite citizens in key states such as Florida. Bush's ascendancy to the presidency was contested all the way to the U.S. Supreme Court. The court engaged in its own state-of-emergency logic to put itself in the position of the electoral process and decide that Bush would become the next president. Bush's foreign policies, especially after September 11, 2001, were premised on active efforts to misinform the public and abrogated democratic decision-making about the Iraq War. His administration's Patriot Act as a way to engage in surveillance against terrorism led to serious intrusions into the basic civil liberties of citizens as well as noncitizens living in the United States. And his reelection campaign in 2004 undermined basic democratic values and procedures in order to ensure his continuation in power. With Bush's presidency, the United States claimed to be taking the necessary steps to spread democracy around the world even while it undermined it at home and replaced it with a state of emergency that represented what we can call "authoritarian populism." Authoritarian populism uses appeals to

Friedrich Nietzsche also saw the real power of sovereignty not as the power to make law and enforce it but as the power to suspend the law if so need be. Or if simply so chosen, even when necessity does not require it. Yet Nietzsche asserted: "The justice which began with, 'everything is dischargeable, everything must be discharged,' ends by winking and letting those incapable of debt go free: it ends, as does every good thing on earth, by *overcoming itself.* This self-overcoming of justice: one knows the beautiful name it has given itself—mercy: it goes without saying that mercy remains the privilege of the most powerful man, or better, his—beyond the law."[36]

Jacques Derrida also argues that the system of justice is founded in extrajudicial acts of force that serve to give the state the ability to impose the "force of law."[37] For Derrida, the very system of legal rights is itself like any closed system founded by the force of a principle that is outside that system. Derrida sees the granting of exceptions as open to being used in a variety of ways, including acts of forgiveness, yet he is at pains to distinguish his analysis of forgiveness from Nietzsche's assertions about mercy.[38] While Nietzsche's mercy is a luxury the powerful can afford to practice at no threat to them, Derrida's forgiving is tainted when it is associated with sovereign power. The power to forgive then is ineliminably tied to the power to judge. What the sovereign gives it can take away. For forgiving to remain untainted, it needs to be disassociated from power.

With Derrida, then, we can imagine that it is the compassion of love for each other as much as the emotions of hate or fear associated with violence that is the outside extralegal force that gives rise to the legal system of rights. It might be better to suggest that the power of the state is a vexed contradiction born of violence but also reflecting the collective capacity to act compassionately toward those who cannot conform to the strictures of the law. It is entirely plausible because citizens have the capacity after a legal system of rights is up and running for granting exceptions, showing

---

mass support so as to legitimize patently undemocratic practices. It is a particularly effective way of legitimating the state of emergency for an undemocratic regime in a democratic society.

36. Friedrich Nietzsche, *On the Genealogy of Morals,* trans. Walter Kaufmann and R. J. Hollingdale (New York: Vintage Books, 1967), p. II: 10.

37. Jacques Derrida, "The Force of Law: The Mystical Foundation of Authority," *Cardoza Law Review* 11 (1990): 5–6.

38. Jacques Derrida, "On Forgiveness," in *On Cosmopolitanism and Forgiveness* (New York: Routledge, 2001).

mercy, providing compensation, and generally engaging in acts of compassion not required by the law or expected with the rights that citizens
receive under the law. The idea that the people as a collectively constituted political community can create a system of legal rights to entitlement is founded on the prior ability to grant exceptions to that system, to
forgive those who have violated its edicts, to show mercy to those who
cannot comply with its strictures, and so on. Derrida writes: "What counts
in this absolute exception of the right of grace is that the exception from
the law, the exception to the law, is situated at the summit or foundation of
the juridico-political.... As is always the case the transcendental principle
of a system does not belong to the system. It is as foreign to it as an
exception."[39] While Derrida writes of a messianic call to recognize our
ability to grant exceptions to the law and forgive law-breakers, his words
have direct relevance to my argument here that people should appreciate
the role of the emotion of love supplementing reasoned legal logic for
deciding what is a just set of entitlement rights.

Agamben agrees in that he seeks a return to privileging politics over law
as a way of resisting the inclusive exclusion that makes the law legitimate.
Through politics, people can resist the arbitrary character of sovereign
power today and choose to override legal injunctions that punish and
marginalize the excluded, all in the name of validating established power
of the included as legal:

> Any interpretation of the political meaning of the term *people* ought to start
> from the peculiar fact that in modern European languages this term always
> indicates also the poor, the underprivileged and the excluded.... The same
> term names the constitutive political subject as well as the class that is
> excluded—de facto, if not de jure—from politics....
>
> The rich nowadays wear plain rags so as to warn the poor that sacrifices will
> be necessary *for everybody*. And yet those who have any lucidity left in them
> know that the crisis is always in process and that it constitutes the internal
> motor of capitalism in its present phase, much as the state of exception is today
> the normal structure of political power....
>
> Such is the sense of the rule of the law over human life in our time: all other
> religious and ethical powers have lost their strength and survive only as indult
> or suspension of punishment and under no circumstances as interruption or
> refusal of judgment.... Nothing manifests the definitive end of the Christian
> ethics of love intended as a power that unites human beings better than this
> supremacy of the law. But what betrays itself here is also the church of Christ's
> unconditional renunciation of any messianic intention.... The task that
> messianism had assigned to modern politics—to think a human community

---

39. Derrida, "On Forgiveness," p. 46.

that would not have (only) the figure of the law—still awaits the minds that might undertake it.[40]

In order to fulfill the law, we need to transgress it, or so said Christ and such is the messianic tradition, as exemplified by Gandhi, Martin Luther King, Jr., and others.[41] Simply insisting on the justice of the law will never be enough; we need to exercise the mercy of love. We need to grant exceptions for those we have left behind by imposing legal standards of inclusion and exclusion. It is already recognized as part of the welfare state that policymakers and administrators have the capacity to grant exceptions to the rules when people's needs are not met. A greater appreciation of the critical role of such acts of compassion in making the welfare state what it is can help usher in a time when we can more readily grant exceptions beyond the law and engage in acts of compensation when the rules fail to produce the justice we think ought to happen. We can supplement justice's entitlement rights based on a rational-legal system with love's compassionate acts of compensation in appreciation of the violence the law does to us.

Take something as mundane, but profoundly critical, as the U.S. welfare system. Today, welfare reform imposes strict penalties on recipients for failure to follow through on plans to move from welfare to work. Nonetheless, like all social welfare policies, welfare reform includes the opportunity for case managers to grant "good cause" exemptions from the sanctions being imposed in cases where the recipient is seen as having

---

40. Giorgio Agamben, *Means without End: Notes on Politics* (Minneapolis: University of Minnesota Press, 2000), pp. 29, 132–35.

41. In some ways, compassionate conservatism shares with compassionate liberalism an interest in rising above the law in order to honor it. Yet, for compassionate conservatism this is done in the name of an adamant refusal to justify its principles via logical argument and instead is premised on a self-righteous insistence that it offers an unquestionable understanding of what is morally correct. Compassionate conservatism rises above the law to insist that we must righteously impose moral standards in ways that foreclose any debate and do not allow for any deviation. Compassionate liberalism rises above the law to allow for rational questioning regarding the imposition of moral standards. For a critique of President Bush's self-righteous thoughtlessness of an unwavering commitment to principles of good and evil, see Peter Singer, *The President of Good and Evil: The Politics of George Bush* (New York: Dutton, 2004); and Philip Green, "Neo-Cons and the Counter Enlightenment," *Logos* 3, 2 (Spring 2004). For a critique of the Bush administration's reliance on philosopher Leo Strauss's veneration of Abraham Lincoln and Winston Churchill's willingness to break the law in order to fulfill some higher moral purpose, see Nicholas Xenos, "Leo Strauss and the Rhetoric of the War on Terror," *Logos* 3, 2 (Spring 2004), http://www.logosjournal.com.

a legitimate reason and thereby justifying the granting of an exception. Social welfare policy is nothing if it is not about granting exceptions. The dirty little secret of public policy is not just the devil in the details but that those details are carried out by administrators who have substantial discretion to grant exceptions and vary and elaborate policy beyond its vague, if originating, specifications to a great extent.[42] It follows that the deviant case always proves the rule in public policy. Like studying the language dysfunction of aphasia to understand the underlying rules that enable language to function, by studying exemptions we learn about policy. The liberal, individualistic welfare state of capitalistic societies is always about deciding who is to be exempted from the expectation of having to work so that they can have their needs addressed by the welfare system.[43] Examining what passes for good cause exemptions tells us much about the built-in biases of social welfare policy, as when employer racial discrimination is not considered a legitimate excuse for failure to secure employment. In fact, most states under welfare reform do not explicitly consider employer discrimination a basis for granting a good cause exemption from being penalized.[44] Instead, it is more often than not something that is left unmentioned to be addressed by case manager discretion. What does that tell us about the built-in biases of welfare reform? By working on what gets counted as a legitimate exception, we can tap into the latent compassion already existing in the welfare state that allows case managers to exercise discretion and commit daily acts of mercy. This is classic social work as a politically inspired practice. The welfare state is vexed, simultaneously regulating the lives of the poor to get them to conform to the existing political economic and social-cultural order that calls for adhering particular work and family values, even while it extends needed aid to those families.[45] The state colonizes a space of compassion. Just as religion occupies the space of spirituality and erases its more pluralistic possibilities, welfare rules do the same to the latent compassion implicit in

---

42. See Michael Lipsky, *Street-Level Bureaucracy: Dilemmas of the Individual in Public Services* (New York: Russell Sage Foundation, 1980).

43. See Deborah Stone, *The Disabled State* (Philadelphia: Temple University Press, 1984), pp. 15–20.

44. Only California, Delaware, Kentucky, Louisiana, Michigan, and Vermont explicitly list employer discrimination as a good cause for an exemption from sanctions. Other states leave this issue to the discretion of case managers. See Center on Law and Social Policy, State Policy Documentation Project (http://www.spdp.org/tanf/sanctions/goodcause2.PDF).

45. See Frances Fox Piven and Richard A. Cloward, *Regulating the Poor: The Public Functions of Welfare* (New York: Vintage Books, 1971).

the very idea of welfare and our implicit commitment to caring for strangers.[46] We can practice a politics of exceptions that moves welfare policy toward a more pluralistic appreciation of all the diverse reasons why low-income single mothers might need to continue to receive welfare, perhaps even to the point of granting them not just exemptions but better and more supportive benefits.

Therefore, perhaps a better formulation is that while violence is the basis of all law, love is the basis of its resistance. We need to look for spaces in the law that love can occupy, so that we can exercise compassion for each other as others. To be sure, Agamben is right and the law is not only founded by violence and not only reiterates each time it is invoked, it is often used as a surrogate for violence, to maintain order, promote stability, regulate the allocation of resources, etc. The law in fact is used to prevent us from exercising compassion for each other and imposes the force of law instead for regulating how we maintain our social bonds.

Agamben insightfully however notes that the sovereign state does not arise out of some preexisting social bonds; instead, there is a political process by which the constituting power that gives rise to the state constructs a nativity to ground its nationality as if to make its *nomos* derivative from some *physis*. Agamben writes:

> It has been rightly observed [by Alain Badiou] that the state is founded not as the expression of a social tie but as an untying (*deliaison*) that prohibits. We may now give a further sense to this claim. *Deliaison* is not to be understood as the untying of a preexisting tie (which would probably have the form of a pact or a contract). The tie itself originarily has the form of an untying or exception in which what is captured is at the same time excluded, and in which human life is politicized only through abandonment to an unconditional power of death. The sovereign tie is more originary than the tie of the positive rule or the social pact; the sovereign tie is in truth only an untying. And what this untying implies and produces—bare life, which dwells in the non-man's-land between home and the city—is, from the point of view of sovereignty, the originary political element.[47]

The power that constitutes the state does so not by superceding some preexisting political community. It does not untie preexisting social bonds, nor does it act to formalize them. Instead, the constitutive power that gives rise to the state is better seen as the more originating political act, politicizing bare life, making the conditions of life itself an issue it was not seen to be before. It is only at this point that the idea of preexisting

---

46. Michael Ignatieff, *The Needs of Strangers* (New York: Viking Press, 1983), pp. 133–42.
47. Agamben, *Homo Sacer*, pp. 83, 90.

community becomes an issue for it itself is retrospectively imagined as the basis for the state. The allegedly preexisting community from which citizens come is an aftereffect of the state-constituted power.

While there is not a preexisting community that is the basis for resisting the state's usurpation of our ability to live as we wish, we can still hold the state accountable for the fantasy it enthralls us with. The law therefore can be bent by the loving compassion we have for each other that expresses if only a wish that we live together in peaceful relations in the imagined community we never had and which only the state has manufactured. That extralegal loving resistance to the communitarian lie of state power needs to be reiterated each time to challenge law's violent birth and the nonloving relations it gives rise to within the legal system. It is important to note that this need not lead to the false idolatry of compassionate conservatism's pretense that we can rely on the primordial community to care for ourselves. Nor should it lead to a naively unreflective support for a more intrusive welfare state that can regulate the basic conditions for life. Instead, we can resist both the pretense that there is a community that forms the basis of the social bond and the idea that the state is its legitimate heir. In so doing, a politics of loving compassion can maneuver within the law and without the worry that it is doing something unnatural to create a more compassionate welfare state, providing increased assistance to all who need it regardless of the limits of legal rights to entitlement at any one point in time.

Hannah Arendt writes: "Aristotle concludes that it is friendship and not justice (as Plato maintained in the Republic, the great dialogue about justice) that appears to be the bond of communities. For Aristotle, friendship is higher than justice, because justice is no longer necessary between friends."[48] Yet, for Arendt and Aristotle, communities do not preexist politics but are an artifact of its creating the means of mutual understanding. Therefore, it may be that there is something to the idea that justice will never be sufficient in itself to serve as a public standard for ensuring that everyone will get that to which they are entitled in order to live decently. Justice needs to be supplemented by the loving compassion that arises from a politics that fosters the emotional bonds such as those associated with friendship and community.

Yet, this is sometimes hard to see. Sometimes, perhaps increasingly so with the emphasis on the new forms of governance, it seems debates about the future of the welfare state tend to pose false dichotomies of public

---

48. Hannah Arendt, "Philosophy and Politics," *Social Research* 71, 3 (Fall 2004): 427–56.

welfare versus private charity that reinforce all of the other related distinctions I have been discussing.[49] Public welfare is based on law, grounded in the logic of legal reasoning as to who is entitled to what, granting them rights supposedly are enforceable in courts for purposes of ensuring justice. Private charity is an act of compassion, based on the emotion of caring for your neighbor, and it is a privilege to receive charity not enforceable under law as a right but instead to be accepted graciously when offered as an expression of love. This false dichotomy operates insidiously to erase from consideration the compassion that we can build into the welfare state by resisting its homogenizing impulses.[50] We need to learn to resist these dichotomies and promote a compassionate liberalism, one not tied to the limits of the liberal contractual order. This compassionate liberalism would not insist on developing entitlement rights as the sole way to provide succor to the poor. Instead, it would be willing to seek more ambitious forms of compensation for those who do not have their basic needs met by the limited entitlement state. It would not wait for the legal logic to be developed; it would rely on our love for each other to compensate for the deficiencies of the welfare state.

Of the dichotomous relationship between the state and international humanitarian organizations, Agamben writes:

> The separation between humanitarianism and politics that we are experiencing today is the extreme phase of the separation of the rights of man from the rights of the state. In the final analysis, however, humanitarian organizations—which today are more and more supported by international commissions—can only grasp human life in the figure of bare or sacred life, and therefore, despite themselves, maintain a secret solidarity with the very powers they ought to fight. It takes only a glance at the recent publicity campaigns to gather funds for refugees from Rwanda to realize that here human life is exclusively considered (and there are certainly good reasons for this) as sacred life—which is to say, as life that can be killed but not sacrificed—and that only as such is it made into the object of aid and protection. The "imploring eyes" of the Rwandan child, whose photograph is shown to obtain money but who "is now becoming more

---

49. For an attempt from the Left to imagine a more ambitious nonstatist approach to the problems of poverty, see Arjun Appadurai, "Deep Democracy: Urban Governmentality and the Horizon of Politics," *Public Culture* 14, 1 (Winter 2002): 21–46. Appadurai details what he calls the "federation model" for building networks of local self-help and advocacy with global links as exemplified by the National Slum-Dwellers' Federation in the city of Mumbai, in the state of Maharashtra, in western India.

50. See Feldman, *Citizens without Shelter*, pp. 132–34, for a critique of Michael Walzer, *Spheres of Justice: A Defense of Pluralism and Equality* (New York: Basic Books, 1983), for promoting an "art of separation" that risks marginalizing compassion to the private sphere.

and more difficult to find alive," may well be the most telling contemporary cipher of the bare life that humanitarian organizations, in perfect symmetry with state power, need. A humanitarianism separated from politics cannot fail to reproduce the isolation of sacred life at the basis of sovereignty, and the camp, which is to say, the pure space of exception—is the biopolitical paradigm that it cannot master.... The [figure of the] refugee...calls into question the fundamental categories of the nation-state,...and...makes it possible to clear the way for a long-overdue renewal of categories in service of a politics in which bare life is no longer separated and excepted, either in the state order or in the figure of human rights.[51]

The biopolitical welfare state increasingly raises the threshold for what is life within that regime, deepening the distinction between life inside and outside the regime, making it harder to overcome the walls that cordoned off life inside the regime from the bare life that is left outside, and leaving it increasingly to extrastate, humanitarian organizations to provide charitable aid in emergencies to those who are left out.[52] In this way, the biopolitical welfare state proliferates new forms of governance that exchange aid for discipline. Rather than providing economic redistribution through state entitlements, the biopolitical welfare state relies on service programs in the private sector, often in the name of charity, increasingly by religious organizations providing "faith-based" services, to inculcate the right values and teach self-discipline as the solutions to poverty and deprivation.[53] The process creates people who, as Arendt has put it, are without "the right to have rights."[54] In this way, the humanitarian organizations become the perfect supplement to the sovereign power of the modern biopolitical welfare state, enabling it to ignore the calamities of bare life that it has excluded from its purview. The supplements these humanitarian organizations provide become the new forms of governance for disciplining populations in an era of globalization.

Under these conditions, compassionate conservatism is a rationalizing agent for the new forms of governance. It helps rationalize the idea that people are without rights to having their basic needs addressed by the state,

51. Agamben, *Homo Sacer*, pp. 129–30.
52. For an analysis of how the rise of contractual discourse in the welfare state produced charity as its marginalized other, see Nancy Fraser and Linda Gordon, "Contract Versus Charity: Why Is There No Social Citizenship in the United States?" *Socialist Review* 92, 3 (1992): 59.
53. See Maia Szalavitz, "Why Jesus Is Not a Regulator," *The American Prospect* 12, 6 (April 9, 2001).
54. See Hannah Arendt, *The Origins of Totalitarnianism* (San Diego: Harcourt Brace, 1973), p. 296.

as Katrina demonstrated. Assistance via the private sector becomes a dangerous form of compassion that compensates for the lack of rights but in a way that continues the denial of those rights. Instead, those in need are left with the options of either the soft love of charity or the tough love of discipline, both provided privately and in ways that reinforce that they do not have entitlement rights. For instance, charitable policies based on compassion for the homeless and punitive policies based on the compassion fatigue that have followed share the idea that the homeless do not have the right to have rights.[55] Only by resisting this diabolical divide that works in tandem to reproduce a state of neglect for human well-being can we begin to bring compassion for life back into the state and the system of rights.

The false dichotomy between charity and entitlement is underscored when we see them both as gesturing toward what Derrida says is the impossibility of the gift.[56] Derrida's analysis of the gift enables us to demonstrate that both private charity and public entitlements are essentially counterfeit gifts that fail to capture the full meaning of giving. Derrida notes that it is more than a coincidence of language that in English the moment in time that we call "now" is referred to as "the present." For Derrida, the ultimate present you can give anyone is time, but not just any time, instead the time to be here now, in the present, free from the debts of the past and without future obligations. To forgive past debts as if to not even know they existed and to give the opportunity to be free in the present without obligations for what comes in the future is to give the ultimate gift. Yet, private charity is no more like this than public entitlements, both of which are highly stylized, one ritualized by customs of private exchange and the other formalized by the rules of law and justice. Both private charity and public entitlements have their own sense of reciprocity. For this reason, they are both at best simulacra of the idea of a gift. Not real gifts, neither is free and neither makes us free. Both need to be supplemented with the compassionate love and mercy that forgives past debts and forgets any future obligations.

One specific mechanism for introducing a more politically effective compassion into the welfare state is to rethink the dichotomy between entitlements and compensation.[57] Entitlements are a form of melancholy, acting proactively to protect citizens from possible risks to their economic

---

55. See Leonard Feldman, *Citizens Without Shelter*, pp. 1–24.

56. Jacques Derrida, *Given Time: I. Counterfeit Money* (Chicago: University of Chicago Press, 1992), p. 29.

57. Ralph Waldo Emerson appreciated the need for compensation. He followed his oft-cited essay on self-reliance with an essay on compensation. See Ralph Waldo

security. Compensation is a form of mourning, granted after the fact as an act of compassionate charity for those who have already been wronged. In the welfare state, entitlements rights are superior to compensation, which is seen as a lesser benefit for those who have not earned the rights to entitlements. Entitlements are seen as national, universal benefits of relatively high value given to citizens on the basis of some criterion that says they have earned the right to that entitlement, whereas compensation is a form of a handout given to people in need, almost as if it were an act of charity extended as a privilege, not as a right. Yet, the example of unemployment benefits is an interesting mixed case, often in the past referred to as both unemployment insurance and unemployment compensation, pointing its indeterminate status as a not quite complete entitlement that is increasingly hard to secure as needed.[58] In fact most entitlements, including Social Security retirement benefits, which are seen as the touchstone for entitlements, are not pure entitlements but have characteristics like compensation, targeting benefits based on need, limiting access to selected populations, conditioning benefits on the basis of behavioral requirements, and thereby undermining that entitlements are extended strictly on the basis of right. Social Security retirees are widely recognized as having an entitlement right to their benefits because they have earned them; however, many retirees receive benefits well beyond what they have paid in. Further, the case could be made that we subsidize Social Security benefits of the retirement population in this way as compensation for their not working in order to create more employment opportunities for the pre–retirement age workers. Therefore, the entitlement/compensation distinction deconstructs and arguably all entitlements can be said to be forms of compensation where we choose to extend aid to people for reasons other than that they strictly have a right to that benefit. Therefore, even the entitlement state can be said to be based on more than rational-legal reasoning but is also animated by the emotional impulses that flow from compassion to help those in need even if they strictly speaking do not have a right to that assistance.

Emerson, *Essays: First Series* (Boston: J. Munroe and Company, 1847). Emerson talks of compensation as a rebalancing of a natural equilibrium that is implicit in the order of things, including the social order. In Emerson's words, this rebalancing is motivated by love of our fellow man. Also see Thomas Dumm, *A Politics of the Ordinary* (New York: New York University Press, 1999), pp. 71–89; and Andrew Ross, *Real Love* (New York: New York University Press, 1998), pp. 189–216.

58. See Michael Katz, *The Price of Citizenship: Redefining the Welfare State* (New York: Metropolitan Books, 2001), pp. 222–31.

The compassionate impulse to compensate is tied to the relationship of the included to the excluded. Phillipe van Parijs takes the idea of compensation a step further when he underscores that the employed class of workers owes a debt to the unemployed and should compensate them via welfare benefits.[59] The employed gain access to wages and social welfare benefits, in the form of privately provided health insurance and pensions and still other subsidies, by virtue of their employment. This employment in benefit-providing jobs is made possible by the regulation of the economy that includes policies designed to ensure economic stability that inevitably prevent the necessary number of such jobs being created for all who need them. Attempts to curb inflation, as well as panoply of other policies that allow employers not to have to create more jobs than are profitable, help perpetuate a chronic shortage of such jobs. As a result, the employed owe a debt to the unemployed and should compensate them for it. Parijs, like a growing number of analysts, proposes a universal entitlement in the form of a basic income guarantee as the way to provide such compensation. The excluded get to be included as possessing an entitlement right by virtue of the need to compensate them for their exclusion. Exclusion becomes the basis for inclusion and the right to entitlement is seen as having been earned because one's exclusion becomes something for which one should be compensated. More than any other proposal, this one by Parijs for a basic income guarantee provides a dramatic example of how the entitlement/compensation dichotomy deconstructs.[60]

On the basis on such compassion, we can practice a politics of harm reduction, granting compensation so as to aid all those who need assistance, and doing so without passing judgment as to whether they bear responsibility for their failure to conform to overly narrow standards of the self-sufficient self. We can do this in ways that incrementally improve social and economic well-being.[61] This is preferable to either falling prey to the pretense of relying on the preexisting community or thoughtlessly

---

59. Phillipe van Parijs, "Basic Income and the Two Dilemmas of the Welfare State," in *The Welfare State: A Reader*, Christopher Pierson and Francis G. Castles, eds. (Malden: Polity Press, 2000), pp. 360–68. Thanks to John Tambornino for suggesting the point that the basic income is a form of compensation that the included owe the excluded.

60. Compensating the "excluded" for serving to make the "included" possible is an ethic consistent with Giorgio Agamben's idea that "the people" are constituted through an act of "inclusive exclusion" at the expense of marginalized peoples, the bandit, the outlaw, the refugee, the homeless, the impoverished, etc. See Agamben, *Means without End*, pp. 29–36.

61. For an analysis that calls for pursuing a "radical incrementalism," see Schram, *Praxis for the Poor*, pp. 101–03.

building a more ambitious welfare state that increasingly arrogates unto itself the regulation of the basic conditions of life.

A Loving Antagonism

Loving resistance to the state's processes of marginalization is therefore its own form of agonistic politics that pushes for what changes in the existing standards of deservingness can be gained at any one point in time.[62] Jane Addams famously argued with John Dewey at Hull House about her refusal to accept the idea that antagonism was fundamental to life and that conflict was essential to getting change.[63] It was her attempt to express a philosophy of love as fundamental to producing social change. She essentially put ethics above politics. Yet, it could be that real love animates an ongoing agonistic politics that resists the processes of marginalization at work in the welfare state.

A politics of loving therefore actually values the role of conflict and antagonism. Antagonism need not involve violence and need not insist on only working for a total overhaul of the existing juridical order. Instead, we must learn to work both within and outside the system simultaneously.[64] This means pushing for more legal rights to entitlements even as we work within the system to make it more likely to allow for acts of compassion that compensate people right now within a system of entitlements that leaves them unable to meet their basic needs. We must work to make incremental reforms possible now in the short run even as we work to produce structural reforms in the long run. While the continuing struggle for a basic income for all is imperative, this needs to be supplemented with building in more compassionate and more generous assistance to those who are currently excluded from the entitlement system.[65] This would be a politics of compassion worth fighting for.

---

62. See Stears, "Challenging Politics: Contention, Coercion and the Study of Political Theory," pp. 19–21.
63. Louis Menard, *The Metaphysical Club: A Story of Ideas in America* (New York: Farrar, Straus & Giroux, 2001), pp. 313–16.
64. A parallel tension is between working in the community to build more collaborative social change organizations versus emphasizing a more disruptive politics of protest at the national level. See Romand Coles, "Democratic Organizing: Between Theory and Practice," *Perspectives on Politics*, forthcoming; and Sanford F. Schram, "The Praxis of Poor People's Movements," *Perspectives on Politics* 1, 4 (December 2003): 715–20.
65. On the push across welfare states for a basic income, see Philippe van Parijs, "Basic Income: A Simple and Powerful Idea for the Twenty-First Century," *Politics & Society* 32, 1 (2004): 7–39.

Such a politics of compassion would work within liberal institutions to humanize them while at the same time plotting to transform them beyond the limits of liberal capitalism. It would practice harm reduction, offering aid without passing judgment, working to incrementally make things better for people even as it planned to overcome the systemic sources that marginalized and oppressed those who did not conform to the standards of deservingness in a society that insisted on particularly narrow understandings of who was a personally responsible, self-sufficient member of that society. This politics of compassion would not be anything like the compassionate conservatism that has been promoted in recent years. It would not be a compassion that can be used to rationalize the substitution of entitlement rights with the disciplinary practices of the new forms of governance that work through civil society to regiment people into the emerging social order. It would instead be a politics that recaptures compassion from those who seek to exploit it to justify painting the welfare state as cold, heartless, uncaring, and not worth fighting for. It would do that in the name of rebuilding the welfare state. And in an era of globalization, this is a most urgent task.

Index

About the Author

Sanford Schram teaches social theory and social policy in the Graduate School of Social Work and Social Research at Bryn Mawr College. He has authored three books and co-edited three others. His first book, *Words of Welfare*, won the Michael Harrington Award from the American Political Science Association. Schram lives in Haverford, PA, with his wife, Joan.